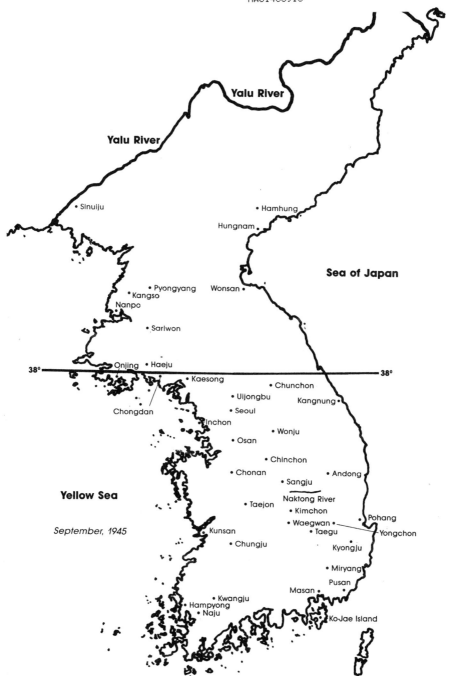

Yalu River

Yalu River

• Sinuiju

• Hamhung

Hungnam

Sea of Japan

• Pyongyang
• Kangso
Nanpo

Wonsan •

• Sariwon

38° Onjing • Haeju   38°

• Kaesong

• Chunchon

Chongdan   • Uijongbu   Kangnung •

• Seoul

Inchon

• Wonju

• Osan

• Chinchon

• Chonan   • Andong

• Sangju

Yellow Sea   Naktong River

• Taejon   • Kimchon

September, 1945   • Waegwan •   Pohang •

Kunsan   • Taegu   Yongchon

• Chungju   Kyongju •

• Miryang

Pusan

• Kwangju   Masan •
• Hampyong
• Naju   Ko-Jae Island •

Beyond the Horizon

Beyond the Horizon

A Pathologist's Life

Joseph Song, M.D.

VANTAGE PRESS
New York

FIRST EDITION

Published by Vantage Press, Inc.
516 West 34th Street, New York, New York 10001

Manufactured in the United States of America
ISBN: 0-533-10992-2

Library of Congress Catalog Card No.: 93-94326

0 9 8 7 6 5 4 3 2 1

In memory of my parents

Contents

Author's Note

Many of my friends, both here and in my native land of Korea, have on numerous occasions urged me to write my memoirs, some of them feeling that I should have done so several years ago. This is the product of their advice.

The purpose of this publication is not to praise any achievements of mine, but to express my undying gratitude to those who offered me a helping hand when I desperately needed it during the dismal, dark days of the Korean War. In spite of my shortcomings and failures, the love and care of my family, mentors, true friends, and guardian angels have continually sustained me.

1
Wake Island

A middle-aged diplomat, assigned to the Japanese Embassy in Washington, D.C., shook my arm and pointed to a small island below. I must have been dozing since we left Haneda Airport in Tokyo.

"What a beautiful and peaceful island!" I said.

"Yes," he replied in a sentimental tone of voice, "but there was a bloody battle here during the latter part of World War II, wiping out the entire Japanese Marine Regiment."

I was only fourteen years old at that time and remembered very little about the numerous battles that had been fought in the Pacific theater.

The Pan American Clipper landed at the Wake Island airfield and slowly taxied toward the hangar for refueling. The passengers, mostly American businessmen returning to the States, Japanese diplomats and their wives, some Japanese students, and I, in my dusty Republic of Korea (ROK) army medical officer's uniform were led into the lounge for soft drinks. Refueling would take approximately an hour, the speaker announced, and our next stop would be the Hawaiian islands.

I hastily wrote postcards to my parents and sisters, who I had left seventeen hours before, and to my best friend, Dr. Charles Kim, still at the aid station in Pusan.

Wake Island, situated midpoint in the Pacific Ocean between Japan and Hawaii, was serenely beautiful. I spotted two small Japanese tanks on the beach and walked toward them. As I sat on one of the ruined tanks, I was struck with the beauty of the huge sun, slowly sinking over the horizon.

Looking around, I failed to discover any significant piece of land or buildings except for the large airfield, worth fighting and dying for. Several other destroyed tanks, scattered over the area, reminded me of the large-scale war still going on in the Korean peninsula, responsible for some 3 million homeless people and countless casualties.

As the setting sun dropped lower, coloring the sky in shades of orange, I was overwhelmed with sadness and a feeling of apprehension,

1

not knowing what to expect when I arrived at my destination: Memphis, Tennessee. Most of my classmates and professors and the senior medical officers in the ROK army had expressed doubts about my success as an instructor and pathology resident at the University of Tennessee Medical School.

A voice from behind, announcing that the plane was about ready to take off, abruptly interrupted my thoughts. "Well, Joe," I said to myself as I slowly stood up, "you pulled all kinds of stunts and strings to come this far. There's no turning back now. Let's go through with it, all the way."

On our continuing flight to the Hawaiian islands, I vividly recalled the smiling face of Mrs. Francesca Rhee, the wife of Pres. Syngman Rhee, whom I first met in 1950. I thought of her kindness and her gift to me of a much-needed new navy blue suit. Just a few days before I left Pusan Military Airfield to catch the DC-9 cargo plane for Tokyo, Mrs. Rhee said to me, "Young man, the task is not an easy one, but you will do all right."

As we flew on, I pictured the tired and wrinkled features of my father, a staunchly anti-Japanese man, who had refused to learn or speak the Japanese language throughout his lifetime. My mother's anxious face kept passing through my mind like a silent movie.

It was June 25, 1952, the second anniversary of the bloody Korean War. I was twenty-five years old.

2
Port of Entry, USA

Our plane left Wake Island, proceeding to its destination, Los Angeles, California, with an intermediate stop in Hawaii. Unable to sleep I took out a letter from Fr. T. Yun and read it for the third time. The son of a wealthy wine merchant in Kwangju, Father Yun had attended the Catholic seminary in Seoul and had received further education in France. He was a linguist, able to speak six languages fluently. He had returned to his home province in Korea to serve as a parish priest.

When my tent was burned by mortar fire from the guerilla forces during my final military service in Hampyong and Naju, I stayed with Father Yun for two nights. As I was undressing in the bedroom we shared, he noticed that I was carrying a small capsule around my neck.

"Captain, what is that you're carrying?" he asked.

"This is a poison capsule, Father Yun. It may come in handy if I'm captured and tortured by the North Korean People's Army [NKPA]."

He snatched the capsule from my neck, threw it away, and said, "Captain, God created you, and your life is not your own to take."

I learned a great deal from Father Yun regarding Catholicism and his philosophy on life. In his brief letter he reemphasized the importance of my serving God and making a contribution to cancer research.

Putting the letter back into my shirt pocket, I also recalled a conversation with Mrs. Rhee at the temporary presidential palace in Pusan. "Why didn't you come to me before you joined the army?" she asked. "I could have helped you."

"I don't mean to sound like a phony patriot, Mrs. Rhee," I explained, "but I felt that I should do my part to end this war."

She nodded. "We need more honorable young men like you to rebuild this country."

The plane touched down at the Honolulu airport. This being a port of entry for the United States, all the passengers had to go through the Immigration Office and customs clearance. With my special passport, I was the first one to clear customs. A husky Chinese porter took my duffel bag and suitcase to the waiting area. Noticing my uniform and the Medical Corps insignia, he said, "There are two Korean organizations in Hawaii, the Korean Friendship Society and the Korean Nationalist Association, just three blocks apart." He suggested that I visit them because we had a layover of approximately three hours.

I took a cab to the office of the Korean Friendship Society, where I learned that this political organization was composed of supporters of Pres. Syngman Rhee, and we exchanged greetings. A short time later I was received by members of the Korean Nationalist Association, but not in the same warm, friendly manner, because they opposed President Rhee to the last man. Most of them spoke Korean with a northern accent, and I discovered that they were from the same hometown as my father. When I explained to them that I had no political allegiance to the Korean Friendship Society, they offered me a cup of tea and biscuit. I understood then why President Rhee had advised me not to listen to some of the Koreans in Hawaii and on the West Coast. This was my first exposure to the fierce underground political fight between the pro– and anti–Syngman Rhee factions.

The plane arrived at the Los Angeles airport at 6:00 A.M. on June 27. I showed a cabdriver the address given to me by my father. The cabdriver shook his head and said something, speaking so fast that I was unable to understand. When he wrote a figure of $40 on a piece of paper, I asked him to take me to the downtown police station instead.

About forty minutes later I was met by Off. William Kravitz. He very kindly took me to a neighborhood restaurant for breakfast and told me that there had been an assassination attempt on John M. Chang, the Republic of Korea's prime minister, by the opposition political party. After breakfast, Officer Kravitz drove me to my destination: 4131 South Catalina Street. This was the main office of a cultural organization known as Hung-Sa Dun, established about fifty years ago by Do San Ahn, the acting head and senior member of the Korean government in exile. Mr. Ahn was a teacher of my father, who had followed him to Shanghai to participate in an independent movement against the Japanese.

An executive officer of the organization, Henry C. Harr, embraced me. "So you're the son of my friend H. C. Song! Welcome to America!"

Mr. Harr took me upstairs to a bedroom, changed the linens, and told me to rest. With that I collapsed from extreme physical fatigue and slept for ten hours straight.

The next morning a member of the organization sent me to a restaurant, two blocks away, run by a Korean immigrant, J. C. Park. Because of my indigestion, I ordered only French toast and a cup of coffee. On the stool next to me lay a Korean newspaper. Picking it up, I noticed the headline: "Skulls of Dead NKPA Soldiers Crying Out Loud." I perused the newspaper and found that it was communistic. I almost fell off my stool in astonishment that this kind of paper would be allowed to circulate. I threw it on the floor in indignation.

Mr. Harr told me later that many political dissidents and unsuccessful businessmen had formed a political organization called the Los Angeles Korean Communist Party. "But they're not really Communists," he said. "They don't even understand the Communist doctrine. They wanted to be identified as an independent political party, neither pro– nor anti–Syngman Rhee."

"Even so," I said, "this is ridiculous. I fought the Communist forces for almost a year and a half, and to find this kind of garbage in a free country makes me disgusted."

That evening I met Louis B. Kang, another friend of my father. Mr. Kang was a self-made millionaire and the owner of a manufacturing company called Lin-Sol Products, which made liquid soap. Mr. Kang took me to his home for dinner and explained bitterly, "We all came together to America years ago to escape from the Japanese and to launch an independent movement, but we split when our leader, Mr. Ahn, died in a Japanese prison. Now there is no unity among us. My suggestion is that you stay away from politics. Study pathology and concentrate your efforts on cancer research." I appreciated his honesty and sincerity.

The next day Mr. Kang bought two neckties for me at Sears & Roebuck and took me to a Seventh-Day Adventist camp meeting in Whittier. He had attended a missionary school run by the Seventh-Day Adventist in North Korea, and he and his family were devout Seventh-Day Adventists.

There were approximately five hundred Korean businessmen in the Los Angeles area, I learned. Mr. Kang introduced me to a brother-in-law of Mr. Ahn, named T. C. Park. He was the owner of a small liquor store in downtown Los Angeles. His wife invited me for dinner at their home one evening.

I stayed about three days in Los Angeles and met many Koreans, most of whom hated Syngman Rhee. Because I owed so much to President and Mrs. Rhee, I felt very uneasy in conversing with these people, so I refrained from expressing my views.

Mr. Harr and some UCLA students taught me elementary American manners, the proper use of tableware, and how to order meals at a restaurant. I recovered from my fatigue and left Los Angeles for Memphis, Tennessee, on the morning of June 30.

5

A tall, heavyset, bald man met me at the Memphis airport, around seven o'clock in the evening. He greeted me warmly. "Welcome to Memphis, Dr. Song! I'm Dr. Coy Anderson. Dr. Sprunt is on vacation, and I'm supposed to take you to the institute and get you settled." Dr. Anderson was associate director of the Institute of Pathology at the University of Tennessee.

"You came with a famous actress," he said. A red-haired film star, Rhonda Fleming, was on the same plane, I learned.

Dr. Anderson and his son Ted drove me around Memphis, and I was impressed with the beauty of the city, the hundreds of automobiles, and the quiet manner of the people. We then went to the top floor of the Institute of Pathology building, where I met Jerry Little, with whom I was to share quarters. Jerry was a student from the University of Mississippi and had a summer job in the autopsy service.

3
Summer in Memphis

During the hot, humid, and hectic days of July, I was introduced to cornbread, buttermilk, beets, and black-eyed peas at the John Gaston Hospital cafeteria. Since I had never been exposed to such suffocating heat and murderous humidity, every day seemed like a lifetime of sweat and endeavor. In Pyongyang, North Korea, where I grew up, the summers were cool and a constant breeze prevailed.

The Institute of Pathology was a new and modern ten-story building for the pathology and microbiology departments of the university. In the fifth-floor office I met my officemate, Dr. Charlie Gilbert Fletcher. He was the son of a Methodist minister in Jackson, Tennessee, and the nephew of a Methodist missionary who had served in North Korea in the early 1930s. Dr. Fletcher asked if my first name was the Korean equivalent of Joseph.

"I suppose so," I said. "It was given to me by my parents without my choice." From that moment on, I was known in Memphis as Dr. Joe Song.

My office was a spacious room overlooking a large private hospital, Baptist Memorial Hospital, and a famous orthopedic clinic known as Campbell's Clinic. Anne McKenzie, payroll clerk at the institute, explained the income tax system and the necessary forms to be filled out before I could receive my monthly paycheck. Dr. Douglas H. Sprunt, the head of the department, was still on vacation in North Carolina.

The food of John Gaston Hospital's cafeteria was inedible, as far as I was concerned, except for breakfast, which I seldom had time to enjoy. My stomach growled continually with hunger and indigestion. Evenings were a nightmare because of the humidity and hot weather. When Dr. Anderson noticed my haggard face and bloodshot eyes, he asked if anything was wrong with my accommodations.

"No, Dr. Anderson, everything is fine," I assured him. "But I need some time to adjust to this new environment, particularly the weather and the food."

7

"We can advance you some money if you need it," he offered.

"No, thank you," I responded. "I still have $110. I just need a little more time to adjust."

The medical school system at the University of Tennessee was quite different from that of other university medical schools. Instead of a semester system, theirs was a quarter system. Medical students had to take twelve quarters to complete a course that lasted for three years and three months, and the Department of Pathology staff had to endure heavy teaching duties for the medical students of the fourth, fifth, and sixth quarters, as well as the dental and dental hygienist students. The students could take three months of vacation for the whole medical course or complete their medical education in just three years. The university graduated from 240 to 300 students a year, inviting the comment: "The University of Tennessee turns out doctors like flies."

I was assigned to the fourth-quarter medical students as a lab instructor three days a week, in addition to my autopsy duties. John Gaston Hospital had approximately a thousand autopsies a year. Our chief resident, Dr. Helen Proctor, performed one autopsy with me and then said, "You're on your own now, kid!" And off she went.

Brooding over the inedible food, sleepless nights, and miserable weather, I said to myself, "I thought I was coming to a land of milk and honey, but I jumped from the frying pan into the fire!"

I was surrounded by intelligent and energetic pathologists at the University of Tennessee: Dr. Russell Jones, a diligent pathologist; Dr. George Changus, an expert in bone pathology; and Dr. J. Walter Scott, a superb surgical pathologist. I felt extremely fortunate to be under the influence of these outstanding men. Not only the senior staff members, but also the clerical staff and students were very kind and willing to help me. This overwhelmed me.

The fourth-quarter medical students were a friendly group. It was a pleasure to talk with them and show slides during the course of their pathology study. Among them, Bruce Walker, Al Rader, Bob Smith, Billy Hightower, and Mort Gubin became my lifelong friends. To provide satisfactory autopsy service, the department hired from three to five medical students during the three months of summer vacation. They were called student prosectors, and they supplemented three pathology residents who regularly performed two or three autopsies a day. Among the student prosectors, Bob Rainey, Jim Meyer, Joe Campbell, Andy Warner, and Jerry Berkley were particularly friendly. I had no problems in communicating with them, but I had a great deal of difficulty in understanding the black maids and orderlies and had to ask Andy to interpret for me.

On July 20, I received a letter from Glen E. Daly, a certified hearing-aid audiologist and head of the Mid-South Hearing Aid Society:

Dear Dr. Song:

It must be a frustrating experience to have difficulty in hearing. I have had a hearing difficulty for the past ten years. Many exciting things are happening in the field of hearing aids, such as an all-in-the ear model that I have been using for the past three months with excellent results. You are invited to see the newest hearing aid on the market today, and there will be a gift for each one who uses this model. Please come in to see us. We will be glad to provide you with a hearing aid consultation at no obligation to you. We also make house calls.

I dismissed the letter without any consideration until I had received four letters in four weeks. Then I showed it to Andy Warner and asked his opinion as to why I was receiving such a letter every week.

Andy read it and burst into laughter. "Joe, they think you can't hear well because you can't understand the people around here."

A week later I received a letter from the president of the fourth-quarter medical school students asking me to be their chaperon for a social function. Again I had to turn to Andy for an explanation. He said, "All they want you to do, Joe, is to come to their party and have a good time on Saturday evening. You may have to send a letter to the Student Center of the university, stating that their class party was conducted entirely in a dignified manner, which may not be true, but that's the price you have to pay."

One of the sixth-quarter medical students called me on the phone that same afternoon and asked me to chaperone their group on the same evening at a different place.

Mort Gubin and Al Rader took me to their party in the western section of Memphis, where there was a stage show and a skit. I really enjoyed meeting the students and their spouses and consumed a great deal of beer for relaxation. Around 9:30 that evening I went to chaperone the sixth-quarter social function and drank a significant amount of whiskey, returning to my quarters about 1:30 A.M.

The department policy in autopsy service, based on Dr. Sprunt's belief that postmortem examination must be carried out immediately after a death, kept us residents busy day and night, At 3:10 A.M. I was

9

awakened by a call from the switchboard for an autopsy but was unable to get up. On the third call, I finally managed to dress and walk down to notify a group of students who were on call with me that night. Four students arrived at 5:00 A.M., but they were equally drunk. We finally completed the autopsy by 6:30 A.M. and went back to bed.

The gross conference (to review the organs and systems to correlate clinical findings) was held at 8:00 that morning. No one was there to present the autopsy findings to the tenth-quarter students, so I was called down to produce the organs. Because of the aftereffects of the previous evening's social functions, we had performed the autopsy but had not saved the organs. I was forced to recover the organs from the garbage to make a presentable case.

When I told Andy about this, he giggled and said, "If the old man finds out, you'll be cooked!" Fortunately, that was the only such occurrence during all my four years of training.

It was not easy for me to distinguish one Western face from another, because the students all had crew cuts and wore uniforms. Since I found it difficult to remember their names, I decided to differentiate the students by the color of their hair. There was an interesting autopsy case in which a fifteen-year-old boy died of a very unusual type of cirrhosis of the liver, and I wanted a gross photograph of the organ. Previously a fourth-quarter student and amateur photographer, Ben Leming had photographed the organs removed at the autopsy table. I distinctly remembered his fiery red hair. As I entered the classroom on this particular day, about seventy students were busy studying microscopic slides. I spotted a student with bright red hair and approached him, asking, "Mr. Leming, can you take a gross photograph on this autopsy case?"

He looked at me, rather puzzled. "My name is McGee, sir." From that moment on, I knew that there was more than one red-haired student in the school.

Room and board and uniforms were provided by the university. I was able to send $150.00 a month to my parents, keeping $47.50 for my own use, which I spent at a downtown Chinese restaurant called Joy Young.

A short time later Paul Finck, of Geneva, Switzerland, and a middle-aged physician, Bengt Larson, from Malmö, Sweden, joined the department as residents, thus completing our UN delegates to the Department of Pathology, University of Tennessee School of Medicine. The *Memphis Commercial Appeal* printed an article titled "The Time Is Reversed," in which Dr. Sprunt commented: "Years ago American physicians had to go to Europe to study medicine. Now Europeans are coming to America to complete their training."

Dr. Sprunt returned from vacation and called me to his office at 9:00 A.M. on August 1. I thanked him for his patience and help in expediting my coming to the University of Tennessee. He then told me that during his fellowship at the Rockefeller Institute he had spent some time in Peking, China, and was exposed to Oriental culture, which he held in high esteem. Dr. Sprunt asked me to let him know if there was anything he could do to help me. He also mentioned that Dr. Hyman, dean of the medical school, had a son, a recent graduate of West Point Military Academy, who was reported missing during the first phase of the Korean War. He suggested that I speak with Dr. Hyman. After doing so, I wrote to Mrs. Syngman Rhee, asking if she could help in gathering information regarding the whereabouts of Lieutenant Hyman, an infantry officer of the U.S. Army's Twenty-fourth Division. Six weeks later I received a reply from President and Mrs. Rhee's secretary, Rev. J. B. Koh. He said that as far as they could tell, the young man was reported missing in action in the vicinity of Taejon around July 25. He suggested that the Hymans get in touch with the commanding general of the Eighth Army for detailed information.

I said to Dean Hyman, "Your son gave his life for my country, yet I am here to study pathology in Memphis."

"He was a professional soldier," Dr. Hyman replied, "and he took his chances."

During the weekly Thursday evening conferences, I was appalled to hear the language used, primarily by Dr. Sprunt, who tended to swear for no reason at all. It was disgusting to listen to the gutter language of some of the American GIs and officers during the Korean War, and now I was hearing four-letter words and profanity from honorable American doctors. I later learned, through Eloise Jones, a pathology resident, that "Sprunt's language probably doesn't mean too much. It's his way of expressing anger or hiding his complex."

Being a medical politician, Dr. Sprunt had many enemies within the department as well as outside. One senior pathology resident hated him with a passion. "There's an ulterior motive in his having you guys in this department," this resident told me. "Doug Sprunt had to go to Germany because many other people went, but he never studied pathology there. He spent most of his time dating American girls in Paris, and he's the only one who can't read or speak German."

I was astonished to hear this comment but maintained my own feelings toward Dr. Sprunt, who had saved me from many ordeals and delays in getting out of the army. The resident, unable to obtain a satisfactory letter of recommendation from Dr. Sprunt, volunteered for the U.S. Army Medical Corps.

Before I left Pusan, Professor Lee advised me to obtain a Ph.D. degree in pathology and return to his department as an assistant professor of pathology. The registrar of the University of Tennessee, Dorothy Woodbridge, explained that it was too late for me to start the July quarter. She suggested that I discuss the matter with Dr. Sprunt and Dr. Nash, dean of the graduate school. Dr. Sprunt felt that I should take pathology as a major and microbiology as a minor in a three-year course of graduate study toward a Ph.D. degree in pathology.

When I registered in September, my officemate, Charlie Fletcher, asked me why I wanted to take on another burden in addition to the duties of pathology residency. When I explained to him that this was the only available and open course for advanced studies in pathology in Korea, he said that a Ph.D. degree means very little and an M.D. degree is far superior to that of Ph.D. or Doctor of Science. To be a pathologist I had to pass the examination given by the American Board of Pathology, and with the title of Diplomat of the American Board of Pathology, I could open every door in the field of pathology practice. Fletcher told me that it was a very difficult examination. Most of the ex-residents from the Institute of Pathology had to repeat the examination, and some of them had to take it three times before they could pass. This was the same, he explained, in every specialist organization, such as the American Board of Medicine, the American Board of Surgery, and the American Board of Obstetrics and Gynecology, to ensure the qualifications of specialists in medicine.

I could not picture myself passing such a difficult examination if so many trained pathologists from the institute failed to pass it the first time. So I dismissed the idea and concentrated on my routine of teaching, autopsy pathology, and the scheduled pathology conferences.

When they found out that I had registered for graduate school toward a Ph.D. degree in pathology, three other residents, Tom Newman, Jim Williams, and Dick Miller, rushed to the registrar's office to sign up for graduate school. When I left Memphis in 1956 with my degree of master of science in pathology and microbiology, none of them had completed their course.

Dr. Anne Dulaney, professor of microbiology, asked me to give a talk on Korea and the Korean War to a group of professors at the student center during their luncheon break. Professor Dulaney was a genuine scholar and a lady who had devoted her life to research in microbiology.

"Certainly, Dr. Dulaney, I'll be happy to do so," I said. "But I must

12

first explain the history and culture of my people, which may be rather boring to you."

"That's all right," she replied. "We would be fascinated by your presentation, I'm sure."

4
My Fatherland

Korea is not naturally divided in two, except by the spine of mountains, the Taebaek Range, that runs from north to south, close to the Sea of Japan. Korea is geographically, strategically, economically, and ethnically a single entity, with each part as necessary to the rest as a man's arms and legs are to his body. Its division at the thirty-eighth parallel was a tragic mistake—a mere military convenience of such minor concern to military historians at the time that Pres. Franklin D. Roosevelt allegedly gave in to the demands of Premier Stalin, although no one today can say for certain just who first suggested it.

The thirty-eighth parallel is not a border in any true sense. It is not militarily defensible, nor does it possess any traditional significance. Koreans who live north of the parallel speak the same language, favor the same clothing and customs, and nourish the same national pride as do those who live in the south.

Korea, despite its history of invasion and enslavement by powerful neighbors, has always existed as an independent nation in the hearts of the people, who for centuries have had a strong and fierce desire to run their own affairs. Its geographic location has made it a battleground for nearly as long as man has kept records of his doings. China, Russia, and Japan have all at one time or another, and in spite of international commitments to the contrary, tried to annex Korea's territory to their own. According to Gen. Matthew Ridgway, the United States made pledges several times to assist Korea in the event of attack but never raised a hand to rescue this tiny, hapless kingdom from its foes next door.

The six-hundred-mile-long Korean peninsula protrudes like a small, fat thumb from the landmass of Asia. It is pointed directly at the Japanese island of Kyushu, offering or inviting invasion across the narrow Strait of Tsushima. It is less than a hundred miles from Pusan, the principal port of Korea, to the Japanese port of Shimonoseki.

The Korean peninsula divides the subarctic Sea of Japan from the subtropical Yellow Sea. Although Korea lies in the temperate zone, in the same latitude as Kentucky, it suffers wintry cold on the craggy six thousand-foot ridges in the north that can reach fifty degrees below zero fahrenheit, while the heat in the south during the summertime can make man gasp. There is also the green of growing fields, so rich and brilliant that it takes one's breath away.

The northern part of Korea, which holds the industrial section, largely depends on the south for its food. The southern part receives supplies of electricity, heavy industrial products, and rich mineral resources from the north. The country as a whole, viewed from the air or while walking among the hills or on its seashores, seems especially blessed with beauty. When the summer fades, the foothills of the spinal range, where hardwood trees grow in profusion, turn golden and yellow and shades of red and brown. The skies are often a clear blue, and the seas on either side of the peninsula stretch out deep and clean. The far north, however, offers a more forbidding prospect, particularly in winter, when storms from the distant Manchurian land, reaching toward the Yalu River, scream down and lay ten-foot drifts on the mountains.

Unlike the terrain, the Korean people are thoroughly hospitable. But they are fierce patriots, who harbor a century-old hatred for the Japanese, whose brutal policies they well remember. Individualistic as the Irish, many Koreans are very temperamental, never willing to submit to enforced Japanese rule.

Ancient Korea, with forty-three hundred years of history, was a united kingdom composed of four major states, according to various historical descriptions. Maps depicting the nation's boundaries in 3,000 B.C. illustrate (1) the Buyo, occupying the lower third of Manchuria, (2) the Koguryo, situated in the northern part of Korea, (3) the Backje, controlling the midbelt of the Korean peninsula, and (4) the Silla, filling the southern part of the Korean peninsula.

The Buyo was subsequently invaded and conquered by the soldiers of the Han nation and absorbed as a part of China, and the Buyo people were forced to move back to the Korean peninsula. Later the Silla annexed the provinces occupied by Koguryo and Backje, proclaiming the United Kingdom of Korea in A.D. 668. Its capital was based at Kyongju.

Silla was constantly besieged by attacks from China over the land in the north and by invasions from Japan across the sea in the south. While repelling all the attacks, Silla succeeded in developing Korean

15

culture to a new height. Great advancement in arts and letters, architectural achievements in the construction of magnificent monasteries and temples, and the flowering crafts of gold, silver, and precious stones were only part of Silla's golden age. The granite tower built in A.D. 647, the oldest existing astronomical observatory, still stands in Kyongju as a monument of stunning achievement. It was from this tower that the astronomers forecast seasonal changes and weather for the farmers.

The "ice house," possibly the earliest man-made refrigeration system, was another accomplishment of Silla. A huge chamber was dug deep in the ground, and a network of narrow canals was built to crisscross its floor. The river water was brought up to flow through the canals, and when the walls of the chamber were sealed and layers of dirt covered its strong roof, the refrigeration system was ready. In the winter, blocks of ice were cut from the frozen river, hauled into the ice house, and stored there. The natural insulation of the earth and the constant flow of the river water kept the ice frozen until the following winter.

The first land reform began in A.D. 700. The civil service examination was inaugurated in A.D. 957, marking the first examination system for employing civil servants and government officials. The well-known printing plate was used in Korea in A.D. 1234, long before the Gutenberg Bible was printed. Furthermore, the Koreans claim that they built the world's first iron-clad warships, which destroyed the combined fleet of Japan in 1592.

The artistic talent possessed by many Koreans is by no means exaggerated, since the children are constantly exposed to the nation's artistic achievement. In ceramics Korea was unsurpassed by her neighbors. During the Koryo dynasty (918–1392) even the Chinese praised Korean pottery, marveling that the secret color of Koryo was the "first under heaven." The secret color was celadon, a haunting shade of pale green applied in rich oil glazes. Breaking from the self-conscious traditions of the Chinese, the Korean potters indulged their own romantic sensibilities, producing elegant elongated vessels. Some bloomed into flowers and animals—a water dropper took the form of a monkey, a tea dish the shape of a water lily.

Other artists began to limn scenes from daily life. In contrast to the sedate, idealized renderings of the Chinese, there is a certain humor, a realism bordering on caricature, in these works: in one, a scholar pulls up his robe to dip his toes in a cool stream; in another, a group of women enjoy their day off in the country. As such depictions of manners and mores demonstrate, the Koreans were survivors who never lost the ability to find pleasure and beauty in the everyday.

One cannot overlook the achievements of the ancient Chinese, whose nation was civilized when the rest of the people of the world were still living in caves. When Confucius taught ethics, Rome was only a village, and England did not exist. Two thousand years later a united China prospered under the Ming dynasty. While Europe was a struggling hotbed of principalities, the Chinese produced paper, porcelain, printing, gunpowder, the compass, the wheelbarrow, and the fore-and-aft rig. Europe produced chocolate and the cuckoo clock.

What are the characteristic differences among the Chinese, Korean, and Japanese people?

When I was growing up in Pyongyang, Korea, I often asked my father to explain to me the basic characteristics of the Asian people. He would take me into his study and say, "Traditionally speaking, Son, the Japanese bring up their boys to become brave warriors and soldiers, to die for their emperor. Chinese youths are taught to become the best businessmen of the world. On the other hand, we train our boys to become educated servants, scholars, or academicians, to teach literature, art, porcelain, and painting." He continued by saying that I should become a professor at the university, or a lawyer, to defend the Korean people against the oppressive Japanese government.

The Kingdom of Koguryo (Koryo), which lasted for centuries, finally replaced the Silla dynasty, achieving one large independent nation. Gen. Sun ge Lee, of humble origin from northeastern Korea, ascended rapidly to become the most able senior general of the dynasty. He revolted in 1392, overthrowing the royal families and killing their most trusted generals, thus ending the Korea dynasty.

When General Lee became king of Korea, he changed the name of the country from Korea to Chosun (Land of Morning Calm), and the capital was moved from Kaesong to Seoul. This was the beginning of the Yi dynasty.

King Lee feared possible assassination or reprisal from his fellow officers of northern stock, so he selected his bodyguard entirely from residents of Seoul or southern Korea, as they were known for their obedience. In fact, King Lee never used or promoted northerners to cabinet positions or upheld them in higher governmental posts or military ranks. This eventually led to the uprising initiated by a northern politician named Hong Kyong Rae. Many cities were taken, but the revolution was unsuccessful. Hong was arrested and put to death.

5
Struggle for Independence

The Korean peninsula, because of its strategic location, was the object of repeated attempts at occupation by three major powers—Russia, China, and Japan. The Imperial Russian Navy, searching for warm ports to expand their naval strength in the Far East, continued their political and military manipulations through the pro-Russian cabinet members of Kojong, the twenty-sixth king of the Yi dynasty. China felt that she must protect the Korean peninsula from the growing threat and expansionism of Japan. The Empire of Japan held the view that it was essential, for their own survival, to take the Korean peninsula in order to search for a new frontier—namely, Manchuria.

Being an underdeveloped land with a weak military system and many corrupt politicians, the Kingdom of Korea was plagued by tempting offers from all three big powers. China had 1,500 soldiers stationed in Seoul to protect their interests and the embassy; Japan maintained a small troop of 140 marines for the same excuse. A core of young Korean radicals, representing a progressive political party, were determined, however, to sever ties with the three big powers to maintain a strong and independent nation.

On the evening of October 17, 1884, the postmaster general, Ry S. Hong, was giving a dinner party in celebration of the completion of the new post office. A handful of young patriotic politicians with a burning desire to drive foreign forces out of Korea launched a military coup, killing several conservative pro-Russian and pro-Chinese cabinet members. Then they marched into Chang Duk Palace for an audience with Emperor Kojong. The king agreed to move to a smaller palace for his own protection.

Members of the group subsequently returned to the palace to declare a new progressive government. This government lasted for only three days, at which time the Chinese troops took command and controlled the city of Seoul, killing most of the japanese soldiers.

The instigators of the aborted military coup were forced to leave the country to seek political asylum in Japan and the United States.

Their leader, Ok Kyun Kim, was accepted by the Japanese government, while Syngman Rhee and Philip Jaisohn So headed for the United States. According to the strict rules for treason and treasonous acts, members of their families were captured and put to death.

Syngman Rhee settled in Boston to study international politics and law at Harvard University. Philip Jaisohn So entered medical school in Philadelphia. Ok Kyun Kim received cordial treatment and protection from the Japanese government until he was assassinated in Shanghai, several years later, on instructions of King Kojong of Korea.

To gain the initiative and eventual control of Korea and Manchuria, Japan launched a war against Russia in Manchuria in 1904, winning several battles there. Because of their internal problems and potential revolution, the Russians agreed to meet with a Japanese delegation to discuss a peace treaty. They met in 1905 in Portsmouth, New Hampshire, with mediation by Pres. Theodore Roosevelt. The peace treaty they signed gave Japan a free hand in her occupation of Korea and Manchuria. It called for the immediate dissolution of all Korean armed forces, against the will of the top-ranking army and navy officers, most of whom took their own lives in protest of such a radical movement. Col. Park Sung Whan, commander of the Imperial Guards' First Regiment, shot himself, resulting in a fierce battle between the remnants of the Korean armed forces and the numerically superior Japanese troops.

Emperor Kojong dispatched three secret emissaries to the international peace conference at the Hague in 1907, to arouse the consciousness of the world and to seek the nations' help in repealing the treaty that the Japanese government had forced him to accept. Due to Japan's strong opposition, the three emissaries were not admitted or allowed to present the letter from the king of Korea. When their repeated efforts to address the conference failed, one of the delegates, Ambassador Lee Jun, committed suicide while there. This incident forced King Kojong to abdicate.

From 1907 through 1910, 141,602 Korean soldiers and armed volunteers engaged in 2,819 battles with the Japanese troops, until all their ammunition was exhausted. The Koreans lost 17,600 in the three-year fight. Many of the former soldiers of the Korean armed forces fled to Manchuria and established a new military academy to train exiled soldiers and their sons. Countless battles were fought there against the Japanese troops by the soldiers of a newly established political party, the Korean Independent Party. The most notable and victorious one was the battle of Chong Sun Ri, in Manchuria. Five thousand Korean soldiers of the Independent Party defeated 50,000 troops, forcing them to leave 3,000 casualties on the battlefield when they retreated.

Japan forcefully annexed Korea in 1910. The twenty-seventh king of the Yi dynasty, King Lee Un, a mere eleven-year-old boy, was moved to Japan. The boy king always wept when groups of Korean nationals or students visited his palace in Tokyo. Upset and dismayed on observing the young king's sorrow, Japanese officials suspected a conspiracy against their government. They isolated the boy's residence, and from that time on no one was allowed to visit the last king of Korea.

Many of the patriots left their country to establish a Korean government in exile in Shanghai, China. The undisputed leader of the nation was Do San Ahn, from the province of Kangso, of Pyongyang Prefecture, in North Korea. My father was born and raised in that same district. Most of the military academy students and conscientious politicians received their education in the twenty-seven schools and universities established in Korea by Presbyterian and Methodist missionaries from the United States. My father was advised to go to a missionary school in Seoul. He was converted to Christianity while attending Bae Je High School, established in 1886 by Presbyterian missionaries. After four years of education, he became a staunch anti-Japanese patriot. He followed Mr. Ahn and his group to Shanghai, with the dream that they would return to Korea in the near future to regain independence for Korea.

Vice Pres. Kim Kyu Shik represented the government in exile to the international peace conference in Paris in February 1910, to plead their cause. Nine years later, six hundred college students gathered in the YMCA building in Tokyo and passed a resolution calling for independence for the Korean peninsula.

The formal Korean government in exile was established in Shanghai in 1919, and new diplomatic efforts were launched to gain support from the Western countries to secure the independence of the Korean peninsula.

Ten years after the forced annexation to Japan, in hundreds of villages, north and south, Korean patriots met secretly to plan their liberation. Thirty-three Korean leaders met on March 1, 1919, at the Bright Moon Restaurant in Seoul for a last meal together. They read the Declaration of Independence aloud, signed their names with a flourish, and called in the police. At the same moment all over the land, 2 million people gathered in the streets to hear the declaration read, then marched joyfully through the villages, carrying the forbidden flag of Korea and shouting for independence throughout the entire peninsula. The marchers were unarmed and threatened no violence. But in the next few weeks, 46,948 were arrested by the Japanese military and secret police, 7,509 were killed, and 15,961 were wounded. The Japanese troops destroyed 715 houses and burned forty-seven churches and two high school buildings to the ground.

Meanwhile, the State Department of the U.S. government was solemnly warning the consul in Seoul that he should be extremely careful not to encourage any belief that the United States would assist the Korean nationalists in carrying out their plans or to give the Japanese any basis for believing that the United States even sympathized with the Korean nationalist movement.

The United States has known of the existence of Korea for a relatively short time and has dealt with her diplomatically. The first treaty between Korea and the United States was drawn up in 1882 in Tientsin, establishing commercial relations between the United States and the Kingdom of Korea. It contained a clause that pledged mutual aid in case either country should be unjustly treated by another. The unjust treatment, however, was open to restricted interpretation. Under the Tientsin treaty, the U.S. government specifically recognized China's sovereignty but studiously avoided giving offense to either China or Japan to control the land of Korea.

In 1894, when the China-Japan rivalry over Korea exploded into warfare, the Americans took pains to choose neither side and confined their good offices to the expression of a polite hope that Japan would not visit an unjust war upon a defenseless neighbor. During the Sino-Japanese conflict, the United States rejected a British proposal that Americans intervene jointly with Britain, Germany, Russia, and France. When Japan won complete control of Korea, the United States once again recognized Korea's "independence" while acknowledging Japanese rights. In the next two decades Americans were twice invited to honor their original pledge to protect Korea from being eaten alive, and twice they rejected the request.

When Japan made Korea a protectorate, Pres. Theodore Roosevelt wrote off Korea: "We can not possibly interfere for the Koreans against the Japanese." This was his reply to the request, made five and six years earlier, that Americans undertake to secure from the great powers an agreement guaranteeing the integrity of Korea.

The sadistic and cruel characteristics of the Japanese race were clearly demonstrated in 1919. All the political parties of the Korean independence movement were outlawed by the Japanese military government, forcing them to go underground in 1931. A vast network of communication, however, was maintained throughout the Korean peninsula and Manchuria.

A water-bottle-shaped bomb was thrown at the ceremonial platform of Japanese military leaders who were celebrating their emperor's birthday, on April 29, 1933, in Shanghai. The bomb killed or maimed many Japanese diplomats and army and naval officers. A member of the Korean Independent Party, Yun Bong Kil, gave his own life in this bombing.

Soldiers of the Korean Independent Party were known for their fierce fighting spirit and ruthlessness toward the Japanese military and secret police. To discipline naughty children, mothers had only to say, "The soldiers of the Independent Party are coming!" My mother tried this several times on me, bringing a chilling effect for better behavior.

When the Sino-Japanese War broke out in 1937, the Korean government in exile was forced to move from Shanghai to Chungking under the protection of the Chinese government. Several thousand soldiers were recruited and trained to fight the Japanese, side by side with Chiang Kai-shek's troops. The Korean government in exile formally declared war against the Japanese empire from Chungking in 1942. Under the Korean national flag, six thousand soldiers, mainly from the Korean peninsula, Manchuria, California, and Hawaii, took part in the Allied forces expeditions in Burma and China under the leadership of Gen. Lee Bum Suk.

My mother's younger brother, Uncle Koh, a former literature student at Yon Hi College, of the American Methodist Missionary Foundation, was taken to the Japanese army. Ordered to guard a railroad in mid-China in October of 1943, he quietly left his sentry post, walked four miles west, and threw himself into a Chinese army regiment. He was sent to Chungking to join a Korean force, along with several hundred Korean students who had escaped from the Japanese army.

My paternal uncle, B. J. Song, was a law student at Seoul Imperial University until April 1943, when he was forced to join the Japanese army. He was sent to northern China after six months of basic training. On the evening of November 2, 1943, he left his Japanese company and hiked ten miles toward the north. He took a wrong turn, reaching the Chinese Communist regiment by mistake. The political officers of the new fourth Corps of Mao's Communist troops sent him to Yunan, the home base of the Chinese Communist Party, for two years of political and military training. When Uncle B.J. returned to Pyongyang, in October of 1945, he was a true Marxist and Maoist, trying to brainwash the students in Pyongyang. Fate was so unpredictable.

22

6
Japanese Occupation

The administrative policies of the Japanese empire in Korea during the thirty-five years of occupation may be summarized in a few words: arrests without warrant, torture, followed by long-term imprisonment or death. The cruelty of the Japanese secret police and military personnel was beyond all understanding. Their so-called emergency decree justified their actions. On the basis of suspicion, rumor, and information provided by their informants, they arrested many Korean intellectuals, professors, artists, and especially ministers of the Protestant denominations. These people were detained indefinitely without justification or proper charges. This relentless oppression by the Japanese, however, created more underground resistance movements and drove many young people toward Communism.

Realizing their shallow culture and the relatively short history of their country, the Japanese officials felt that the creation of Japanese history would serve as the foundation of their nation. According to Japanese history books, a goddess named Amaterus descended from heaven to the Japanese mainland, which was very dark and uncivilized. She had to chastise her mischievous brother but gave him three sacred articles that she had brought with her from heaven—a golden dagger, a mirror made of metal, and a pearl necklace. Before she left for heaven, she declared her brother the governor of the Japanese island.

During my primary and secondary education under Japanese rule, we students were told repeatedly that the sacred Japanese mainland was indeed the creation of their goddess, and the three sacred articles representing their national treasure and heritage were kept in the central Shinto shrine in Tokyo. Most of the Japanese teachers, I believe, were not convinced of the story's validity, although they were forced to repeat it. None of the Korean students were impressed with this creation theory, and they tended to laugh behind the backs of their Japanese teachers.

A famous and honest historian, Professor Tsuda, published a monograph challenging the national view of the creation of Japan. He stated that such a fairy tale would not serve any purpose in establishing historical facts. He emphasized that they had to face the scientific fact that the island of Japan was discovered by Indians who crossed the Bering Strait and settled on the Japanese mainland approximately two thousand years ago.

A fanatic right-wing politician, Mr. Ashida, with military backing, made a formal accusation of treason against the Japanese government and brought Professor Tsuda and his publisher, Iwanami, to the high court of Japan. The trial lasted for more than one year, as Professor Tsuda prepared well for his own defense, based on historical facts and his investigations. The statute of limitations ran out, and the professor avoided a long prison term, although he lost his position as professor of history and was unable to find suitable employment before he died.

The Japanese are fanatic people and tend to build more Shinto shrines than are needed, I believe Shinto shrines are located in the major cities of Korea for worship of imaginary ghosts, representing Japan's famous but notorious warriors, generals, emperors, empresses, and great ancestral figures. The Pyongyang shrine was located on high land overlooking the Dae Dong River and its cherry-tree-covered banks. All the students were forced to worship by climbing to the top of the Shinto shrine six times a year. Twelve Methodist and Presbyterian ministers refused to attend the morning worship at the Shinto shrine and were subsequently arrested and tortured. Five of them received unspeakable punishment and died three years later.

Against the Japanese policies for destruction of Korean heritage, artistic culture, and traditional customs, a group of academic leaders established the Korean Language Research Institute, in 1921, to preserve the national heritage and the Korean language.

The Japanese secret police continually harassed the editors of the Korean language newspapers, *Dong A Daily* and *Chosun Ilbo*. Two of the Korean-language magazines were forced to discontinue publication long before 1941, when Japan entered World War II. The two daily newspapers were subsequently outlawed by the Japanese government.

During my six years of primary education at Chong-Ro Grade School, in Pyongyang, the Korean teachers continued teaching our language until the fifth grade, although we were warned not to speak Korean at school outside the classroom. About one-third of the Japanese teachers were genuine educators, but they were constantly pressured to emphasize their creation theory, which none of the students believed.

The Japanese government adopted a policy of hiring Korean people as civil servants, engineers, teachers, and high government officials, based on their ability to manage the Japanese language. My father, who refused to learn the language, used to call an interpreter when the Japanese teachers visited our home during my primary education. He was prohibited permanently from holding any jobs or positions because of his unwillingness to learn the Japanese language.

When I was born in Pyongyang in 1927, my mother, who was converted to Christianity through the Presbyterian church, had me baptized at a suburban Presbyterian church and gave me the Hebrew name Joseph. She often repeated the Old Testament story of Joseph, who was sold by his brothers to a caravan, ascended to the position of prime minister in Egypt, and was able to help his own people. I protested on numerous occasions as I was growing up, because of my odd name. But she never would consent to changing it to an ordinary Korean name. She told me that I should grow up like Joseph of Egypt, to help my people. I intensely disliked my name throughout my primary and secondary education, because I was always ridiculed by the Japanese teachers for having such an unusual first name.

When I entered the Second Pyongyang High School, there were two Japanese army officers to give the students military training, with the ultimate goal of preparing us to die for their emperor on the battlefield. They stressed repeatedly that our remains would be placed in the Yasukuni shrine in Tokyo, to be worshiped by millions of people. None of us were serious about receiving military training but had to go along with their fanatic ideas in order to graduate from high school.

The Korean people traditionally are bound to their national heritage and customs and feel that it is their supreme duty to carry on the family name for generations to come. They so adhered to their surnames that even married women never took their husband's names, although the offspring were raised in the husband's tradition and family units. It was a serious insult if one said to another, "A man like you should change your last name." I overheard my mother saying several times, "If I do this [or accept this offer], I will change my last name."

The Japanese administration forced the Koreans to change their names to Japanese names, not realizing the importance to the Koreans of preserving their surnames. Those students who wanted to go to college or to receive higher education suffered discrimination by the college and university officials because of their lack of Japanese surnames. Many Koreans found it necessary to change their last names so that their children could attend college. Some found a loophole in the new system by adopting Japanese pronunciation of the Korean name without actually changing it, thus deceiving the officials.

I never keenly felt the effects of the discrimination exercised by the Japanese government until I reached my senior year in high school and was preparing to enter college. It became obvious that the barriers set by the Japanese government for the Korean students to overcome to achieve a higher education were indeed very high. Every college and university, except those established by missionaries, set a quota system, restricting Korean students to less than 20 percent of the enrollment. More than 80 percent of the seats were occupied by Japanese students, who had no problem being admitted to the school.

As the Pacific war followed the course of disaster after disaster in 1943, even the most fanatic Japanese students had second thoughts about being drafted and dying for their emperor. They had no desire to go to the Pacific theater to be slaughtered by the superior U.S. forces. Most of the soldiers sent from Japan to defend the worthless islands were drowned as their ships were torpedoed by American submarines. Many of the Japanese students frantically sought sanctuary at medical and engineering schools for the duration of the war.

The college in Pyongyang that I entered during the latter part of World War II reserved 80 percent of its seats for Japanese students, leaving 20 percent for selected Koreans. Out of six thousand applicants, only twenty students were selected and admitted for the first year of college.

Severance Union Medical College, in Seoul, founded by Methodist missionaries, had a reverse system, admitting one hundred Korean students and twenty Japanese. Most of the Korean students admitted to that college, however, were sons and nephews of Methodist ministers and high-ranking church officials, leaving very few openings for non-Christian Korean students.

At my college a group of highly select and intelligent Korean students always held the top 5 percent of the positions in the class, based on their academic performance. It was the policy, however, that the president of the class should be a Japanese student. I was appointed by the Japanese teachers to serve as vice president.

In my class were many Japanese students who had come from mainland Japan to avoid the continuous B-29 raids. They told us that it was futile to continue the war against the United States. Some Japanese professors who had been educated in the United States criticized the madness of the Japanese government in launching such a destructive war, saying that those blockheads of the Japanese military system would never understand their way of thinking. There were many informants at every level of society. Some of the professors lost their positions, and a few were imprisoned by the Japanese secret and military police.

7

Liberation Followed by Political Chaos

The first announcement of future Korean independence was made in Cairo, Egypt, in December of 1943, during a conference attended by Franklin D. Roosevelt, Winston Churchill, and Gen. Chiang Kai-shek. This was reaffirmed by open avowals at Potsdam stating that Korea would become a free and independent nation following the Japanese surrender. The Soviets agreed to enter into the Asian war from Manchuria to defeat the Japanese in the summer of 1945.

For a week's battle the Soviet Union gained a vast amount of territory in Manchuria and North Korea, moving through Manchuria with only token resistance by the skeleton Japanese troops, until the atomic bomb explosion on Hiroshima on August 7. Most of the Japanese troops had been moved from Manchuria to the Pacific islands prior to Soviet intervention. Masses of T-34 tanks and Soviet infantrymen swept through Manchuria, reaching the Yalu River in a matter of one week.

At the Potsdam conference, Truman agreed that the Russian troops would occupy the northern part of Korea for the purpose of disarming the remaining Japanese troops, while the southern part would be controlled by the U.S. Army for the same purpose. The demarcation line, the thirty-eighth parallel, indeed indicated a temporary settlement to receive the official surrender from Japan in both northern and southern Korea. The division based on the thirty-eighth parallel line was to be removed after the general election to establish the central government of Korea.

The basic mistake of letting the Soviets into the northern part of Korea sealed the destiny of the unborn republic of independent Korea. When this was agreed upon, we are told, the U.S. president was ill and unable to insist that the whole Korean peninsula should be under the temporary control of one nation. Neither part, north or south, can survive without the other.

In December 1945, officials from the United States, Great Britain, and the Soviet Union met in Moscow to discuss the Korean problem and agreed to assure Korea her independence after a five-year trusteeship under the Soviet Union, Great Britain, China, and later the United States.

The first Soviet troops arrived in Pyongyang on September 15, 1945, with several fighter planes and bombers, followed by a mass of infantrymen with rugged T-34 tanks. The North Korean people were soon dismayed to find that the so-called peace-loving Soviet troops were a bunch of savages, raping women in broad daylight, looting, and killing people indiscriminately in the streets of Pyongyang. The hardcore Communists and left-wing politicians explained that these soldiers were ex-convicts from Siberian prison camps and did not represent the cream of the crop. The Soviets, however, began dismantling most of the industrial factories and shipping all the heavy machinery and equipment to Russia, beginning in October 1945. Many of the Soviet troops and commanders were diverted from the German battlegrounds to establish new military commands and naval ports in North Korea, and political officers were arriving weekly to round up landlords and rich civilians.

In early September, American soldiers of the Twenty-fourth Division, commanded by Lt. Gen. John R. Hodge, arrived at the port of Inchon and proceeded to the city of Seoul. Originally the Twenty-fourth Division was committed to invading the island of Kyushu during the month of August, but it was diverted to occupy South Korea following the Japanese surrender. The division found itself unexpectedly in charge of the southern half of the Korean peninsula, with little planning and without reckoning of the consequences, to fulfill its obligation under a trusteeship that had never been approved by the Korean people.

According to Gen. Matthew Ridgway, the United States made a major blunder almost at once, costing it the confidence and cooperation of the Korean people, by confirming the offices held by the despised Japanese administrative officials. Alarmed at the prompt outburst of indignation that followed this move, the United States then compounded the mistake by hastily phasing out the Japanese and filling their posts with well-meaning but wholly unqualified American civilians who had no knowledge of the language or understanding of the problems posed by a need to formulate banking and currency policies for a newborn republic. Failure to reach an overall agreement with the Soviet Union aggravated the crisis and left both Moscow and Washington accusing each other of devious activities directed by one against the other.

The Korean people seethed with unrest and began to turn violently against both sides, whom they suspected of preparing to renege once again on their oft-ruptured promise of independence. The proposed five-year trusteeship touched off riot after riot by the indignant Korean people, who were dead set against having such an arrangement.

The Soviet Union had no intention of honoring the agreement reached in Cairo and Potsdam to make Korea a free and independent nation. Instead they kept sending Communist leaders (Korean nationals, trained in Moscow) to organize a separate Communist government in North Korea. Gen. Mu-jong Kim, who participated in the Long March with Chinese Communist troops, was to head the military organization of the North Korean regime.

A mass demonstration in opposition to the proposed trusteeship was organized in the large border town of Shiniju, with thousands of high school students participating. Similar demonstrations followed elsewhere in North Korea.

The middle of December of 1945 was a sad period for the Korean people, when most of the demonstrating students were arrested by Soviet troops and their secret police. More than eighty senior high students went to prison and were later transferred to Siberian concentration camps, and approximately twenty students were killed in the streets.

The brutality demonstrated by the Soviet troops and the secret police drove many young students into the underground anti-Soviet movement throughout North Korea. A high-ranking official of the Ministry of Education came to our school and openly wept with the students, denouncing the trusteeship. But a week later he became a staunch supporter of the trusteeship, presumably under pressure of the Soviet administration in North Korea.

Despairing at last of winning Soviet cooperation in setting up the trusteeship, the United States turned the problem over to the United Nations, which prompted the Soviet Union to charge a betrayal of the original agreement. The United Nations moved to conduct free elections in both zones, but the Soviets refused to permit the UN Temporary Committee to enter the Soviet zone, north of the thirty-eighth parallel. They had earlier insisted that only those political parties might participate in the election, which had given full support to the Moscow agreement on trusteeship. This disqualified practically all the parties in the American zone, the southern part of Korea, where freedom of speech had allowed openly expressed dissatisfaction with any postponement of independence, trusteeship or not.

At noon on a cool autumn day in September 1945, a lone assassin gunned down J. H. Hyun, the head of the newly formed Nationalist Communist Party, on a Pyongyang street. Hyun was a scholar and educator, a graduate of Imperial University, in Seoul, who had spent fifteen years in a Japanese prison because of his socialistic and communistic activities. Following the Japanese surrender, when he was released from prison, he became the instigator of a new political party of the Communist and nationalistic doctrine and refused allegiance with Moscow. Huyn's assassin escaped and was received by the Soviet secret police in Moscow, we were told.

The Soviets then brought in a thirty-seven-year-old guerilla leader from Manchuria by the name of Sung Chu Kim and installed him as head of the Communist Party in October 1945. The Soviets must have felt that in order to gain popular support from the North Korean people, he should take the name of Gen. Il Sung Kim, a legendary leader of the Korean resistance against the Japanese regime. General Kim had, according to many historians, outsmarted the Japanese officials by sneaking into Manchuria and returning to a Taebaek mountain ridge to form his regiments to fight the Japanese. Sung Chu Kim thus changed his name to Gen. Il Sung Kim and later became premier. In January 1946, Premier Kim persuaded his former high school teacher, Rev. R. O. Kang, a Methodist minister, to accept the position of first secretary of the Labor Party, representing the Communist political organization. A grenade was thrown into Reverend Kang's house at 5:00 one morning in the middle of January, killing his three children. Massive and ruthless retaliation followed, purging many patriots, Christian leaders, and even a well-known Communist Party leader. Prof. D. B. Kim, a Korean-language scholar and friend of Chairman Mao for more than twenty years, did not escape the purge. Professor Kim and his followers from Yunan, China, established a unification Communist Party in Pyongyang before they were executed.

The first phase of land reform changed our family copper mine in Kangso Province to a people's copper mine. Approximately fifteen hundred acres of producing land were also confiscated and given to the peasants. Without the copper mine and the land, my parents were still well off, owning several office buildings, a large general store, and a medium-sized hotel, which occupied a whole block in Sonkyo-Ri, a suburb of Pyongyang, which was at that time a city of approximately one hundred thousand.

My mother managed the hotel. She was an entrepeneur and an exceptionally keen businesswoman who built a small fortune from nothing. As far back as I can remember, there were always several servants attending my three sisters and me. It was not necessary for me to lift a finger, as everything was prepared and cared for by the servants. My parents were generous, giving me 30 percent more than the usual allowance. My father always told me that I had to entertain my friends when they invited me to their homes for a meal. "You must repay their kindness with your own money," he said.

The political chaos in South Korea was even worse than that in the northern part. Syngman Rhee, ending his long exile in the United States, returned to Korea in September 1945 and settled in Ewha Mansion with his wife, Francesca, and their secretaries. Mrs. Rhee was a native of Austria whom Syngman Rhee had met in Europe years before, when he was pleading the cause of Korean independence. They were married in Vienna while he was attending a political conference there. Syngman Rhee was instrumental in establishing a new political party, called the Korean Democratic Party. Dr. Philip Jaisohn So, a physician from Philadelphia, accepted the position of consultant to the military governor of South Korea, Lt. Gen. John R. Hodge, and occupied an office in the Central Government Building in Seoul.

Kim Koo, head of the Korean government in exile in China, returned in Seoul in late 1945 and founded the Korean Independent Party. H. Y. Park, representing the leftist organization, became the leader of the Communist party called the Southern Labor Party. W. H. Ryo, who was assassinated two years later, became the head of the Korean Socialist Party.

All the leaders of the various political organizations and their members were opposed to the trusteeship agreement reached by the three statesmen representing the United States, Great Britain, and the Soviet Union. H. Y. Park, however, made a 180-degree turn to become a staunch supporter of the trusteeship regime, on instructions from Moscow. As usual, many promising young politicians in both wings were assassinated because of their potential threat to the older members of the political movement. It was rumored and whispered in the streets of Seoul that these assassinations were manipulated by Syngman Rhee, although there was no concrete evidence to support such a theory.

8
Escape from North Korea

It was December 7, 1945. All the students of the college were assembled to hear a Soviet political officer tell of the achievements of the Soviet people, the Soviet military complex, and Comrade Stalin in liberating the Korean people from oppression by the Japanese government. Through an interpreter the major spoke for more than an hour, emphasizing the struggle of the working class against the capitalists and the upper class. I was stunned to hear such a radical speech and saw the need to adjust my way of thinking in a Communist territory.

We were interviewed individually by the political officer. He tried to probe my attitude toward the Soviet government, Comrade Stalin, the meaning of democratic society, and the necessity of a forthcoming revolution by the working class. He was rather severe in denouncing Christianity, exploitation of the working and poor classes by the upper middle class, and landowners. He stressed the need for adaptation of the Soviet system in both governmental and agricultural structures.

He had a complete dossier on my family and me. He said that religion is like opium, as far as the Soviet government is concerned, and I should change my first name from a Christian name to another one. The interpreter added that I should take notes on the conversations of my fellow students in regard to their feelings toward the Soviet Union and the heroic Korean freedom fighters, just returned from Manchuria. The Soviets endeavored to set up a vast network of informants, watching one another and reporting to the political officer.

Most of the premedical students in my class were the offspring of upper-middle-class or high-class Koreans, possessing a significant amount of assets in either liquid form or real estate. None of us had previous experience for the new regime.

In order to enlarge the class from forty-five to eighty students, the college admitted a large number of unqualified students representing the working class, laborers, interpreters, and guerrilla fighters from Manchuria. They constituted the major structure of the communication network—a large spy system.

I confined myself to my two best friends since high school days, B. J. Park and C. H. Choi. We students were sent out in groups to persuade the peasants to increase their rice production and crops for the North Korean regime and the Soviet Union. Each group was dispatched to the northern area for a week to stay with peasant families, educate them, and form close-knit Communist cells.

A group of eleven students was arrested upon their return to Pyongyang and detained in prison for five days, based on the suspicion that some of them were counterrevolutionary, which was subsequently proven to be false. This, however, drove many students to join underground movements to print anti-Soviet leaflets for distribution among the people.

In North Korea, the stronghold of the Presbyterian denomination, many church gatherings were held every week as the people sought God's guidance for their future. Thousands upon thousands of Christians, singing and praying, filled all the churches in North Korea for the Palm Sunday service. Alerted because of a possible conspiracy among the Christians, Soviet troops and North Korean secret police surrounded the central and largest Presbyterian church in Pyongyang to disperse the thousands of people. Despite threats and possible imprisonment, the congregation stood firm, and there were clashes between them and the secret police. Many Christians were imprisoned, but there were no casualties.

I was unaware of the fact that we were continually followed by disguised secret police for approximately two weeks. On March 14, B. J. Park and C. H. Choi felt that we should move the printing equipment from the subbasement of my home to B.J.'s house, not knowing that each of us was under surveillance by the secret police. At 3:00 on the morning of March 15, they raided B.J.'s house, confiscating all the printing materials and papers from his basement. Both B.J. and C.H. were arrested and herded to the detention center.

From up the hill to the street of B.J.'s home came the rising whine of an engine as the driver of a gray canvas-covered Soviet truck downshifted on the steep grade. Brakes squealed and the truck slowed to a halt. Troops spilled from the rear of the truck in a clatter of boots and weapons. To the accompaniment of whistles and shouted orders, soldiers were fanning out, blocking off the street. Weapons were ready and soldiers ran toward the front gate of B.J.'s house. It was a raid routinely practiced by the Soviet secret police force to round up suspected counterrevolutionaries and political dissidents. These raids were always held at 3:00 A.M.

Both B. J. Park and C. H. Choi were asleep and dreaming. They didn't hear the brief squeal of brakes of the Soviet trucks. Had they heard, the sound might have carried a subconscious warning, for only the Soviet troops and North Korean secret police forces drove cars in the streets on Pyongyang, North Korea. A Soviet captain, the commander of the raid party, was a big man with short, bristly hair. He struck both boys hard in their faces. Their eyes flew open, their cheeks flaring red from the blow. A husky soldier stepped forward and drove a rifle butt into B.J.'s stomach, doubling him over. Two other soldiers drove their fists and elbows into C. H. Choi's body. C.H. could hear himself gagging and gasping with shock and pain. B.J.'s parents were also pushed back by rifle butts as their younger children started screaming. The soldiers dragged the boys from the house to their truck, pulling them to their feet. C.H. cried out in agony as a dagger of pain stabbed the right side of his chest. His ribs were broken and he sank to his knees. Dizziness rolled over him in waves. B.J.'s mother screamed at the top of her lungs, begging the Soviets take her instead of the boys.

The soldiers confiscated the printing materials and more than two hundred anti-Soviet leaflets yet to be circulated. Printed in large block letters, slogans read: "Pro-Soviets go to Russia, pro-Americans leave for the USA. Only patriots remain in Korea."

The shrill ringing of the telephone on the nightstand shattered the silence in my home at 5:00 A.M.

"Get your boy out of the house now!" the shouting voice of B.J.'s father rang out, confusing my parents.

"What are you talking about?" asked my mother, trying to control her emotion.

"My son B.J. and his friend C. H. Choi were arrested an hour ago and taken away by Soviets. You had better hide your son before they can make connections."

"What is going on, Joe?" inquired my badly shaken father.

When I briefly explained to my parents what was going on, my mother started weeping.

"Why did you get yourself involved in this futile movement?" my ashen-faced father asked as he tried to control my hysterical mother. He started cracking his knuckles, a nervous habit of his.

"It's a little too late to worry about that. What are we gong to do now?" said my mother.

"We must go to Reverend Park to seek his help. Start packing, Joe."

"I will go with you to our church," my mother said as she went to get dressed.

I went to my room and retrieved my winter clothes, overcoat, and several books in a bag. Only thirty minutes had passed since B.J.'s father had called, but to me it seemed much longer. I pounded down the tight stairs to the ground floor, missing a step in the semidarkness of the stairwell and nearly falling. I took a deep breath and opened the front door, half-expecting to come face to face with the Soviets.

A cold trickle of sweat ran down over my ribs as I stepped out onto the sidewalk, but the street was deserted. I went down on one knee and tightened a shoelace, holding my mother's hand. As rapidly as we could, we walked down to the town's square and reached our Presbyterian church in twenty minutes.

Rev. Gene Park was conducting the morning prayer session, with about ten people attending. My mother and I silently joined the prayer. After the initial shock, Reverend Park took me to the attic of the church and found a place for me to hide.

"I will send up your meals and some books to read. But you must keep quiet." With that remark. Reverend Park returned to his manse.

The next evening, while Mrs. Park was preparing a pot of jasmine tea at Reverend Park's residence, my parents and older sister listened attentively to our minister.

"North Korea, under the tight control of the Soviet Union, is no longer safe for Joe to continue his education. We must get him settled in Seoul, South Korea, as soon as possible and before those two boys talk."

"Reverend Park, they would never betray me; I know they wouldn't," I insisted.

Ignoring my remark, Reverend Park continued. "I understand how you feel, Joe. But everyone breaks at some point. The problem is figuring out how to get you across the thirty-eighth parallel to reach Seoul safely. The border is guarded by Soviets day and night."

My parents started blaming me for having been involved in such a dangerous and reckless movement run by a bunch of hot-headed kids.

The minister intervened, "It's too late to accuse Joe now. Let us try to solve our problems."

"My friend Kyonja Kim works at the refugee center in the downtown office receiving several hundreds of Manchurian refugees and repatriating them to South Korea and Japan. Why don't I ask her to include my brother?" my elder sister suggested.

"Well, that is an excellent idea, Aida, if you can persuade your friend to provide a paper certifying that your brother is one of them going back to Pusan." Reverend Park's eyebrow's rose.

"Joe is our only male heir for this family. I will have to go with him!" insisted my father.

My mother broke the silence, saying, "The long-term absence of the head of the household would invite unnecessary inquiries from the neighbors and may arouse the suspicion among Communist informers. I will take Joe to Seoul, where I may locate a distant cousin."

Ten days later my sister was able to obtain two false papers certifying me and my mother were refugees from Manchuria trying to resettle in their hometown: Pusan, South Korea. Miss K. Kim, who issued two forged papers, insisted that she would go with us to Seoul to unite with her younger sister. She was patiently waiting an opportune time to cross the thirty-eighth parallel line border.

My mother and I had come through an underground passage from the Pyongyang railway station to an arcade, and as we ascended the stairs to the upper level, we heard the crowd noise spilling from the hall above us. At the top of the stairs we stopped, momentarily taken aback by the milling mass of civilians and Soviet soldiers thronging the station's concourse.

"What's happening?" my mother gasped.

"They must be loading the troop trains," I said grimly.

"Where are they sending so many soldiers? They must be intending to reinforce the border patrols," my mother said tensely.

I felt a hard knot in my stomach when I saw two security control gates leading to the station hall adjacent to the boarding platforms.

North Korean security police at the gates were holding back the civilians to make way for the troops being marched out to the platform area, and it was impossible to estimate how long it would take us to reach our train.

"We will miss our train," I said tightly.

"The train will probably be delayed," my mother said quickly.

The confusion in the station did not deter the security police from carefully checking the papers and luggage of each passenger passing through the railway control.

I was disguised as a refugee from Manchuria with my face unshaven for ten days and torn, dirty clothing, and my mother wearing a cheap blouse and an unclean skirt, had been waiting for forty-five minutes in one of the long, ragged lines. We were close enough to observe the procedure.

37

Because of the crush of people, a temporary wooden barricade surrounded the central area. Civilians were admitted at intervals in groups of thirty. Normally, Soviets and Koreans worked together in pairs at security checkpoints, but now the security police on duty were being aided by additional Soviet military police. Hovering close behind the security police were men in civillian clothes with restless, alert eyes.

My mother said something to me, but I didn't hear clearly.

The Soviet military police in front of the barricade were pushing back the crowd and removing a section of the barricade to allow a large Soviet contingent through. As the last of the Soviet soldiers marched through the opening in the barricade, the crowd of civilians pushed forward restlessly. Arguments and some angry shoving broke out as tempers flared. Fatigue, frustration, and the heat generated by the press of bodies were repugnant.

"I will go through first," I said. "If I am not stopped or caught, we will know that my friends have not given them my description."

"No, Joe, we will go together," insisted my mother.

The security guards were preparing to admit a fresh batch of civilians to the platform, and we were jostled from behind as more people pressed forward. I reached out to take my mother's arms and discovered she was no longer at my side. In the momentary confusion she had passed through the security gates and stood waiting for me to join her. While the Korean secret police guard took an additional three minutes scrutinizing my paper, my mother was carried away by human waves to the platform. When the police waved me through, my mother was nowhere to be found. I looked around to spot my mother, oblivious to the people moving past me.

"Joe, Joe, I am here; please hop in."

I raised my head to see the waving hands of my mother through a window of the second passenger car. At least seventy passengers were blocking both doors, trying to get aboard. In desperation I jumped into the nearest passenger car just before the train moved out, only to find the car full of Soviet soldiers. They started shouting at me to move on to forward sections with hand signs to get out. One Soviet officer brusquely waved me off. Fifteen minutes later, I finally joined my mother at passenger car no. 2.

The train left the Pyongyang railway station about two o'clock in the afternoon, headed for the southern port of Haeju, just above the thirty-eighth parallel, a journey of no return toward South Korea and the city of Seoul. About two hundred Japanese refugees from Manchuria, many merchants going south, several young students, presumably escaping from the Soviets, and approximately a hundred soldiers heading for the border patrol filled the twelve passenger cars being pulled by an old steam locomotive. The train moved slowly until it stopped to take on water at the Sariwon station. This was indeed checkpoint 1 for the Soviets and North Korean secret police patrols to inspect papers. When one pair boarded the train from the front and another from the rear, my muscles began to tense, first in my stomach and then in my legs. A chill passed down my spine.

We were standing in the aisle, since there was no place to sit. The first police patrol come through, staring at me for thirty seconds and passing without a word. My mouth went dry and sweat soaked my armpits. As the patrol came near, I became terrified, shaking uncontrollably. My mother was equally frightened by their threatening shouts and the rattling of rifles. Murmuring prayers as a last resort, we both felt that this was the end of the line.

The patrol discovered a young high school student six persons before us escaping from the Soviets with a forged paper. He was handcuffed and immediately removed from the train. I will never forget the determined look of the student and the triumphant air of the two policemen as they marched him to the platform of the Sariwon railway station.

The wind was picking up, and gusts of cool, moisture-laden air swept across the platform. I tightened the waist belt of my jacket. After about twenty minutes, the train started off before the patrol returned to continue their miserable job. My mother breathed an inaudible sigh of relief. The old steam engine, pulling its twelve passenger cars, slowly climbed the steep hill that was covered with blossoming cherry trees and wildflowers. I smiled an immense relief.

"Hello, Joe, traveling south, are you?" The voice was barely above a whisper.

I turned around in astonishment to face a bearded man in his fifties with a thin smile. I felt sweat beading my forehead and running down over my ribs beneath my loose cotton shirt. *Oh, my God, my cover is finally blown. Now I am dead meat*, I told myself.

The man got up and approched my mother. He led her to his vacated set and motioned for her to sit down. "I am a friend, Joe," he said in a low voice. I suddenly felt my knees buckling. "I know your father well, Joe. I am also escaping from the Soviets. I have been a history professor at Sun-Sil University in Pyongyang. My name is Sam Hong."

"I have heard about you from my father, Professor Hong. Why are the Soviets after you?" I whispered back.

39

"I was the secretary of Mr. J. H. Hyun until he was assassinated last September. I was forced to go underground then."

I vividly remembered the assassination. At noon on a cool autumn day in September of 1945, a lone assassin gunned down J. H. Hyun, the head of the newly formed Nationalist Communist Party, on a Pyongyang street.

"You see, Joe, Soviets were determined to eradicate the Korean Nationalistic Communist organization by arresting all the members. Most of them were already purged by the Soviets. A few of them remained underground."

I sighed dejectedly, then asked, "Professor Hong, whatever happened to your brother, General Hong?"

"Well, Joe, when Japan colonized the Korean kingdom in 1910, they transferred all the cadets of the Korean Royal Military Acadamy to the Japanese military institution."

I nodded as Professor Hong continued. "My brother, with his characteristic enthusiasm and perseverance, was made lieutenant general of the Japanese army."

"Yes, I know," I acknowledged. "He was the only one who held a high-ranking position."

"But the Japanese were such cunning and sneaky bastards. They made sure that my brother was always bypassed whenever top-secret documents were circulated. His rank had no privilage. When he was ordered to become the commandant of the prisoner-of-war camp in Manila, Philippines, in December of 1944, he asked me what he should do. His close friends and I advised him to join the Korean army in Chunking, China.

"But he was afraid for his family. He knew the Japanese needed a scapegoat when they lost the war for mistreating Allied prisoners, Americans, Australian, and British soldiers," the professor continued.

"Why didn't he denounce his position then?" I was curious.

"Well, his defense lawyers provided by American troops suggested that he should tell them he was a puppet manipulated by the Japanese army, but he declined. He told the court that he was responsible for the prisoners who died from starvation and disease. He was hanged in January of 1946." Professor Hong looked the other way with bitterness.

I could not suppress a flash of fury. The muscles in my face went taunt as I gazed pensively over the passing hills.

The train finally arrived at Haeju around eight o'clock in the evening. There refugees were met by a guide who was a true Christian gentleman. Addressing the crowd of three hundred people, he said,

"We have prepared some food and drink for you before you start walking toward the thirty-eighth parallel around ten o'clock this evening. By the time you reach the border, it will be almost midnight, and the Soviet guards will be sleeping after drinking much vodka and whiskey. You will have approximately one hour to cross the border, and with God's help you will be successful. When you reach your final destination, think about the suffering that our Lord endured just before he was crucified. Try to live with his love and the truth of the Bible." He wished us good luck and gave a broad smile. He was one of two decent human beings we met on our escape from North Korea.

After the light supper of salty chicken soup and rice, we followed the guide who had been hired by the group. Around midnight my stomach growled for food, but it was the fierce, suffocating thirst that tortured me most. I cursed myself for not having had the wits in the last moments before starting out walking to clip a canteen on my belt. The crescent moon gave us enough light to see the silhouettes of several ox carts carrying many pieces of luggage.

About two hours later the guide stopped and gestured for the group to keep absolute silence, as we were about to cross the thirty-eighth parallel. Suddenly a big black dog appeared from a housing area on the hill and began barking loudly. A man stepped out to take the dog inside, waving at us to hurry.

We had almost crossed the border when my mother pulled my arm and said, "I have stomach cramps. I must rest." She sat down on the grassy road.

I whispered in the guide's ear, telling him of my mother's sudden pain and suggesting that they go ahead without us.

The guide and Professor Hong pointed to a low hill on the left. "About a mile farther down from that hill is an American army observation post. If you make that, you will be safe. Good luck!" The guide said and off they went with the remaining refugees.

The dog's barking must have aroused some of the Soviet soldiers, as one of them struck out in our direction, carrying his machine gun. I took my mother and moved quickly into the bushes, and we held our breath. The soldier was drunk. Veering off to the left and kicking at the wet grass, he looked around and up the hill. A call came from the guardhouse, apparently telling him to return. I heard a dry rustle and saw a match popping into flame. The dead match fell to the ground, and the husky soldier inhaled heavily and went on. I stared at the match, my eyes filling with tears.

We finally reached the observation post around 5:00 A.M. and were met by a tall, thin American soldier—the first American I had ever seen. He asked us what we were carrying, and I explained with gestures that we were on our way to Seoul for a new life. He was very gentle and kind and gave me a cup of hot coffee.

Directing me to the road that would take us to Chongdan, The American soldier said, "From there you can catch an afternoon train to Kaesong. Good luck to you!"

As we slowly approached Chongdan, the rising sun suddenly splashed a burst of gold against the sandy soil of the low hill with gnarled trees clinging to its side. I inhaled the fresh morning air deeply with a tremendous feeling of joy and hope.

At the Kaesong railroad station we cheered each other for being on the verge of breaking out of North Korea. We finally reached the city of Seoul at dusk on April 17.

In 1948, I accidentally met an older sister of B. J. Park, Yong Hee, who successfully escaped from North Korea with her two sons and settled in Seoul. She told me that C. H. Choi died soon after they arrived in Siberia. B.J., with an inborn toughness, was able to survive and subsequently transferred to a camp in Tashkent. There he tried to escape to Afghanistan on foot but was executed by an NKVD (later to become the KGB) firing squad. He was betrayed by a woman informer working in the kitchen. B.J. was twenty years old. As I tried to avoid Yong Hee's sorrowful glance I somehow felt guilty of deserting two of my best friends in the hands of brutal Soviet soldiers.

The weather in Seoul was a blessing. Mid-May was the height of the South Korean spring. The mountains were bursting with color. Azaleas and rhododendrons tumbled down the stony slopes, and masses of iris displayed their cobalt flags. The air was soft with the fragrance of oleanders and roses.

Our hostess, a distant cousin of my father, was a widow who took advantage of our situation. Upon arrival, at her request, we gave her all our money to place in a safety-deposit box. She told me that her relative Dr. Choi, who was the dean of Severance Medical College, would be in a position to help me continue my medical education. But it was the middle of the semester, and he could not arrange any transfers at that time.

Since the money was gone, according to our hostess, I found myself in the streets of Seoul, a city of six hundred thousand, seeking employment. It was difficult for me to adjust to such an abrupt change in lifestyle, descending so rapidly from the high cloud of opulence to the real world of poverty and hunger.

When Mother crossed the thirty-eighth parallel in the middle of June, returning to Pyongyang, the North Korean border patrol took her for questioning at their barracks, two miles north of the border. During the interrogation by a young lieutenant, it became apparent that he had been a high school classmate of mine, who had lived in our district of Pyongyang. Lieutenant Ahn treated my mother with the utmost courtesy and arranged transportation for her to Pyongyang.

Meanwhile, Premier Kim of North Korea solidified his position, purging most of his opponents from northern China and Manchuria who once led troops against the Japanese army. Premier Kim's propaganda continued to advocate North Korea as a paradise for workers and intellectuals.

When Gen. John Hodge's assistant took the Soviet commander to the Kaesong railroad station to view the massive exodus of intellectuals, scholars, and businessmen fleeing from oppressive North Korea, the Soviet shook his head and said he could not understand. Approximately 2 million refugees poured into South Korea from 1945 through 1949.

My mother returned to Seoul in the latter part of September with more capital to open a small business to sustain my education and living. She rented a store, thirty by twenty-five feet, converted it into a bakery, and hired a baker who had never baked anything in his life. He immediately built a huge dough box, eight feet long, four feet wide, and four feet deep. Sacks of flour were poured into the box and mixed with water and yeast. I was so excited that night, having high hopes for a successful bakery business that would finance my schooling.

Early the next morning, with great anticipation, the baker, Mother, and I opened the dough box. We were astonished to find that the dough had not risen. Instead, it had sunk one centimeter below the pencil mark that was left the evening before. Panic swept over Mother and the baker; nevertheless, he attempted to made two hundred rolls. But all of them were returned by the restaurant owner, with a nasty note saying that they were the heaviest and hardest rolls he had ever tasted.

Around two o'clock in the afternoon the disaster became obvious. In despair my mother went to the next-door neighbor, borrowed a cart, and asked me to take the two hundred rolls to the amusement park and sell them.

The park, called Chang Kyon Won, had been converted from the king's courtyard to a public park years before and was located across the street from Seoul University Hospital. I pushed the cart, loaded with the rolls in a wooden box, for two and one-half miles and finally arrived at the park around four o'clock in the afternoon. I was fortunate enough to find a small spot among the vendors of vegetables, fruit, and cotton candy. At closing time hundreds of people streamed out of the park, passing by the lemonade and vegetable stands.

A vendor told me that I had to shout something like, "Two for ten cents! Two for ten cents!" I tried but found my vocal cords not functioning. At any rate, I sold about a hundred rolls and then began thinking. What if some of the people would return for their money after they tried to eat those hard rolls? I ran home, pushing the cart, with more than a hundred rolls left.

The bakery business was a complete disaster, wiping out our meager remaining funds. My mother, a determined, strong-willed woman, decided to return again to Pyongyang to raise more money. She left from the Seoul railway station a week later. Just before the train departed, she said to me, "Son, the lease of the store runs out in December. You must stay and make the best of it." As I watched my mother walk away, a chill passed down my spine, and I felt a sudden urge to run after her.

In the middle of November it was cold during the night. I tried to sleep on the dough box, huddled under a thin gray U.S. Navy blanket. The wind sweeping through the hastily installed doors of the store was merciless. I shivered all night long, unable to sleep a wink. I thought about my boyhood in Pyongyang—the happiest time of my life. Riding my bicycle, with a fishing pole in my left hand, I often went to the riverbank and spent a considerable amount of time there fishing and singing. Wrapped in my thin blanket, I cursed the Soviets and the Communists from Manchuria and China for driving me into such misery and hardship. At dawn my joints were stiff and half-frozen. I was barely able to get up and prepare my breakfast of chicken noodle soup.

The South Korean school system made a radical departure from the customary April to March semester system. All grade schools, high schools, and colleges and universities traditionally admitted their students during the month of March. Classes began in the first part of April and continued through the end of March of the following year. With the American system, all the classes started in September and were completed in early June of the next year. Consequently, I had to wait four months before resuming my studies in medicine. After a vigorous written examination, followed by a penetrating oral interview and tests, I was finally accepted by Seoul University School of Medicine for the class of 1946, which was to begin in September.

The political chaos apparently created fertile soil for the growth of Communism and anarchism throughout South Korea. The campuses of Seoul University School of Medicine and many other colleges were full of Communist agitators and socialist students. The creation of Seoul National University, absorbing many small colleges, was indeed the most effective and advanced decision made by the military government. The loss of identity of the small colleges was, however, used as a political tool by the Communist agents and sympathizers to launch a general strike against the regime of the U.S. military government. The agitators and radical members of the Communist and socialist parties distributed leaflets among the neutral students, appealing to their indignation at losing the identity and traditional values of each college.

School registration began in the early part of September. When I arrived at the front gate of the administration building, there were twenty-five to thirty agitators. I pushed through the human barricade, with name-calling, shouting, and catcalls filling the air. I shouted back, "If you love Communism, why don't you go to North Korea and taste some of the real Communist doctrine and methods?" I was appalled to see the excessive degree of freedom enjoyed by the left-wing political parties and students, causing disruption after disruption in the operation of schools and government organizations.

Thirty-eight students in all forced their way to the hall to register. When I finished registering as a freshman in the college of medicine for the semester that would begin in September, I found four other fellows who had followed me through the barricade of agitators. We introduced ourselves and headed for a restaurant for supper. Charles Kim was from Nampo, North Korea, C. W. Lee, age thirty-two, had been a grade school teacher before medical school; he was from Wonsan, North Korea. B. L. Roh came from Hungnam, North Korea, and T. J. Park's home was in Pohang, South Korea. We were a group of poor students, except for T. J. Park, whose parents ran a textile mill.

On the first day of school only five students came to the physiology lecture, which was promptly canceled because of lack of attendance. Thereafter all classes were canceled; thus the general strike began in September 1946. Frustrated by the continual agitation and strike, I approached Professor Yun, chairman of the first pathology department, in the study of experimental pathology, and asked him to create a small corner where I could study and work with the assistant residents for the duration of the strike. He was kind enough to instruct his residents to take me under their wing.

9
Introduction to Medical Research

By the middle of October 1946, the general strike by students and professors finally ended. Several radical students and a few left-wing professors were expelled.

The chief resident in pathology, Dr. H. S. Han, asked me to help him in his research dealing with the injection of treated human sera in rabbits in order to study the controlling mechanism of temperature regulation. Fascinated with the opportunity to participate in experimental medical research with Dr. Han, I performed the procedures outlined by him on a seven-day-a-week basis. After a full day's lectures and laboratory exercise, I would rush back to the Department of Pathology to carry out my assignment.

Early in 1946 the Hung Han Foundation was created by a successful businessman and entrepreneur, Hung Shik Park. Mr. Park had very little formal education, but he built a vast fortune and a gigantic corporation throughout Korea. His strong desire was to help promising young students at the university level, and he appropriated sufficient funds for medical research projects.

An administrative assistant to the dean of the medical school, C. Paik, sought me out in the hallway during class intermission. He wondered why I had not filled out the application form for the scholarship offered by the Hung Han Foundation. I was not aware of the notice of this scholarship. Mr. Paik advised me to make application for the series of written and oral examinations by the board members. He then asked me if I was a Christian, because of my first name, and informed me that he was a Presbyterian minister's son from North Korea. I felt keenly Mr. Paik's willingness to help and his friendship and immediately applied for the scholarship. Six weeks later the foundation notified me that I would receive a monthly stipend of 3,000 won (equivalent to $50 a month), beginning in January 1947.

I was also assigned to two assistant residents of the Department of Pathology, Drs. S. J. Hong and K. S. Lee, who taught me routine histology technique, how to make a thin section from a tissue specimen, preparation of hematoxylin and eosin solutions, and description of postmortem examinations. Dr. Hong was a warm, kind person with a burning desire to restore full pathology at Taegu University School of Medicine.

There were many cases of cirrhosis of the liver and hepatoma (liver cell cancer), comprising about 30 percent of the autopsy cases, which ranged from 100 to 160 per year. I was curious to know why there was such a high incidence of cirrhosis, or hepatoma, and approached Prof. J. K. Lee, who was head of the second pathology department, dealing with morphologic studies of the cells. He gave me several textbooks to study in preparation for presenting a seminar on liver disease.

On March 22, 1947, my father and a friend arrived at Inchon Harbor with a shipload of lumber and bamboo from North Korea, representing a large investment. The cargo was unloaded and sold to wholesale merchants, bringing a significant profit. Sufficient funds were deposited in the bank account for me to continue my medical education.

I was able to pursue my study of cirrhosis of the liver under Professor Lee's direction. His opinion was that highly spicy food may cause cirrhotic changes in the liver. He advised me to obtain six rabbits for long-term feeding of black pepper mixed with ordinary rabbit food or injecting a watery form of pepper into the stomach.

The rabbits would not eat their food simply because it was too hot. We soon found that to introduce a significant amount of genuine hot pepper, we had to use a catheter to inject 20 cc. of watery pepper directly into the stomach. One rabbit died of perforated gastric ulcer, and four survived for six months. One of four rabbits showed changes of early cirrhosis, with a massive necrosis (cell death) of the liver and a considerable degree of fibrosis surrounding the necrotic zones.

I submitted gross photographs illustrating early cirrhosis of the liver to the Hung Han Foundation in hopes of receiving a sizable research grant. Appearing in the office of Dr. Myron Lee, a Yale University graduate who was secretary to the military governor, I emphasized the importance of the project and the need for a research grant.

Dr. Lee studied the photographs for a few minutes, then shook his head, saying that as a layperson he would not be able to evaluate the changes of the liver or the importance of research. But he submitted the photographs and several slides of the rabbit's liver to staff members of Severance Medical School for their opinion and evaluation.

I made four trips to Dr. Lee's office during the following two months. He suggested that I make a written request for the research grant. This was in December 1947. Obsessed with my research in liver cirrhosis and cancer, I spent most of my meager funds on acquiring more animals and histology slides. Later Dr. Lee's secretary informed me that Dr. Lee was impressed with my enthusiastic approach and persistent drive for research, but he said that I had to do something to repair my torn overcoat.

In March 1948, Professor Yun, dean of the graduate school of Seoul National University, returned from a trip to Cornell University Medical School, in New York. He brought with him a bottle of a carcinogenic hydrocarbon, 20-methylcholantrene, and several cages containing thirty C3H, CBA, and C57 mice, donated by Jackson Memorial Laboratory, of Bar Harbor, Maine.

I immediately approached Professor Yun about sponsoring several research projects, including one of cirrhosis of the liver, and discussed with him the possibility of receiving a grant from Hung Han Foundation through Dr. Myron Lee, who later became the Korean ambassador to Great Britain.

On my fifth visit to Dr. Lee's office, I handed a typewritten research grant application to his secretary, who promised that they would discuss the application at their next board meeting, in May 1948.

For my experimental production of liver cancer in rats and mice, I began reading about the work of Dr. Harold J. Stewart. It was the first time I had come across the name of Dr. Stewart, who had produced many excellent articles in the field of cancer research. Dr. Stewart embedded cotton swabs soaked with 20-methylcholantrene into the wall of the stomach of mice and rats and was able to produce an adenocarcinoma of the stomach, which I believe was the first most significant piece of work in the field of cancer research.

What was happening in Pyongyang, North Korea, during this time? Upon his return to Pyongyang, my father was summoned to appear before the People's Committee to explain his trip to South Korea. He informed them that his son needed funds to continue his medical education. To his surprise, he was well received. In December 1947, however, he was served notice from the People's Committee requesting his written application to dispose of his properties and real-estate holdings. All the rental properties and the hotel building were confiscated by the People's Building Committee in March 1948 and assigned to working-class people for occupancy.

48

It soon became obvious that my family members would not be able to survive under such a regime, so they quietly began packing to come to South Korea. My parents and my two younger sisters left home, one by one, with a permit to visit my older sister in a small town thirty-five miles south of Pyongyang. They each carried only two suitcases, to avoid the suspicion of the secret police. Then they diverted to Haeju, hired a boat to take them to Inchon, and finally reached Seoul in the latter part of June. With the help of my mother's friend, we were able to rent a small house in a suburb of Seoul.

In July of 1948, Mr. Paik again called me to his office and asked me to apply for a tuition scholarship reserved for the two top students of each class. I was deeply grateful for his assistance. The scholarship enabled me to lend money to Charles Kim, who was cut off completely from his hometown in North Korea, and it was an enormous help to him.

To support my two younger sisters in their high school education, I decided to seek additional employment through the help of a friend of mine, T. S. Kim, who had been ahead of me in high school. The family of a new textile tycoon, Y. H. Park, interviewed me for the position of private tutor for their son. For teaching this high school student every evening I received enough money to pay for my two sisters' education.

During the annual meeting of the Korean Medical Association's scientific sessions in October 1949, I presented a short article titled "Cirrhotic Changes Induced by Long-Term Pepper Feeding." The senior members of the hospital staff and the professors bombarded me with questions. I was able to get through those merciless questions and comments purely because of my being a senior medical student instead of a more experienced scientist.

On November 1, 1949, I learned that the research grant application had been approved by the Hung Han Foundation for the sum of 50,000 won (equivalent to $1,700). Professor Yun received a check for the purchase of a sufficient number of mice for the experimental cancer research.

When I received my first payment for tutoring, my close-knit group of friends insisted that I treat them. That evening we wined and dined at the best restaurant in Seoul, then headed for a theater to see the movie *Suspicion*, directed by Alfred Hitchcock. I blew 5,000 won that evening but remembered only these phrases from the movie: "trial of Richard Palmer" and "arsenic poisoning." The film was a classic, starring Cary Grant and Joan Fontaine, but except for those few words, I was unable to understand their dialogue.

Mr. Park's foundation assured me that there would be future regular funding as long as the cancer research was making some progress. This required more attention and continued effort on my part, and it was impossible for me to maintain my tutoring job. I asked Charles Kim to join me in the department as a student assistant and share the responsibilities of the research. He obtained permission from Professor Yun.

Following the last lectures of each day in medical school, we rushed back to the Pathology Department to measure the tumor size in the mice and to devise new research plans. We stayed until 8:00 P.M. Every Wednesday evening, after our research work, we strolled down the shopping street, called Myongdong, for window-shopping or a cup of tea. Under the full moon we walked slowly past the men's clothing shops, discussing our future plans and making frequent stops to examine the fancy suits and white shirts, although we were unable to purchase anything. Neither Charles nor I paid much attention to the way we dressed, but we would not miss any good movies if we could possibly afford to buy tickets.

During the latter part of 1949 the chief pathology resident, Dr. Han, suddenly dropped out of sight for several weeks. We were told later that he was detained by the police for his subversive Communist activities. Three weeks later an assistant professor, Dr. W. K. Park, disappeared; he later surfaced in Pyongyang, in February of 1950, as a professor of pathology at Kim Il Sung University. The well-organized Communist political network in South Korea made a promise and moved him and his family, with their household goods, to Pyongyang by truck.

Two months later another assistant professor, Dr. C. S. Chung, was dismissed from his position because of his indiscreet speeches praising the achievement of the North Korean Communist government. Dr. Chung was a coward, giving lip service to the leftist group but afraid to take any action for them against the South Korean government. He later became head of the pathology department in Taegu.

The Department of Pathology was falling apart because of unrest and political turmoil involving the senior staff members, creating a very unfavorable atmosphere for research or investigative work. But these conditions never deterred us in our determination to continue the research that we had launched sixteen months previously. There was no slowing us down in the field of cancer research, perhaps because we were both poor and could not afford to waste our time in completing our medical education or research.

During the month of February 1950, I was summoned to the office of the department chairman. He told me to prepare four abstracts of cancer research papers to be submitted to the Fourth International Cancer Congress, which would be held in Paris July 18–22, 1950. He then left for a cocktail party given by political analysts and newspaper reporters at Mijang Lounge, in the middle of Seoul.

Neither Charles nor I had any experience in writing an English abstract of cancer research papers. We needed help from the senior members of the staff, and there was no one available. Using several English dictionaries and other books, we hastily summarized our results and tabulated them to make a draft.

Two weeks later the department chairman's secretary told me where to find the professor to show him the drafts. He was at Mijang Lounge, half-drunk, chatting with politicians in a smoke-filled room. After handing him the drafts of the abstracts, I turned and left the scene in disgust.

I had a sudden urge to attend the cancer congress in Paris and present the papers myself. Charles agreed with the idea, because we had done all the research work from the beginning. Professor Nam, chairman of the Physiology Department, agreed with Charles that I had made a tremendous effort to complete several abstracts on cancer research and that I should attend the meeting. I became obsessed with the idea of going to Paris, hoping to meet the famous cancer researchers of the world, including Dr. Stewart of the National Cancer Institute (NCI), and to learn their methods and the results of various phases of cancer research.

To seek funds for my travel expense from Seoul to Paris, I paid a visit to Dr. M. M. Lee, who was secretary of the commission established by the United Nations for the election of the Korean government. He called Dr. Y. S. Koo, minister of health of the Republic of Korea. Dr. Koo, according to Dr. Lee, was a North Korean orphan who had been brought to the States by Methodist missionaries and sent to Emory University Medical School. On receiving an M.D. degree, he took residency training in pediatrics in Baltimore, Maryland. Then he returned to Seoul to accept a cabinet post as head of the Department of Health.

After listening to my explanation, the story of my background, and my analysis of the status of my cancer research, Dr. Koo turned from the window and nodded, indicating that he understood. When I tried to explain how difficult it was for us to obtain sufficient funds to carry on our cancer research, he interrupted me, saying that my case was nothing compared with that of two Franciscan nuns sent to North

Korea to conduct a medical mission in Sungho Ri, thirty miles west of Pyongyang.

"Young man," Dr. Koo said, "these two nuns, who received their M.D. degrees from Women's Medical College of Philadelphia, were determined to establish a medical clinic as their mission, against the unfriendly Japanese government and the officials who did their best to keep them away from the ordinary Korean people. The Japanese Health Department officials then insisted that the nuns take written examinations in basic science and clinical medicine in Japanese, which neither was able to understand or write. The two nuns went to language school for six years to learn sufficient Japanese to pass the written examinations in basic science and eleven subjects of clinical medicine. They finally obtained their medical licenses eight years after their arrival."

Dr. Koo promised that he would study my situation and talk with me at a later date. I was deeply impressed with the story of those nuns who undertook such a seemingly impossible task as overcoming the barriers built by the Japanese officials. I know nothing about the fate of those two brave women following the Korean War, but I shall never forget the story of their determination, dedication, and perseverance.

On the last day of final examinations my friends and I decided to celebrate at a restaurant. We pooled our resources for a dinner party and a movie. During the celebration we discussed plans for our future after medical school. C. W. Lee, on the recommendation of his uncle, a professional soldier and division commander, had decided to enter the army Medical Corps. B. L. Roh had applied for a residency in surgery at the University Hospital. Charles Kim and I would stay on as residents in pathology following graduation in May. The newest member of our group, H. C. Kim, from Seoul had decided to take a residency in obstetrics and gynecology. T. J. Park was to be married to his high school sweetheart during the early part of June. They planned to spend a month in Masan, a famous resort area known for its hot springs; then he would begin an internal medicine residency.

On the morning of April 10, Charles told me to go immediately to the department chairman's office. When I arrived, the professor said that I should take a cab and report to Rev. J. B. Koh, secretary to Pres. and Mrs. Syngman Rhee, at the presidential mansion. I had no idea why I was being summoned there.

Charles stopped me, fountain pen in hand, and stained a couple of white spots on my coat. Then he handed me 300 won for cab fare.

52

Kyong Mu Dai, the presidential mansion, stood on a hill overlooking the Central Government Building. The one-hundred-acre grounds were beautifully landscaped with cherry trees, roses, and tulip gardens. I arrived at the front gate at 12:30 and was directed to a waiting room inside.

Forty-five minutes later I was ushered into a large reception room in the mansion. There I met the secretary of the interior, S. W. Paik; director of the Information Bureau, Dr. T. S. Kim; and Mrs. Thompson from Boston, Massachusetts, secretary to Mrs. Rhee. Then the mayor of Seoul, K. B. Lee, reached out his hand to shake mine. Mayor Lee later became the secretary of defense and finally reached the position of vice president of the country, just before the revolution. I was shocked to hear, in 1959, that his oldest son shot all the members of his family when they were pushed into a corner during the revolution.

In the rear garden of the presidential mansion Pres. Syngman Rhee and his wife received me, with Secretary Koh standing beside them. Mrs. Rhee praised my performance and insisted that I should be allowed to go to the Paris cancer congress for my abstract presentation. I was astonished at how much she know about my background and the cancer research projects. President Rhee nodded several times and assured me that he would see what he could do. Five minutes later I was ushered out.

Reverend Koh advised me to go to the Health Department to receive instructions from Dr. Koo. I walked all the way to the Department of Health building, in downtown Seoul, to see Dr. Koo. It was he who had informed Mrs. Rhee about my cancer research and my hope of attending the Paris meeting. I thanked him and expressed my deep appreciation, then went on to my father's office to tell him the good news.

Charles could not believe what had happened at Kyong Mu Dai. He spread the news all around the Department of Pathology.

Many years later I finally conceded that I did several things wrong and made some mistakes. First of all, I was not supposed to go over the head of the professor and chairman by seeking help from Dr. Y. S. Koo. The elderly Koreans always said that Confucius taught them to follow their teacher six feet behind, not step in his shadow. They quoted Confucius as saying that the wise man stays away from the dangerous mission. Furthermore, according to Confucius, the wise man checks the stone bridge three times before he crosses it. In a way, Confucianism, making the Koreans such a docile people, probably caused the downfall of the Korean kingdom.

I was so obsessed with the idea of attending the cancer congress in Paris that I could not see the traditional way of obeying my professors and teachers, without any question. I still cannot understand this way of thinking.

In Memphis, when I published three papers in three months I was criticized for being exceedingly aggressive. I would always reply, "It's in my blood. I can't help it." Raising my voice, I would say, "If I hadn't been aggressive, I could have died in the Korean front lines or in a Siberian concentration camp!"

10
Graduation

On a warm, sunny spring day, May 13, 1950, my classmates and I finally received our medical degrees. At the graduation ceremony the American ambassador, John Muccio, delivered a touching speech, which I still remember, reminiscing about his boyhood life in northern Italy.

It was ironic that I met Mr. Muccio's sister in North Providence, Rhode Island, in 1957, through my friend Pauline Lombardi. We recalled the trying days of the infant Republic of South Korea and the enormous personal efforts by Mr. Muccio, who was at that time ambassador to one of the small South American countries.

A cocktail party given by C. W. Lee's uncle was a farewell for C.W., who was to begin his military training the day following graduation, to become a career army medical officer, and also a celebration of T. J. Park's forthcoming wedding.

I proudly showed off my new impeccably tailored, custom-made navy blue suit, donated by Mrs. Francesca Rhee through Mayor K. B. Lee. According to him, she guessed that I had worn my blue coat for a number of years, as it showed wear and tear in various places.

A second drinking party at Mijang Lounge lasted until 10:00 P.M.

The following morning I took my parents to Reverend Han's breakfast prayer meeting at 6:00 A.M. Overwhelmed with emotion, with tears in my eyes, I thanked God, my parents, and my many friends for the accomplishment of my medical education.

It was very difficult to obtain a suitable residency position for special training because of the limited number of residencies offered by Seoul University Hospital. We were envious of B. L. Roh's appointment, out of twenty-two applicants for the same position, as a junior assistant resident in the second surgical department at Seoul University Hospital. B.L. was to begin his residency in surgery on June 1. Receiving no stipend from the hospital, he had to earn his living by working part-time as a high school teacher. H. C. Kim was to become the lowest man on the totem pole in the Department of Obstetrics and Gynecology at Seoul University Hospital.

Charles and I decided to remain in the Pathology Department as junior assistant residents, receiving a meager stipend from the research grant. We concentrated our efforts on completing the five cancer research papers to be presented at the Fourth International Cancer congress in Paris. When we finally finished typing the manuscripts and abstracts, on May 20, we sent copies to Dr. Koo and Dr. Myron Lee. Mrs. Rhee received copies of our abstracts from Dr. Koo.

I was busy making final preparations for the forthcoming trip to Paris, with frequent discussions and meetings with the Department of Education officials and Dr. Koo's secretary. The Hung Han Foundation made an additional grant to support ongoing cancer research projects.

11
The Korean War

In a speech before the National Press Club on January 12, 1950, Secretary of State Dean Acheson ticked off the U.S. defense perimeter in Asia, excluding South Korea from the U.S. defense line. His speech was indeed a direct invitation for the North Koreans to invade South Korea.

When Premier Kim, of North Korea, received a translation of Acheson's speech from his intelligence service in Pyongyang, he summoned an interpreter, who translated the articles from the *New York Times* and the *Washington Post*. Not totally convinced of the validity of Dean Acheson's statement, Premier Kim ordered the translator to obtain papers from the neutral countries to confirm the statement. When this was done to Kim's satisfaction, with the complete statement abstracted from the Swiss and other European newspapers, he began exchanging his views with officials of the Soviet Union. A secret pact was signed subsequently by Premier Kim and Molotov, in Moscow, for the purpose of achieving the complete communization of Korea by invading South Korea during the month of June 1950. Acting under directions from Moscow, Premier Kim undertook massive preparations with his five-hundred-thousand-man army to strike to the south on June 25.

By the end of 1947, the American-trained Korean constabulary in South Korea had an authorized strength of 20,000 men. The aid program was stepped up the following year, and arms and equipment were provided for an army of 50,000. Soviet forces withdrew from North Korea in 1948, leaving their arms behind for the newly trained NKPA.

In the first months of 1950, just prior to the eruption across the thirty-eighth parallel, the Soviet Union supplied the NKPA with large quantities of modern arms, including heavy artillery, 242 T-34 tanks, trucks, automatic weapons, and about 180 new aircraft, of which approximately 40 were YAK fighters and 70 were attack bombers. Before the NKPA invaded South Korea, they could field eight infantry divisions, all at full strength, two divisions at half-strength, a motorcycle reconnaissance regiment, an armed brigade equipped with T-34 tanks, and five brigades of border constabulary—a total strength of 135,000.

Premier Kim also requested the return of two crack divisions composed of Korean veterans, which had been on loan to the Red Chinese army since World War II to complete their revolution. These veteran Korean soldiers were then reassigned to the thirty-eighth parallel for a full-scale invasion, scheduled for June 25, 1950. Divisions and other large units in the NKPA were commanded largely by men who, as junior officers, had served with credit in the Soviet army during World War II. Each NKPA division had assigned to it approximately fifteen Soviet army advisers.

The preparation of the U.S. and ROK army's defense against the NKPA was indeed a joke, with outdated equipment of a 65,000-man constabulary and a 4,000-man Coast Guard with requisite vessels. Four of the army's infantry divisions had only two instead of the normal allotment of three infantry regiments, and the entire army had only ninety-one 105-mm. howitzers. The ROK army had no tanks and no fighter or bomber planes. They had artillery that far outnumbered and outranged those of the enemy but no gun capable of slowing a tank. It was as if a few Boy Scout troops with hand weapons had undertaken to stop a panzer unit, according to General Ridgway.

The existence of the powerful striking force in North Korea and the massing of troops near the border were not secrets to U.S. intelligence. It was their evaluation that was at fault, guided by their conviction that the Communist forces in the world were not ready to risk atomic war by resorting to armed aggression. Limited war was a concept still foreign to them, except in the sense that all wars are limited by the willingness of the participants to pay the price required.

In the spring of 1950, the Central Intelligence Office of the ROK army had forwarded a formal report to General Headquarters (GHQ) in Tokyo, describing a large-scale military maneuver in North Korea, with the deployment of numerous T-34 tanks and heavy artillery along the thirty-eighth parallel, and warned of an imminent invasion by the NKPA. Report after report describing the NKPA movements toward the border, with continuous transportation of heavy equipment and tanks, was completely ignored by General MacArthur's headquarters. In fact, much reliable information was not taken seriously, which raised the question, Why did they suppress concrete evidence of the forthcoming invasion?

Only six days before the NKPA crossed the border in force, a Central Intelligence field agency reported extensive troop movements north of the thirty-eighth parallel, together with evacuation of all residents from the northern side of the parallel to a depth of two kilometers; suspension of civilian freight service from Wonsan to Chorwon and the reservation of this line for transporting military supplies only; movement of armed units to border areas; and movement of large shipments of ordnance and ammunition also to border areas. How anyone could have read this report and not anticipated an attack is difficult to understand. Yet this report was not used as a basis for any conclusion by G-2 at GHQ in Tokyo, and it was forwarded to Washington in routine fashion, with no indication of urgency. Later GHQ was to disclaim all responsibility for failure to interpret these almost classic preparations and to insist that it had forwarded all the facts to Washington. But this does not explain the fact that, six days before the NKPA struck, GHQ sent an interpretive report to Washington that stated: "Apparently Soviet advisors believe that now is the opportune time to attempt to subjugate the South Korean Government by military means."

The failure to assess properly the high level of the combat effectiveness that the NKPA had attained eventually was inexcusable. A senior American officer, John E. Baird, informed the newly appointed ambassador to Korea, John Muccio, that the type and quality of material available to the ROK army was not sufficient to maintain existing borders. Baird reported that the outnumbered ROK army troops were thoroughly outgunned by the NKPA, who had 122-mm. guns with a range of roughly seventeen miles, as against the American-supplied 104-mm. guns with effective range of about seven miles. He urged that the ROK army be given some means of defense against air attack, recommending that they be supplied with F-51 aircraft. His urging went unheeded.

Civilian voices, too, and President Truman's, had earlier spoken out against the rapid dismantling of the U.S. war machine and mothballing of the army industries. Those voices were drowned out by Congress and the press; so when the big guns finally did signal the eruption of full-scale warfare in Korea, the baby republic they had created found itself completely unready to offer more than token resistance, and the U.S. government was militarily unprepared to implement its agreement for mutual aid.

The ROK army troops were totally unprepared for such a full-scale invasion. None of them had ever received antitetanus or antigangrene toxoid injections. This proved to be a fatal mistake, causing many to die needlessly in hospital beds at a later time. Many of the senior high school students who volunteered to fight were wounded and hospitalized in the Pusan area and died of lockjaw. Most of them could have been saved, had they received antitetanus and gas-gangrene toxoid prior to the so-called police action in Korea.

I kept working seven days a week in both schooling in medicine and carrying out my cancer research. Sufficient funds were provided by the Hung Han Foundation to obtain shipments of mice from Maine for the experimental production of hepatoma (liver cancer) by the application of 20-methylcholanthrene. A previous conversation between Dr. Stewart and Professor Yun had indicated that Dr. Stewart and his associate were unsuccessful in producing hepatoma by means of 20-methylcholanthrene.

After incising the liver tissue with a sharp scalpel and covering it with thin gauze, I introduced a minute amount of the powdered form of methylcholanthrene directly into the liver tissue. Another method I employed was the introduction of a cotton ball soaked with benzene solution, containing 0.06 percent methylcholanthrene, into the deep liver tissue. Subsequently the mice all became infected and died. The methods of introduction of the carcinogenic material into the liver were changed, with an injection of solution through the needle of the syringe into the deep liver tissue. To enhance the production of possible liver cell cancer, I then removed the spleen from all the mice except the control groups. As the spleen is the source of the immune system, producing antibodies against any foreign material causing infection or neoplasm, this did indeed make some sense.

Dr. Myron Lee of the foundation was very understanding and provided additional funds as they were needed for the experimental cancer research studies.

The month of June 1950 was eventful—from a happy wedding for Dr. T. J. Park to full-scale war in Korea.

Bringing wedding gifts, we all attended T.J.'s wedding in Pohang except for C. W. Lee, who was training at the army medical school and then was stationed in Uijongbu with the Seventh Division. Two days later, after seeing the newlyweds off for their honeymoon in the Pusan area, we returned to Seoul.

On June 18, I completed my passport application form at the Foreign Ministry and proceeded to the Budget Bureau of the Department of Health to discuss my forthcoming trip to the cancer congress in Paris.

On the same day John Foster Dulles arrived in Korea and visited Uijongbu to inspect the ROK army line of defense against the NKPA. Mr. Dulles then gave a speech before the National Assembly, explaining the new policy adopted by the United States in regard to the defense of the Republic of Korea. He stated that the United States would come and help the infant republic, should it be attacked by foreign powers.

At 9:00 A.M. on that day, Maj. Y. B. Chu of the NKPA, an officer from the Second Engineering Corps and a Russian language expert, was summoned to the office of Colonel Dolkin, a Soviet military adviser. The colonel demanded Major Chu's sworn statement that under no circumstances would he reveal to anyone the contents of the documents that he was about to translate. These documents contained operational orders for the invasion of South Korea on June 25, plans worked out by Soviet brigadier general Pordoll and approved by the Defense Ministry of the North Korean People's Republic. Major Chu completed his translation into Korean, took a pertinent portion of the document concerning the duties of the Corps of Engineers for the forthcoming invasion, and returned to his battalion.

Alarmed by the statement and the new development since the arrival of John Foster Dulles, members of the cabinet of Premier Kim held an emergency meeting at the premier's office at 1:00 A.M. June 19 to discuss military strategy based on the development in Seoul.

It was the unanimous opinion of Premier Kim and his cabinet that it was too late to change the military situation and call off the invasion, which was scheduled to begin at 4:00 A.M. on June 25. Most of them were convinced that the Dulles comment was probably an offhand remark, without support from the U.S. government, to placate Pres. Syngman Rhee's desire or his nagging demand to unify the entire Korean peninsula by force. They decided to execute the invasion plans as scheduled.

Following the departure of John Foster Dulles to Tokyo, members of President Rhee's cabinet, politicians, and high-ranking military officers were jubilant at having received the promise from Dulles concerning the defense of the infant republic against its foes. They held numerous parties in celebration. The chief of staff of the Korean army gave a lavish dancing party for his subordinates and high-ranking officers, which lasted until 2:00 on the morning of June 25. Most of the soldiers defending the thirty-eighth parallel, division officers, and members of the top brass were given a three-day pass from the evening of June 23 through midnight of Sunday, June 25.

The commander of the ROK army's Third Division was a nonpolitical soldier and a prudent man, with 9,388 men under his command. Alerted by unusually heavy traffic and movement of the NKPA along the Chunchon-Hongchon defense line, he put out a general alert denying the three-day pass to his division, and this was the only exception among the ROK troops defending the thirty-eighth parallel line.

At 3:00 A.M. on June 25, Maj. Gen. K. S. Yu, a 105th tank commander of the NKPA, reinspected his troops and ordered them to start the engines of the T-34 tanks, fully loaded with ammunition. He gave an impressive speech to his men, saying, "Two regiments of ROK soldiers invaded North Korea, and it is our duty to repel the enemy, to unify the whole Korean peninsula."

At 4:00 A.M. on Sunday, June 25, 182,000 NKPA soldiers invaded the one-hundred-mile front with heavy artillery and Soviet T-34 tanks. This marked the first day of the Korean War.

The First and Sixth NKPA Divisions, with the 206th Armored Regiment, forty T-34 tanks, and 21,000 troops, swarmed over the Onjing–Munsan–Kaesong defense line, overrunning the ROK First Division, composed of 10,161 soldiers with light weapons, mostly M-1 rifles and machine guns. The ROK soldiers had nothing to match the enemy's howitzers and T-34 tanks but stood bravely, with 40 percent casualties. Colonel Chun himself fired a 57-mm. antitank gun with no effect on the T-34 tanks. Volunteers were called to destroy enemy tanks with grenades, rocket launchers, and dynamite strapped to themselves. They destroyed a few tanks but gave their own lives.

Capt. C. H. Ahn of the Medical Corps, a 1949 graduate of Severance Medical School, while leading forty-three wounded soldiers toward Seoul diverted them into a cornfield for rest. Most of them died early on the morning of June 26 in the field; the rest were killed by friendly fire on the same day. Captain Ahn asked an engineering soldier why he was digging a deep hole. The soldier replied that he had been ordered to dig a hole from which to destroy enemy tanks with a Molotov cocktail. With the remaining platoon, Captain Ahn took an M-1 rifle and climbed the hill to wait for enemy tanks to appear. He and his men destroyed four tanks but lost their own lives.

At 9:30 A.M. the city of Kaesong fell. Colonel Chun was wounded, his face severely disfigured. Colonel Chun was a veteran going back to 1943, when he fought the Japanese with troops trained by the government in exile in Chungking, China. He was indeed a nonpolitical, truly courageous soldier, who had no fear of death. Against the advice of his subordinates, he made no effort to remove his family from Kaesong to a safer place, and they were massacred by the NKPA political officers in early July.

Soviet tanks penetrated the city of Munsan, which was defended by a small force headed by Lt. H. Kim and his three noncoms, all of whom were refugees from North Korea. When they exhausted their ammunition, against the order to withdraw to the south, they killed themselves.

The dock area was a scene of chaos, with hundreds of wounded soldiers and refugees seeking ferryboats to cross the river. More than half of the soldiers killed themselves with grenades when they saw no way out, yielding the ferryboats to the thousands of refugees fleeing from the Onjing and Kaesong area.

The massive NKPA troops, made up of 34,000 men, with eighty T-34 tanks, marched down to take Uijongbu, an important city in the defense of Seoul, the capital of South Korea. The Seventh Division of the ROK army with Molotov cocktails and grenades successfully counterattacked on the morning of June 26, killing 1,580 NKPA soldiers and destroying fifty-eight tanks. Each ROK army soldier had only fifteen rounds of ammunition. In desperation, Major General Chae, chief of staff of the ROK forces, decided to throw in the entire Student Corps of the military academy to defend Uijongbu. Seventy senior students and eighty-two junior-class cadets were overrun by the T-34 tanks, which penetrated the city of Uijongbu at 1:00 P.M. on June 26, threatening the defense line of Seoul.

My friend C. W. Lee exposed himself to enemy fire when he treated wounded soldiers and students of the National Military Academy. There was nothing C.W. could do to save the lives of so many who were hit by the tanks and heavy artillery. As the students died, one by one, with mutilated intestines, torn extremities, and hemorrhagic brain tissue herniating from the skull, C.W. wept, ordering ambulances to take them to Seoul.

Back at the university hospital in Seoul, Dr. B. L. Roh, a new junior assistant resident in surgery, was working around-the-clock with the incoming wounded of the ROK Seventh Division. He operated and assisted for thirty-six hours straight, without any break, and finally collapsed on the floor.

The eastern front was likewise a one-sided victory when the NKPA's Second and Seventh Divisions, with 23,000 men and 40 tanks, attacked the ROK Third Division, consisting of 9,388 men, inflicting 50 percent casualties on the ROK army forces. The Third Division commander was a dedicated and experienced veteran with a fierce fighting spirit. His men destroyed three tanks with grenades and Molotov cocktails. Sergeant Cho, a brother of my classmate Kevin Cho, destroyed a T-34 tank with sticks of dynamite strapped to his body.

The NKPA suffered 40 percent casualties, but the Third Division had to withdraw when Kangnung fell.

Two battalions of the NKPA Marine Regiment had previously landed on two beaches south of Kangnung and marched toward the north. The NKPA Fifth Division, 666th Regiment, comprised of 22,000 men, attacked Kangnung from the north. The ROK Eighth Division, made up of 900 men, fought a fierce battle to defend Kangnung, but with orders from GHQ they had to retreat to Wonju and farther south to Chaechon.

During the afternoon of June 27, Charles and I were called to the Department of Surgery, as they needed every available hand to attend to the wounded. I telephoned the Department of Health and the Department of Education in hopes of obtaining a passport to leave. All government office buildings were closed, and there was general chaos among the ROK government officials.

We went home on the evening of June 27 to discuss our future plans. The noises of cannon fire and the explosion of shells grew louder as time went by. The city of Seoul fell to the NKPA at 11:30 A.M. on June 28, 1950, with most of the citizens remaining in the city because of false radio broadcasting and strict government regulations to remain calm.

At the UN Security Council's next meeting, they determined that the NKPA was an aggressor and demanded withdrawal of its forces to the original line established before June 25, 1950. When this failed, the council voted to organize the UN Forces for Korean Political Action. They made Gen. Douglas MacArthur the supreme commander of the UN forces in Korea. Under his command were the U.S. armed forces, the air forces of Australia and South Africa, one regiment of British troops, frigates from both the Netherlands and New Zealand, volunteers from Canada, and a token strength of troops from Turkey and the Philippines.

On July 1, Task Force Smith, commanded by Lt. Col. C. B. Smith and consisting of 406 men, was airlifted from Japan to Taejon and advanced to Osan to engage in the first battle with the NKPA. The task force was composed of two rifle companies, two platoons of 4.2-mm. mortars, one 75-mm. recoilless rifle crew, and six 2.36-mm. bazooka teams. When thirty-three T-34 tanks of the NKPA 107th Tank Regiment appeared on July 5, the task force found that their weapons were no match for the tanks. Many soldiers ran, leaving officers and noncoms to reload and fire their mortars, destroying one truck. Task Force Smith paid a high price to hold back the NKPA advancement, with five officers and 150 soldiers killed and twenty-six missing. The gallant stand of the panic-stricken Task Force Smith earned a precious seven hours, during which time they were able to withdraw and retreat to Chonan.

The troops of the Twenty-fourth Division, under Maj. Gen. William F. Dean, had no fighting spirit, putting up only a token resistance to the advancing NKPA tanks. It was tragic to picture the soldiers of the Twenty-four Division, trained for Japanese occupation, fresh from idleness and luxury of peacetime Japan, where they had lived on delicacies and whiled time away with their girlfriends. There was panic and much confusion, and the soldiers withdrew in disorder, receiving heavy casualties. They looked around for respite and found none. They sat and waited to be taken as prisoners of war. The city of Taejon was abandoned on July 20, with many thousands of American prisoners taken by the NKPA.

The performance of the First U.S. Cavalry Division was equally dismal. When we heard, through the underground radio, that the First Cavalry Division had made a successful landing at Pohang on July 16, everyone exchanged smiles, with a feeling of joy and expectation that the tide of war against the NKPA would change. The Twenty-fourth Regiment of the division, under the command of Major General Kean, was composed entirely of black soldiers, except for a few senior officers. Out of 109 soldiers of Company C, only 17 stood to fight, and Pohang fell to the NKPA. The Twenty-fourth Division sustained very heavy casualties.

A report on the psychological condition of American prisoners during the Korean War was so shocking that it was kept top-secret until five years after the war. When it came out, it was a great jolt to the American conscience. Seven thousand U.S. prisoners were taken captive by the Communists during the first three months of the Korean War. Of these seven thousand, over three thousand died in captivity. A shocking percentage—far higher than prisoners of other Allied nations taken by the same enemy. It was not that the Americans were treated any more harshly or even differently than the others. It was the way in which the American prisoners treated one another! After questioning of every one of the surviving prisoners when the war was over, it was discovered that the Americans who had died had not perished due to enemy cruelty, but because they did not care about each other while in prison. One burly bully made headlines and got his picture in the papers because he was tried and convicted for murder while a prisoner. He had thrown two sick prisoners out into the snow in thirty-degree-below-zero weather to die. Forty-four other Americans in the same hut passively watched him do it and did not go out to help the other two back in. They all said in effect, "It was none of our business." This case apparently was typical.

In contrast, 229 Turkish soldiers were taken prisoner and held in the same compound under like conditions. They helped one another, scrounging food for the weakest, keeping them warm at night, and giving up their blankets for those who needed them most. Every one of the Turks survived.

T. J. Park and his bride were completely lost by the full-scale war, which disrupted their honeymoon. They drifted from one hospital to another in Pusan. Unable to return to his home in Pohang, with the frustrations of continuous defeat suffered by the UN forces and the Korean troops, T.J. volunteered for the Eighth Division Medical Corps. He received five days of military training and was assigned to the regiment Medical Corps of the division. His wife volunteered to work as a nurse's aide at the Fifteenth Army Hospital in Pusan.

High-ranking government officials and their families fled Seoul for the south on June 26 and 27, before the bridge over the Han River was blown up on the evening of the twenty-seventh. Approximately three hundred thousand Seoul citizens, unable to cross the Han River, reluctantly returned to their homes to endure the hardships that would no doubt be brought upon them by the NKPA. Most of the residents stayed in their basements and missed the opportunity to flee to safety because of continuous false government broadcasting, citing many victories by the ROK army, who were supposed to march toward Pyongyang. While the citizens of Seoul were listening to the broadcasts, cannon shells began falling in the vicinity of Seoul. From that moment on, most South Koreans were suspicious of government actions and announcements. On the morning of June 28, NKPA troops marched into Seoul with their impressive weaponry, including tanks and heavy artillery.

My plans to attend the Paris cancer congress abruptly became nothing but a romantic dream. About 10:00 A.M. on June 29, I visited Professor Lee to ask his advice concerning the 120 mice and the ongoing cancer research. He advised me to sacrifice all the mice and the cancer research instead of my own life and he told me not to report to the department for the time being. I was grateful for his straightforward advice, which may have saved me from falling into the hands of the Communist troops and agitators.

Most of my classmates were forced to stay at the hospital, operating on or treating wounded soldiers, and were caught by the victorious

NKPA when they brought truckloads of their comrades for medical treatment. B.L. had been operating for forty-eight hours straight, trying to save the lives of ROK army soldiers, when he was ordered to appear at the Central Office. A major of the NKPA was waiting there for all the physicians. He demanded all available beds for his wounded men. When told that the beds were occupied by dying soldiers of the ROK army, he pulled out his pistol and ordered that all the wounded be taken out to the backyard of the hospital immediately. There they were shot and their bodies left unburied, thus making available twenty-seven beds for the NKPA soldiers.

When I heard this story from B.L., I found it difficult to believe such barbaric action and inhuman treatment of people of the same race. But it turned out to be true. My sister came home and described a horrible scene of many bodies lying unburied and emitting a stench in the whole university campus area. B.L. was able to sneak out of the hospital and come to our house to stay for two days.

My father decided to move his family to a friend's home in the crowded central district of Seoul, to avoid possible arrest or execution by the NKPA. We hastily moved, on July 1, and began life underground, hoping to endure for a period of time. My father hoped that I would be as safe as a needle in a haystack, mixing with thousands of people in the central part of the city, but he was too optimistic. Two security police officers, accompanied by four left-wing students, ransacked our former house, looking for me, and made several inquiries of our former neighbors regarding the location of my hiding place, which they did not know.

By mid-July of 1950 the administrative system became more organized, with newly arrived political officers from the north. Teams of security and NKPA officers began to search for hiding ROK soldiers and government officials. Security officers visited individual homes around 10:00 each evening, and many of the soldiers and politicians were taken out to prison. To avoid the nightly search, I asked Dr. S. Kim, a famous Korean surgeon with a large practice, if I could stay during the night at his clinic as an assistant surgeon. He obtained for me a Civil Defense Medical Member certificate, on which was inscribed my medical license number.

By the end of July, so-called people's trials had become common scenes in Seoul. From thirty to fifty people would hold a trial, accusing anyone of alleged misconduct as a government official or police force member under Pres. Syngman Rhee's government. An accused person was not allowed to speak up or to present a defense. A five-minute trial always brought a guilty verdict, and the suspected person was immediately hanged from a nearby telephone or utility pole. It was indeed a reenactment of the French Revolution, but fearful people would not speak out to challenge the kangaroo-court decision.

There was nothing but dismal news regarding the war. The Han River hardly slowed down the enemy. The ROK infantry on the south bank, disintegrating quickly under heavy artillery fire and tank advancement, was forced to withdraw farther south.

A 1949 graduate of Seoul University School of Medicine, Dr. W. H. Sohn, was passing through the Capital Theater area, where radical students and political officers were making an appeal to students and young men to volunteer for the NKPA's partisan guerrilla force. Dr. Sohn accidentally dropped his grocery bag, revealing a small whiskey bottle. This roused the suspicion of security police, who demanded to see his papers. Having no solid proof that he was a Communist Party member or sympathizer, Sohn was taken to the detention center and forced at gunpoint to join an eastern group of the guerilla force. His sister, who went out to search for her brother, was also caught by a group of radicals and was drafted as a cook to support a partisan guerrilla force on the western front. Seventeen months later, when the partisan groups were captured by the ROK army and sent to a prison camp on Kojaedo Island, the brother and sister accidentally met in the prison compound. They embraced and wept for over an hour. It would be impossible to list all the tragedies created by the Korean War, but this story is a typical example of the human misery brought on by the Korean police action.

On the morning of August 15, all the American, British, and French missionaries and Franciscan nuns were rounded up by the NKPA and forced to march toward Pyongyang, the capital of North Korea. They rested in the daytime, because of frequent bombings by the U.S. forces, and walked from ten to twenty miles at night. Among them were Miss Tyler, a Methodist missionary who was head of a girls' high school in Kaesong, and Mrs. Park, a German woman who was married to a violinist. The ladies became very good friends during the ordeal, which eventually took them to Moscow. Miss Tyler, a U.S. citizen, was placed in the custody of the U.S. embassy in Moscow and eventually sent back to North Little Rock, Arkansas. Mrs. Park reached West Germany but was unable to prove her German citizenship because of lack of papers and certificates, so she was sent to a West German detention camp. Later Miss Tyler invited Mrs. Park, a woman without a country, to come to North Little Rock and help her operate a gift shop. Mrs. Park would spend the rest of her life there.

At our dinner table in Little Rock, Arkansas, in September of 1963, we listened until two o'clock in the morning to the fascinating story of Mrs. Park and Miss Tyler's trip from Seoul to Moscow. Miss Tyler told us that on the train to Moscow they saw several wives of high-ranking Soviet officials with fur coats and diamond rings. It was interesting, she said, to observe such opulence in the classless society of Soviet Russia. The two ladies were at that time, in 1963, quite happy operating their small gift shop in Arkansas.

Making rounds with Dr. Kim for his twenty-seven patients at the clinic, I met a middle-aged tank commander, Colonel Choi, who reached the West Gate Prison in Seoul early on the morning of June 28 and opened the doors to release the prisoners. He was shot by a guard and brought to Dr. Kim's prestigious surgical clinic for immediate medical attention. Colonel Choi had been trained in North Korea and China, along with Mao's Communist troops, and was a hard-core Communist soldier and leader of his tank regiment, which swept through the northern part of Seoul. After a brief conversation, he noticed my northern accent and was curious to know when I came down to Seoul and how I happened to be in Dr. Kim's clinic. Dr. Kim stepped in and explained to him that I had been in school in Seoul prior to August 15, 1945, saving me from embarrassing and frightening inquiries. Six weeks later Dr. Kim's clinic was taken over by the NKPA and all the private patients were sent to other facilities. This took away my only sanctuary from the nightly search by the security police.

On my way home from the clinic I heard someone calling my name and turned to see a young man who had been a key member of the Communist circle at a Pyongyang college before I escaped from the Soviets. He was carrying piles of papers and was obviously in a hurry, but he shook my hand and told me, with a sarcastic smile, that I should learn my lesson by joining the student's club of the Communist army. I was paralyzed, fearing that I would end up in the detention center of the security police, but he shook my hand again and went off to his headquarters. Once again I was saved, although the encounter left me terrified.

12
Underground Life in Seoul

Gen. Douglas MacArthur was not merely a military genius; he was a brilliant advocate who could argue his point so persuasively that men determined to stand up against him were won to enthusiastic support. The Inchon landing (Operation Chromite), the daring 5,000 to 1 shot that restored the initiative to the UN forces in Korea and kept them from being pushed into the sea, was a typical MacArthur operation, from inception to execution, that began on June 28, and continued through September 25, 1950.

General MacArthur persuaded many skeptical generals and admirals to execute the Inchon landing, despite strong opposition expressed by the navy staff, who insisted that the receding thirty-foot tides would leave a tight and twisting channel through mile-wide mud flats to ground navy vessels and turn them into artillery targets. Admiral Doyle and Gen. Oliver Smith presented an alternative plan to land at Kunsan, a southern port, where pressure might be more quickly felt by the enemy on the Pusan front.

The successful Inchon landing and retaking of Seoul, on September 28, saved thousands upon thousands of prisoners—intellectuals, professors, and scholars—from slaughter by the NKPA. Not many people failed to realize the importance and significance of the Inchon landing, which saved many of the intellectuals of South Korea. If the UN forces had landed at Kunsan, it would have taken them at least two months to reach Seoul, with virtually no hope for the prisoners to survive under such tyranny. The Korean people were so grateful to General MacArthur for his landing at Inchon and retaking Seoul that they erected a bronze statue, which is still standing today at Inchon Harbor.

By the end of July 1950, the internal security forces of the North Korean government had established a system of food rationing for the residents of Seoul. The food supplies of most households were exhausted by the middle of July, and people were existing on a starvation diet, because the black marketeers had disappeared rapidly when the city fell into the hands of the NKPA. Meat and poultry products were sent to feed the advancing North Korean soldiers, and malnourished children soon appeared on the streets of Seoul. To receive food ration cards, the people were forced to submit their classification (intellectual or laborer) and self-criticism under the government of Pres. Syngman Rhee. When this was approved by the security police, they could obtain a meager amount of food. The system flushed out hiding politicians, engineers, physicians, civil servants, and university professors.

Professor Lee and several of my classmates in order to feed their families were forced to appear at the office building in the central district to fill out the application forms and required documents. Prof. S. J. Sou, of Seoul University Medical School, was selected by the security force to check the validity of the documentations made by physicians seeking food rationing. He was able to feed his five children but intensely disliked his job.

Professor Sou and his senior residents were finally rounded up during the early part of September and forced to go to Pyongyang in a truck, which was spotted by a U.S. Fifth Air Force fighter plane. All the detainees were scattered throughout the hills, about thirty miles north of Seoul. Some of them escaped and made their way back to Seoul, but Professor Sou was caught and put in a truck to continue to Pyongyang. When his second escape attempt was unsuccessful, the security police told him that if he tried again, he would be executed. Two days later, when he was caught during his third escape attempt, they shot him on the spot, forty-seven miles north of Seoul. He was a genius in the field of pharmacology, highly respected by his students and colleagues. Many high-ranking professors and engineers lost their lives needlessly during the month of September.

Through the underground radio we heard that General MacArthur's troops had landed at Inchon on September 25. We looked at one another with a sigh of relief, realizing that there might be a slim chance of survival when the city of Seoul was taken by our troops.

The announcement of increased food rationing enticed technical people who held a neutral political view, to cooperate with the North Korean security police. Most of these technical people were detained and taken to North Korea. When the security police failed to secure transportation and were forced to abandon all prisoners because of the advancing U.S. Marine Corps, well-known architects, science teachers, physicists, chemists, physicians, and musicians were taken to the city parks, with their hands tied behind them, and shot. Many intellectuals survived such ordeals, however, and were rescued by the advancing soldiers of the ROK Division and later reunited with their families.

The nightly search for hidden politicians, engineers, and professors was frequently interrupted by air raids, and people were able to catch up on their sleep at those times. I was tempted to surrender to the security police in order to receive food rations but gave up the idea on the advice of my parents and Charles.

The house where we were hiding was next door to one occupied by twenty-five young female members of the security police force. When the western suburb of Seoul was occupied and secured by the UN forces, that house was set on fire with cans of gasoline. The fire spread quickly, consuming all twelve houses in the block. We had to escape from the fire at two o'clock on the morning of September 28.

The defense of the city by the NKPA was fierce, inviting continuous bombing by the Fifth Air Force, and some of the bombs fell in the Central District of Seoul. My parents, one sister, and I sought refuge in another section of the city through a difficult passage over brick and concrete rubble. We heard low moaning and a chorus of pain, punctuated by intermittent screams of the wounded, as we passed. People were running through fire and a hail of bullets to search for members of their families. The heat of the flames from burning houses and stores was intense, reaching every corner of the streets and creating an inferno. Water hydrants were malfunctioning, and no fire trucks were available. Oxygen bottles were popping off, and bomb explosions threw limbless bodies hundreds of feet into the air. A large office building, two blocks away, blew apart from the basement upward and outward, its walls disintegrating and rubble flying, spewing in all directions. The roof lifted, toppling, shrouded with dust and engulfed in flames. It was a living hell that I cannot forget.

13
Last Stand in Taegu

"No more retreat! We will stand here to defend the city to the last man!" angrily exclaimed Lt. Gen. Walton H. Walker, commanding officer of the U.S. Eighth Army.

ROK First Division soldiers continued the bloody fight with the NKPA Thirteen and Fifteenth Divisions, which launched a frontal attack at Hill 303 on August 15, 1950. The next day, ninety-eight B-29 bombers of the U.S. Fifth Air Force dropped 960 tons of bombs around Hill 303 with no significant results. General Walker subsequently threw the U.S. Twenty-seventh Regiment in to defend Hill 303 against the numerically superior force. On August 18, during the night, the NKPA soldiers attempted for the seventh time to take Hill 303 with hand-to-hand combat. With 3.5 inch antitank rockets the ROK First Division destroyed most of the T-34 tanks, while the remaining Soviet tanks were knocked out by land mines. Three days later the NKPA First Division repeated the night attack and finally penetrated the U.S. Twenty-seventh Regiment's defense line to fourteen kilometers from Taegu. The ROK Ninth Division counterattacked the infiltrating NKPA First and Thirteenth Divisions in the vicinity of Taegu when the U.S. Seventh Cavalry Regiment retreated, opening a wide road for the NKPA to advance.

General Walker, known as "Bulldog" Walker, was fiercely courageous soldier, who ordered the First U.S. Cavalry division to fight at the front in Taegu or die. He refused to see his division commanders returning from the front lines, insisting, "I won't see you unless you're brought in a coffin." Indeed, General Walker saved the city of Taegu.

C. W. Lee was almost killed by a tank cannon shell that exploded near his medical aid station, instantly killing two of his corpsmen. C.W. then removed fifty-seven wounded soldiers to safety but exposed himself to the front line assault. Two days later he was promoted to captain of the Medical Corps of the ROK First Division.

The eastern front, where Dr. T. J. Park was serving as a regimental medical officer, also faced crisis after crisis. The ROK Eighth Division, unable to hold Mount Bo Hyon, had to retreat to defend Yongchon against the NKPA Fifteenth Division. Lt. Gen. Mujong Kim, of the NKPA, issued a stern order to the Fifteenth Division commander to take Yongchon within forty-eight hours or he would be tried at the People's Court. On September 5, at 3:00 A.M., the NKPA Fifteenth Division reattacked the ROK Eighth Division, finally took Yongchon and continued to march toward Kyongju. On September 10 the ROK Eighth Division and the U.S. Twelfth Tank Regiment counterattacked, retaking Yongchon for the second time, destroying the NKPA Fifteenth Division. Remnants of the NKPA Fifteenth Division, leaving three thousand dead and all their equipment, fled to the north.

During that fierce battle, T.J. operated on dying men for forty-eight hours straight without any sleep or rest. His division commander, Col. S. K. Lee, and the regimental commander, Lt. Col. Y. B. Kim, fighting in hand-to-hand combat along with their enlisted men, boosted the morale of the soldiers, despite lack of food and ammunition, and they finally secured the city of Yongchon.

T.J., who successfully defended his medical aid station and transferred his hundreds of wounded men to a safe place, later received the highest military citation and medal for his performance above and beyond the call of duty.

North Korea's Premier Kim visited Kumsong, headquarters of the NKPA, and reshuffled the commanding generals. He gave strict orders to take to conquer Taegu and Pusan by September 25, the target date for reunification of North and South Korea.

It was impossible to stop the advancing NKPA tanks, and the UN forces were compelled to retreat toward the south. The U.S. Twenty-fifth and First Cavalry Division withdrew farther south when the city of Taejon fell, on July 20.

C. W. Lee was reassigned to the newly organized regimental Medical Corps of the First Division and thrown into Sangju to face the NKPA Fifteenth Division. When Sangju fell, the First Division had to retreat to the Naktong River, where it was relieved by the newly formed Capital Division and reassigned to defend the east coast.

Under the command of Brig. Gen. S. W. Kim, the Chinchon operation was launched to retake the city of Chinchon. With a burning desire to defend their fatherland, 102 senior high school students volunteered. They were given old Japanese rifles and a limited amount of ammunition to face the advancing T-34 tanks. The students refused to withdraw and were all killed by Soviet tanks during eight hours of fierce fighting. They were buried in a mass grave, known as the Unknown Students' Tomb.

I was distressed to hear these facts from C.W. But I was more shocked to notice the change in his facial lines after seeing so much human suffering, when he visited me briefly on October 20, 1950. He was on his way to join his outfit to march toward Pyongyang. C.W.'s once handsome face had changed dramatically, with deep lines etched in his forehead and around his eyes and his jawline square and hard.

During the battle at Andong, according to C.W., all the cooks, corpsmen, and even medical doctors had to take up arms to stop the T-34 tanks. He himself fired several antitank rockets and disabled some of them. After receiving heavy casualties in the Andong battle, his division was forced to retreat down to the Naktong River, C.W. treated thousands of refugees seeking medical care. Having been a grade school teacher, he was particularly concerned about the children and other young people who were victims of such a tragic war.

I listened to C.W.'s account with tear-filled eyes, cursing the short-sightedness of the politicians and the incompetent U.S. infantry soldiers and their officers. In contrast to the low opinion we held of the U.S. infantry, we had high praise for the performance of the Fifth U.S. Air Force.

We asked C.W. about the whereabouts of T. J. Park after he volunteered for the army Medical Corps. C.W. told us that T.J. was assigned to the regimental Medical Corps of the ROK Eighth Division, facing the NKPA Fifth Division on the east coast. During the battle of Pohang, T.J.'s hometown, sixty-seven senior high school students volunteered to defend the city against the NKPA Fifth Division and their Soviet tanks. The students held out for one hour at the Pohang Girls High School building, until three T-34 tanks penetrated and diverted into the left flank, killing all of them. On August 15, Pohang fell to the NKPA, and the dead students were buried in a mass grave. When Pohang was retaken by the ROK Eighth Division, the city was a shambles.

One cannot read Korean War history without emotion on learning that 650 students, representing the second generation of Koreans in Japan, volunteered to defend their fatherland from the invasion. These students could have lived peacefully in Japan, with a university education, but they landed at Pusan to fight. Most of them died in the ensuing battles with the advancing NKPA.

On September 18, 1950, alerted by an intelligence report, ROK air force colonel Y. H. Kim and his F-51 fighter squadron were ordered to attack one thousand NKPA soldiers stationed around Temple Hae Inn, one of the oldest Buddhist temples in Korea, built more than twenty-five hundred years ago. When Colonel Kim spotted the NKPA soldiers and tanks near the temple, he decided not to bomb it but attacked with machine guns instead, to save the priceless art, porcelain, and national treasures kept there.

When the squadron returned to their base, Colonel Kim faced an angry American military adviser, Colonel Compton, who asked, "Is an old Buddhist temple more valuable than your nation? Why didn't you bomb and destroy the temple?"

With dismay, Colonel Kim told the American, "It is our duty to save and protect our national heritage and treasures from this senseless, destructive war. A thousand NKPA soldiers and their tanks are of temporary existence in the history of the Korean nation, and we will survive this war. If you had even the slightest cultural background and taste, you would understand why Paris was declared an open city in World War II to save it from wholesale destruction. At the end they were able to save their proud city from the Germans."

Minutes later Colonel Compton appeared in Colonel Kim's office, saying, "Colonel, I apologize for my ignorance and short temper."

Both sides apparently were careful not to destroy their national treasures even during the fiercest battles of the Korean War. This is indeed an indication of the long cultural background of the Korean people—their love of artistic achievement and desire to protect their national heritage.

Charles Kim was very unfortunate during the latter part of September. Against my advice, he went back to the Department of Pathology at Seoul University School of Medicine to check the animals and several other things. To his surprise, he was well received by the cadre of left-wing professors and his schoolmates. Around 3:00 P.M. on September 23, 1950, he was summoned to the dean's office on the first floor at the Basic Science Building. There he was told that all basic science professors and assistants were being drafted into the North Korean army Medical Corps on the spot. Twenty-seven teachers, including Charles, were herded into a truck, to be sent to North Korea. No one was allowed to make stops or send messages to their families. They reached Wonsan, North Korea, on September 28. On the way Charles heard the news that the UN forces had landed at Inchon and were marching toward Seoul.

Just north of Wonsan, the U.S. First Marine Division captured a large number of prisoners of war. Among them were Charles Kim and several other professors of medicine from Seoul, who had been forced to treat the sick and wounded NKPA soldiers. Because of the increasing numbers of disabled and desperately ill, Major Zimmerman, a battalion commander, asked if there were any physicians among the prisoners. Charles raised his hand, dragging with him a hesitant Dr. Seo, an assistant professor of microbiology, saying Dr. Seo, "This may be our way out."

Later Charles told me that while he was trying to remove shrapnel from a wounded NKPA soldier's thigh, he was terrified to feel the earth trembling because of massive bombing and shelling from the warships in the Hungnam area. Both Charles and Dr. Seo worked diligently to save the lives of dying prisoners. Their efforts were noticed by Major Zimmerman and his assistant, Captain Thompson, who learned of their unfortunate circumstances, having been taken from the medical school compound in Seoul by the NKPA.

When the Chinese troops intervened in the Korean War and forced the UN troops to evacuate from Hungnam Harbor, it became obvious to Major Zimmerman that the fate of Charles and Dr. Seo would be dismal, and he determined to save their lives. He asked his assistant to bring them to his tent, where he told them that he was going 150 miles south immediately and would like to take them with him. They hopped into the backseat of the jeep, and off they went, reaching Pusan three days later. At the Pusan port Major Zimmerman gave them new fatigues to wear and shook their hands. Charles visited me at the Fifth Army Hospital on that same day, his voice choking as he told me how a kind and compassionate American had spared his life.

Anthony Quinn, the American actor, once said on public television, "It is no secret that Americans are suffering from a severe inferiority complex because of their lack of culture." It may seem so to Anthony Quinn, but I saw many Americans who demonstrated more humane feelings than so-called sophisticated and cultured people.

When Pres. John F. Kennedy said in his inaugural address, "Ask not what your country can do for you; ask what you can do for your country," I was touched but wondered how many Americans would understand what he was saying.

I once had a low opinion of the American infantrymen's fighting capabilities, based on my experience during the first part of the Korean War. Much later, however, I understood that their method was the most effective way to damage and destroy the enemy with minimal casualties. They did not waste human lives if the infantry positions were supported and covered by superior firepower; they saved lives and still accomplished their goal.

J.W. Lee, the nineteen-year old younger brother of C. W. Lee, refused to join the NKPA and was imprisoned for approximately three months. Just before the UN forces entered Wonsan, all the prisoners were rounded up and marched toward the Korean–Soviet border. Because of the frequent bombing raids by the U.S. Air Force, the NKPA decided to liquidate the prisoners on a hillside forty-seven miles north of Wonsan. They ordered the prisoners to dig a large hole in the ground, about five feet deep. When that was completed, they were forced to stand at the edge. J.W., an intelligent young man, sensing his destiny, fell two seconds before the machine guns were fired. The first one to hit the ground, he was covered with corpses and stayed down without moving. Approximately twenty minutes later, he heard a loud noise. He was able to distinguish from the sound that U.S. Army trucks, not Soviet-made ones, were approaching. Covered with blood, he dug himself out and was saved.

The Americans, acting with great humanity, took J.W. to the Hungnam port, where the evacuation had begun several hours prior to their arrival. All the LSTs were moving out to sea. J.W. jumped into the water and began swimming. He was sinking fast, just thirty yards from the last LST, when he yelled for help. A line was thrown out to him. He grabbed it and was hoisted up. The GIs gave him a new uniform that was much too large. They laughed at little J.W. in his oversize fatigues and embraced him.

Some time after that, I saw J.W. in Pusan, where he was attending Seoul University College of Biology. Seven years later he went to the University of Arkansas, in Fayetteville, to major in biology and anatomy. His brother, my good friend C.W., was reported missing around Pyongyang and never returned to the south. He was presumably killed in action.

Nine days prior to the Inchon landing by General MacArthur's troops, the U.S. Eighth Army launched a fierce frontal attack to destroy the NKPA. The Eighth Army recaptured Waegwan, Kimchon, Taejon, and Chonan by September 19, 1950.

My friend T.J. was transferred to the ROK Third Division, which destroyed the NKPA Fifth Division and recaptured Pohang. When they entered the city, T.J. began searching for his parents and brother in the central district of the city. The houses were completely destroyed or burned to the ground, and T.J.'s home had not escaped such disaster. T.J. learned from the neighbors that the North Korean security police took his parents for interrogation, and no one saw them return to their house. They also told him that his younger brother volunteered to fight in the Eighth Division of the ROK Army and was presumably killed in battle. T.J. wept when he visited the Unknown Students' Tomb, not knowing where to turn. His frantic search for his family failed, and he presumed that they were executed either by Communist sympathizers or by the North Korean security police. Stricken with grief, T.J. consumed a large amount of alcohol to overcome his depression and get some sleep.

The U.S. First Cavalry Division and the ROK Second Corps kept marching northward and captured a large number of prisoners, among whom was Col. H. K. Lee, the highest-ranking NKPA prisoner of the war. Colonel Lee gave valuable information to the UN forces.

On September 25, 1950, the U.S. First Cavalry Division reached the suburbs of Seoul and finally linked with the X Corps, which landed at Inchon on September 26. The ROK Second Corps moved quickly to take Chungju and Wonju. Reaching Chunchon on October 2, they halted their advance just before the thirty-eighth parallel.

T.J.'s outfit, the ROK Third Division, made rapid advancement, retaking Yongduk, and reached the thirty-eighth parallel on September 30. General MacArthur, astonished by the rapid movement of the ROK Third Division foot soldiers, told reporters, "The pace of the advancement of the ROK Third Division soldiers exceeds the speed of the North Korean air force."

The UN forces took thirteen thousand NKPA prisoners during the frontal attack on the Pusan perimeter and sent a message to Premier Kim of North Korea on October 1 advising him to surrender.

Seoul was secured on September 28, when General MacArthur and Pres. Syngman Rhee made a triumphal entry, traveling by motorcade to the gutted capital building. In a brief ceremony before American and Korean soldiers and officials, MacArthur symbolically returned the capital to Syngman Rhee and assured him that complete liberation of his homeland was near.

B.L. Roh, hoping to reach his hometown, Hungnam, North Korea, volunteered and joined the Capital Division, which was to take Wonsan Harbor when they crossed the thirty-eighth parallel. Unlike most Koreans, B.L. never brought his emotions to the surface. He had excelled in his academic studies, taking each subject with cold, methodical efficiency, seeming not to work at all. B.L. was the undisputed genius in our class; mediocrity had no place in his mind. He was a born surgeon, with slender, beautiful hands, and he quickly gained experience in general and traumatic surgery. He stopped to say good-bye to my parents and me around the first of October.

I returned to the pathology department on September 29, trying to salvage some of the equipment and instruments. All the experimental animals had died of starvation, and most of the sophisticated instruments and microscopes had been taken by the NKPA. I discussed future plans with Prof. Lee. He advised me to be patient for at least one month before resumption of the pathology departmental functions.

Early in the morning of October 1, 1950, the ROK I Corps crossed the thirty-eighth parallel to about five miles north of the line and waited for further orders from the U.S. Eighth Army. The United States sought a specific UN directive that would permit punitive action against North Korea and achieve unification of Korea in accordance with the UN resolutions. On October 7, the General Assembly approved a resolution calling for destruction of the North Korean armed forces and the liberation of North Korea.

The U.S. Eighth Army had already crossed the thirty-eighth parallel on October 5, and on October 14 the U.S. I Corps penetrated the defense line of Pyongyang. The ROK First Division reached the suburbs of Pyongyang, showing that their foot soldiers were faster than the U.S. trucks, and took the city on October 19. The ROK I Corps, Seventh Regiment of the Sixth Division, finally reached the Yalu River at the border town Chosan on October 26.

October 14, 1950, was an eventful date in Korean War history. On that day about thirty Soviet technicians, utilizing thirty-two Soviet vessels, laid two thousand mines at the entrance of Wonsan Harbor. On the same day 180,000 Chinese soldiers of the Fourth Field Red Army crossed the frozen Yalu River to intervene in the Korean War. Their strength was subsequently increased to three hundred thousand. Also on the same day General MacArthur arrived at Wake Island for a conference with Pres. Harry Truman and Ambassador John Muccio. MacArthur told Truman that as far as he was concerned, the Korean police action was almost complete, and American soldiers would probably go home by Christmas.

There were two television specials in the mid-1950s on the Wake Island meeting of President Truman and General MacArthur. Both programs depicted the general's behavior toward Truman as insulting. A one-man movie starring James Whitmore also tried to discredit General MacArthur. The two television programs were based on Merle Miller's interview with Truman and with his physician, Dr. Wallace Graham. According to William Manchester's book *American Caesar—Douglas MacArthur, 1880–1964*, Dr. Graham said, "MacArthur deliberately tried to hold up his landing so that we would go in and land ahead of them. Harry caught it right away and told MacArthur, 'You go ahead and land first. We've got plenty of gas. We'll wait for you.' " Truman said to Miller, "I knew what he was trying to pull with all that stuff about whose plane was going to land first, and I wasn't going to let him get away with it."

"All of this," Manchester continues, "is specious." Dean Rusk, who was with Truman, told Manchester, "The account given by President Truman in his interview with Merle Miller simply represented a very old man's faulty memory."

The U.S. ambassador to Korea, John Muccio, who was on the same plane with MacArthur, added that the intimation of rudeness on Mac-Arthur's part is "pure fiction."

I remember very vividly the scene on television played by E. G. Marshall, acting as Harry Truman. When President Truman's plane landed and taxied to the gate, he refused to deplane because General MacArthur was not there. "Hold on, boys! We will wait in the plane until MacArthur shows up."

The fact of the matter was that MacArthur had arrived several hours before Truman, slept, bathed, shaved, dressed, and breakfasted and was on the field at 6:00 A.M. on October 15, ready to greet President Truman thirty minutes before the *Independence* landed.

On October 31, the Chinese soldiers of the Fourth Field Red Army made a sudden attack on the ROK Second Corps and destroyed the Seventh and Eighth Divisions. The ROK Second Corps had to retreat, receiving heavy casualties from the Chinese forces. Task Force Smith, from Osan, South Korea, again engaged in a tank battle in November 1950, thirty-one kilometers south of Sinuiju.

In the meantime, the Capital Division of the ROK army, to which B.L. was assigned, made further advancement toward the northern border dividing Manchuria from North Korea, liberating town after town. Six thousand political prisoners from various labor camps crowded the medical camp. Men, women, and children with sunken faces and stooped frames limped about, seeking food and medical attention. B.L. later told me that their arms and legs bore signs of rat bites. Typhus was rampant, and all the patients were quarantined. Food rations were handed out, and adequate bathing and toilet facilities were provided. The healthy were disinfected with DDT and issued fresh clothing, and those for whom it was too late continued to die.

Among the prisoners was an elderly gentleman with erect posture and dignified bearing who came to B.L. and asked if he knew his son, C. W. Lee. When B.L. replied that C.W. was one of his closest friends, the old man collapsed. C.W.'s parents had been detained by the North Korean security force for repeated interrogation concerning their political activities helping the South Korean army. C.W.'s mother, unable to endure the continual torture and questioning, died in the camp a week prior to liberation by the UN forces. B.L. asked C.W.'s father about his youngest son and learned that he was taken by the NKPA at the beginning of September. His whereabouts were unknown, as he never returned to his parents. Under B.L.'s tender care, C.W.'s father regained his strength and recovered rapidly from his fatigue and malnutrition. C.W., with the First Division's regimental Medical Corps, was at that time about to enter Pyongyang.

14
Yalu River to Pusan

When the UN forces reached the Yalu River, people of both North and South Korea were jubilant, dancing in the streets, shouting, "Now our country is unified!" There was no way to know that their wish for complete unification of Korea was soon to become just a dream, because of the intervention of massive numbers of Chinese troops, shattering most of the ROK army divisions and the UN forces.

B.L. finally located his parents, who had been hiding for more than three months under the protection of Catholic priests and nuns of the Hungnam Catholic church. When B.L. was able to visit his family briefly at Christmastime, it was an emotional reunion. They had been separated since 1948. B.L.'s elder brother, T.C., an electrical engineer, had been stationed by force at a gigantic hydroelectric plant on the Yalu River, which was bombed and destroyed during the Korean War. During the commotion he was able to sneak out and made it to Hungnam but was arrested in the street and sent to a detention camp. When the camp was liberated by the UN forces, T.C. was elected to head the reception committee to welcome them and be temporary chairman of the governing committee until a central government could be established for North Korea.

The abrupt retreat by the UN troops, forced upon them by three hundred thousand Chinese, was a genuine tragedy of the Korean War. The political leaders, intellectuals, and members of the clergy who had been underground surfaced during the brief joyful moment to resume their political activities to establish new governing bodies for North Korea. They were forced to escape from the advancing Chinese troops and the NKPA. Most of them had to flee on the spot, without even having time to say good-bye to their families, let alone take their families with them. While the wives were packing their valuables, the U.S. trucks and LSTs left. Many of the family members were executed by the NKPA when Hungnam was recaptured by Chinese volunteers and North Korean troops.

The U.S. Navy performed a miracle, taking out the Tenth Corps, consisting of 10,500 soldiers, 17,500 vehicles, thirty-five thousand tons of equipment, and ninety thousand refugees, including B.L.'s family, on December 24, 1950. T.C., B.L.'s brother, was trying to locate his family, not knowing that they were already in the LST with other refugees. When he was unable to find them at the Catholic church or the city hall, T.C. tried to reach his daughter's high school, asking people if they had seen his family. About an hour later, after a futile search, he climbed a rope-net ladder into a landing craft that was moving out of the docks. Two weeks later he was finally able to locate his family in the port of Pusan.

When the First Division took Pyongyang, my former professor of surgery, Dr. K. R. Chang, was asked to reorganize the Methodist Missionary Hospital, which had escaped damage during the fierce battle. While he was working on the organizational chart with members of his staff, an army officer rushed in to tell them that there would be a temporary setback, forcing them to evacuate the hospital for about twenty-four hours. All of them climbed up to the army vehicle and crossed the Dae Dong River bridge in the confidence that they would return the next day, not knowing that the so-called temporary setback was to become a continuous retreat all the way to Pusan.

Many of the educators and political leaders were also separated from their families in the belief that they would return to the city in a day or so. The very next day the bridge was destroyed by the fleeing UN forces to stop the advancement of the Red Chinese troops.

Many of the wives left behind were captured and tortured by the NKP security police force, and some of them were executed. The UN troops were again forced to retreat from the Yalu River to Naktong.

A dark cloud hung over the Korean front when Lieutenant General Walker was killed in a jeep accident during the retreat.

On a freezing day in December 1950, we saw long lines of refugees carrying household goods, children, and old people on their backs. We wondered what we had done to deserve such misery and suffering.

I decided to volunteer to fight. My mother was against my joining the army, because I was the only male in my generation to carry the Song family name, but my father understood and agreed with my decision.

The army sent seventy-five Medical Corps volunteers to school in Pusan on January 1, 1951, for ten days of military training. During those few days of training we were taught the basic principles of infantry maneuvers, each of us with a heavy M-1 rifle and ten rounds of ammunition. I was astonished to find that all the ammunition had been made in 1942 and 1943, during World War II, and began wondering if Korea was the dumping ground for surplus weapons and ammunition. That question preyed on my mind until much later, when I reached Memphis, Tennessee.

On completion of my military training, I was assigned to the clinical laboratories of the ROK Fifth Army Hospital, in Pusan, as of January 15, 1951.

A general frontal attack was launched by the Chinese troops on January 1, and once again Seoul, the capital city of South Korea, fell into enemy hands. It was the darkest day of the Korean conflict—being forced to evacuate from Seoul for the second time.

My friend T. C. Park and his outfit were completely cut off from their division headquarters, and the whole regiment was surrounded by Chinese troops, with heavy casualties, including the regimental commander. They buried him in deep snow and retreated to the south. Many soldiers suffered severe frostbite, losing their toes and feet. T.C. was hospitalized during the month of February for frostbite, which necessitated the amputation of all his toes in April. B. L. Roh's Capital Division also received heavy casualties from the attacking Chinese and was forced to retreat to the Kangnung area.

I heard through a friend that my parents and one sister had reached Taegu safely with other refugees and were staying with my father's minister friend, Reverend Kim, at a small Presbyterian church in a suburb of the city.

My father had returned to Pyongyang in the latter part of October 1950 and tried to recover some of the family's lost property. He had almost succeeded, after piles of paperwork, when the cannon fire of the Chinese artillery could be heard in the distance. He and my oldest sister and her family hitchhiked from Pyongyang to Taegu to find brief respite. I brought my sister's family from Taegu to Pusan in June 1951, to a small house in a suburb that I found to rent.

Charles Kim was employed by the UN Relief Program as a physician at a refugee camp on Ko-Jae Island. I saw him in May 1951 at the Pusan dock just before his ship sailed for the island.

Men, women, and children from Seoul continually streamed down to the city of Pusan, trying to get away from the Chinese, to escape the terrors of Communism, and to cling to the freedom so briefly known.

On March 15, 1951, the U.S. Eighth Army moved in and once more raised the ROK flag over the ancient and battered city of Seoul. There to greet them were the remnants of the population, ragged, hungry, sick, and frightened. What had originally been a city of one million inhabitants was reduced to approximately two hundred thousand.

Looting by soldiers in war is a universal phenomenon. When the American soldiers tried to loot in the captured city, they did it on a grandiose scale. Pfc Jack Wright found a couple of soldiers who, while going through the rooms in the capitol, came across one where medals were on display. When they got back to the platoon, they looked like a couple of Soviet generals.

The marines came and took Seoul, and when they left they took Seoul with them. S. Sgt. Chester Bair, of the Heavy Tank Company, Thirty-second Infantry Division, discovered a brewery near the railroad station. After dumping the water from their five-gallon cans, he and his men filled them with beer. Next they drove around the neighborhood bank and blew open the front door. The vault was also locked. They fired an armor-piercing shell into the vault door. They found nothing but some papers that they could not read. The perfect bank robbery, but the robbers left without any valuables.

Back at the Fifth Army Hospital in Pusan, I was asked to attend to some of the young soldiers, mostly high school volunteers, in a branch hospital three blocks away. Separated from their families, with no idea of their whereabouts, they died of tetanus in spite of massive antitoxin injections into the spine. Each time a handsome young boy died, I cried, thinking of the parents who had proudly repeated his first words and read his first school papers and who, if they knew, would feel a wrenching, insatiable sense of loss. I cursed the politicians in Washington, D.C., who had neglected so much for so long.

In June 1951, Jacob Malik, Soviet ambassador to the United Nations, indicated that it was not impossible to negotiate a cease-fire in the Korean peninsula.

15
Army Medical Corps

The ROK army hospital in Pusan was a flagship hospital for the entire armed forces in Korea, with first-class facilities in surgery and medicine. I was assigned, as a first lieutenant medical doctor, to the clinical laboratory, an excellent department with a well-trained staff. My duties were to supervise the hematology laboratory and educate our Medical Corpsmen in elementary hematology. I was also ordered by the commanding officer of the hospital, Col. T. H. Paik, to supervise the building of an autopsy room, which was completed in approximately two weeks. As I carried my abstracts of five papers and a bottle of the carcinogen 20-methylcholanthrene with me constantly, I found a small empty space in the basement of the hospital and tried to continue my cancer research.

In June 1951, as I was discussing blueprints for the autopsy room with the maintenance people, I was told that I had a visitor. In walked B.L., in rumpled clothes but wearing a brand-new captain's insignia. From his haggard appearance, I knew that he had gone through rough duty in the field with his Capital Division. He had been transferred to the Seventh Division and was given a week to visit his parents, his brother's family, and his sister, living in Pusan. B.L. urged me to go with him to visit T.J., at Miryang Army Hospital, and I was able to obtain a three-day pass.

When we arrived, T.J. was not particularly happy to see us, after having lost all of his toes because of frostbite, and was very depressed. His wife was sitting by his side. When we told him that he still had his life to live, he answered with a sigh, "Well, it may be so for you guys, but I'm through."

About half an hour later we gave T.J.'s wife our gifts and started to leave. She walked to the entrance with us, tears in her eyes, saying that she did not know what to do to boost her husband's morale. We encouraged her to stick with him in the hope that he would snap out of his depression in a short time. Unlike B.L., T.J. had never gone

87

through any hardships before and intended to become discouraged when difficulties arose.

On returning to Pusan, I found an emergency order that had been cut that evening ordering me to join a newly created division as a medical officer. Unable to comprehend such an order, I discussed the validity of it with my roommate, Eugene Kim, a microbiologist at the laboratory. He suggested that I approach Colonel Paik, the commanding officer.

Colonel Paik's house was in an expensive suburb, set well back from the road in a carefully tended area of shrubs and trees. Colonel Paik scratched his head, showing a twinge of irritation, trying to keep ordinary annoyance from building into rage. He told me that the order must have been an administrative error, because a combat division doesn't need a pathologist but requires a well-trained, experienced general surgeon or orthopedic surgeon. The colonel advised me to wait for three days, until he was able to straighten things out with the bureaucrats of the ROK army surgeon general's office.

Five days later I was summoned to Colonel Paik's office and found him sitting behind a mahogany desk. He explained that although it was an error, since the order had been cut, I had to follow it, not to a newly created combat division, but to the Twenty-seventh ROK Army Hospital, in Taegu.

I left the next day with my gear and arrived at Taegu the following morning. I was assigned to a small branch hospital to the Twenty-seventh Army Hospital, about twenty miles west of Taegu, to set up a clinical laboratory for that separate unit. The hospital accommodated about 350 wounded, with three general surgeons attending.

The following Sunday I attended church at the chapel of the U.S. Fifth Air Force headquarters in Taegu. There I spotted the son and daughter of Professor Park from Seoul National University, and we had coffee together in the fellowship hall following the service.

I was trying to hitchhike back to my unit, looking for army jeeps or trucks heading for the west, when a blue 1950 Studebaker stopped. The driver asked me to come closer to the backseat. There sat the secretary of defense, K. B. Lee, formerly mayor of Seoul. He stretched out his hand to me, asking me about the situation regarding cancer research. I was overcome by his warmth and friendliness and his remembering all the events that had taken place in April of 1950 at the presidential mansion. He said he would be more than willing to help me in reestablishing a cancer research program and told me that I should have sought his or Mrs. Syngman Rhee's help before I joined the army. I thanked him for his kindness and explained that I felt I should do my part to help in the bloody and destructive war.

When B.L. and I had visited T.J. in the hospital following his amputations, B.L. mentioned briefly the possibility of my going to the National Cancer Institute to continue experimental cancer research and urged me to seek the aid of Mrs. Rhee and Dr. Koo. I dismissed the idea of bothering them in the middle of our country's struggle to survive, feeling that I should pay my dues like anyone else.

According to Gen. Matthew Ridgway, the United Nations had never committed itself to a forceful reunification of Korea. And only in the first great surge of optimism after the Inchon landing had any serious thought been given to operations above the thirty-eighth parallel, bent on destroying all hostile forces. In the days immediately preceding the removal of General MacArthur, on April 11, 1951, a stalemate seemed to be what they would soon have on their battlefront. The offensive was still moving ahead, but the attacks planned were all of the limited-objective type.

On March 20, 1951, the Joint Chiefs of Staff informed General MacArthur that the State Department was planning a presidential announcement. This was to the effect that the United Nations was preparing to discuss settlement conditions in Korea. By March 24 the announcement was almost in final form. It would make clear their willingness to settle on the basis of a return to the general lines of the prewar boundary.

Pres. Syngman Rhee was unalterably opposed to any negotiations at all, and he said so loudly and often. General Ridgway relates that he never could hold in his heart anything but admiration and sympathy for this gallant old man. Uncompromising in his hatred of Communism, bitterly prejudiced in favor of his own people, persistent in asking the impossible, Syngman Rhee was still moved by nothing more than a deep love for his own country, to whose cause he had devoted his long years of exile and all his waking hours since his return to his homeland.

Despite bitter objections by President Rhee, both sides began exchanging their views concerning an armistice in June 1951. Bitterly disappointed by the persistent rumor that there would be a cease-fire in the future, the Korean people did not hide their feelings.

In April of 1951 I wrote a long letter to Dr. Harold L. Stewart, chief of the pathology section at the NCI, giving him a detailed picture of the Korean War and the status of my cancer research. One day a messenger from the ROK Fifth Army Hospital came to the western compound of the Twenty-seventh Hospital, bringing me a letter from Dr. Stewart. After going to two physicians in New York City, where I thought the NCI was located, my letter had finally reached him at Bethesda, Maryland. Dr. Stewart wrote that he was very glad to hear from me and the titles of the papers submitted from Korea were interesting. It was a great misfortune, he said, that we were not able to attend the cancer congress. He wished that a favorable military decision would be reached in our country so that the South Korean scientists could reestablish their cancer research, which had gotten off to such a good start before the brutal attack launched by the Red Army of North Korea.

Six weeks later, several reprints of Dr. Stewart's research work came in the mail, and I digested all of them overnight. I was excited and greatly encouraged on receiving Dr. Stewart's letter and the papers, which boosted my morale tremendously.

During the month of July 1951, I thought much about my future and the continuation of my cancer research and came to the conclusion that I should go to NCI for further study. In order to try to make arrangements, it was necessary for me to transfer to Pusan, where all the government offices were located. So I submitted a request for transfer from the Twenty-Seventh Hospital to the Fifth Army Hospital, in Pusan. When I received word that my request was rejected, I walked fourteen miles to army headquarters to confront the paper shufflers in the surgeon general's office, with no positive results. During the following six weeks I sent three more requests for a transfer, all of which were rejected. Annoyed by my persistent, nagging requests, they transferred me to the Chunchon area—frontline duty—in order to get rid of the nuisance of one first lieutenant medical doctor. I submitted my transfer request three more times. Finally I was summoned to appear before Lt. Col. H. Y. Hong, chief of the Personnel Section, Surgeon General's Office, in Taegu. He was a professor and acting chairman of the Department of Pathology at Severance Union Medical College before the war, and I knew of him slightly.

"What the hell's eating you?" was Colonel Hong's first remark when I stood in his office the following week. There was a slight smile on his face.

The colonel listened to my story for over an hour. Then he nodded and told me to go back to my outfit and wait for an order to be cut in the near future. I was so impatient that I made a telephone inquiry once a week from the battalion headquarters. His answer was always the same: "Just sit tight."

After six agonizing weeks of waiting, I finally received an order to report to the commanding officer of the Fifth Army Hospital. I gathered my gear and all my papers and hitchhiked to Pusan, arriving on August 5.

I was trying to arrange my transfer to Pusan, the first call for an armistice was delivered on Sunday, June 23, 1951, by Jacob Malik, the Soviet delegate to the United Nations. There was no official announcement, however, for the ROK troops, perhaps because of their policy to uphold the fighting spirit. The Chinese Communists soon seconded Malik's suggestion, and many voices in the United States began to call for peace.

General Ridgway made a broadcast to the Chinese high command on June 30 stating that if they were ready for a cease-fire, the UN command would be willing to send representatives to discuss an armistice. It took a few days to make contact and agree upon a meeting place—the west coast town of Kaesong—with Vice Adm. C. Turner Joy representing the UN forces and the chief Communist negotiator, Lt. Gen. Nam Il, representing the NKPA.

The Americans, obviously not familiar with the Communist tactics of trying to wear down an opponent through endless and pointless arguments, did not anticipate that the talks would last more than two years. Both sides had immediately agreed that hostilities should continue during negotiations. In the war's second summer, while the negotiators droned on in a teahouse at Kaesong, foot soldiers fought over trackless hilltops and climbed painfully up granite ridges to take or retake positions the enemy would not let go.

On August 6 I reported for duty to Colonel Paik, at the ROK Fifth Army Hospital, through his adjutant, Capt. C. S. Kim of the Medical Service Corps, and the administrative officer, Lt. S. K. Park. To my surprise, I was ridiculed by these two men, who remarked sarcastically that I was not in my own private army, being transferred back and forth at my own will.

The very next day I received an order to join the ROK First Division, which was assigned to destroy large bands of guerrillas in South Korea, particularly in the mountainous area northwest of Chungju, where they had taken refuge after the Communist retreat. I was supposed to leave on the afternoon of the same day. Enraged by such an unreasonable order, I demanded to see Colonel Paik.

When Lieutenant Park questioned my reason to see the commanding officer, I said, "Look, I just got here from the front lines. You have plenty of medical officers hanging around here. Why don't you send one of them instead of me? I'm not going!"

The adjutant, Captain Kim, stepped in. "Lieutenant, this is an army order! You must obey!"

"This is ridiculous!" I shouted. "I've just arrived for duty. There should be military courtesy. *I'm not going!*"

"Are you saying that you are disobeying a military order?"

"I'm just saying that this is a ridiculous and unreasonable order for a tired officer to follow."

"In that case," Captain Kim calmly stated, "we have no alternative but to turn you over to the military police for a court-martial."

Angered by his statement and sarcasm, I said, "You do that. I don't care." I stalked out of the room and headed for the laboratory to see Eugene Kim.

On that afternoon four medical officers and ten corpsmen left the Pusan railroad station, without me, headed for Kwangju, regional headquarters for Operation Ratkiller.

After visiting my parents and sister, I came back to the hospital, about 4:30, to see Maj. T. S. Kim, the officer in charge of the clinical laboratories. He expressed deep concern about my refusal to obey a military order and asked me to reconsider. I was adamant, repeating my previous statement—that this order was very unfair to a tired soldier who had just arrived from the front.

I went down to the officers' mess for supper. Eugene Kim joined me. "Joe," he cajoled, "I know your intention for your future, but if this goes on your record—a court-martial for disobeying a military order—you'll be finished! Why don't you leave tonight and catch up with your main group at Taejon tomorrow morning?"

Although I nursed a steady anger at Captain Kim and Lieutenant Park, I felt deep inside that Gene was genuinely concerned about my future, and I decided to take his advice. So I left Pusan on the 10:00 P.M. train for Taejon and arrived at 6:00 the following morning. While I was having breakfast, I noticed my colleagues who had left the day before approaching the cafeteria. They stared at me and then laughed in a friendly manner.

Being a latecomer, I was given the worst assignment—to a remote area where a large band of Communist guerrillas with mortars and machine guns was controlling the sector during the night. I was awakened about 4:30 A.M. by shells exploding around our hastily set up tent and bullets crossing above. This was the first time I had been exposed to an attack by Communist soldiers.

My corpsman, M. Sgt. K. Cho, a twice-wounded, highly decorated infantryman who had recently transferred to the Medical Corps, shook me. "Lieutenant, we're under attack! We must hide!"

I followed him, crawling for about ten minutes. Then we ran into the woods. He whispered in my ear, "We must go into the forest and hide until help arrives."

Trees rose high above us, with ferns and foliage thick around the trunks. The area evidently was not used much, as vegetation flourished close to the path. We held our breath as we listened to the thud of Communist guerrillas' footsteps, the splashing of water, and the scraping of branches as they brushed past. Somewhere in the distance a bird was singing.

An hour later we took a path to the side and reemerged into a field leading up to the hill. The mist was lifting, and it looked as if the sun would soon break through the low, skirting clouds. It was a bright, crisp morning. The leaves on the trees were a translucent green, and the sun warmed us gently. After about an hour we were rescued by soldiers from the ROK First Division and taken back to the unit headquarters.

While I was sweating under the bushes, a fierce battle continued in the eastern sector. The Bloody Ridge was held by the ROK First Division, U.S. Second Division, and U.S. Marine Division, repelling the NKPA forces, which finally collapsed on October 5, 1951, with thirty-five thousand casualties. Our side took fifty-six hundred dead and wounded to maintain an advantageous terrain to defend.

B. L. Roh was transferred to the Seventh Division and assigned to the Thirty-sixth Regimental Medical Section. Most of the extensive fighting took place in the vicinity of the Punchbowl, or the Iron Triangle, with perhaps the most blood spilled in trying to seize and hold the hills.

In the battle of Hill 1052, according to B.L., the Chinese and NKPA started frontal attack on October 13, determined to take the hill and hold it. The sandy hill took so much blood from both sides that the surface soil became red clay. One of B.L.'s colleagues, Lt. H. Y. Lee, while he was treating wounded prisoners as well as his own troops suddenly stopped to stare at one of the prisoners. He was stunned to find that he was face to face with his older brother, from North Korea. They embraced and wept. This type of meeting was not unique. There were many, many cases in which brothers were fighting against brothers on the battlefields.

Following completion of my duty as a dispatched medical officer, I returned to the Fifth Army Hospital to discover that I was promoted to Captain, Medical Corps, effective September 15, 1951. During a celebration dinner given by Maj. T. S. Kim and Capt. Eugene Kim, I confessed that I had been wrong in refusing to obey a military order and I was ashamed of being arbitrary so many times. Later that night I confided to Gene my intention of going to the NCI. He advised me to seek help or at least understanding from Mrs. Francesca Rhee, who might remember me.

Instead of going to Mrs. Rhee, I visited the former minister of health, Dr. Koo, who was practicing pediatrician in Pusan. He encouraged me to approach Dr. Stewart about resuming my cancer research in the United States. "Young man, neither side can win this war, and the truce negotiations are still going on. A cease-fire will be signed sooner or later. You shouldn't waste your time here."

Encouraged by Dr. Koo's advice and Gene's suggestion, I visited Secretary Hwang at the presidential mansion. He urged me to initiate all the paperwork with the hospital's commanding officer and the army headquarters. When the papers arrived, Secretary Hwang would expedite the administrative procedures for me to go to the NCI.

When I returned to the hospital, I was summoned to the office of the new commanding general of the Fifth Army Hospital, Brig. Gen. S. M. Kim. As I stood at attention, General Kim told me that I was being dispatched to Chaeju Island, where the First Infantry training school was located, to bring nine hundred patients to the Fifth Army Hospital for treatment. I explained to the general that I was engaged in a planning session for my future and would rather not go at this time.

He interrupted me. "Captain, there will be no argument in this outfit. You will either go or end up in the military police station."

The next morning I left for Chaeju Island with three other medical officers and six corpsmen. The C-47 was delayed in taking off because of the weather. When we finally arrived at Chaeju Island, the patients had already been evacuated, taken the LST to Pusan.

During our stay at the infantry school compound, I briefly mentioned to one of the medical officers my intention of going to the United States to study cancer research

"Stop talking nonsense," he said. "You're crazy! How do you expect to go to the States during this hot war? You'd better start reading the infantry manual and military books to become a better soldier."

From that moment on I had a reputation for being the craziest, most hotheaded and arbitrary kid in the ROK army.

In August 1951, I was ordered to receive medical supplies for the Twenty-seventh Army Hospital and its satellite clinics from the ROK Army Medical Depot, located in Pusan Harbor. After the supplies and equipment were loaded onto the truck by the corpsmen and noncoms, we went on to my temporary home in Pusan for a brief visit with my family. Following the delicious lunch prepared by Mother for my noncoms and me, I inquired of my father concerning the whereabouts of Reverend Ro, a Princeton-educated Presbyterian minister and teacher of an English Bible class at the Fifth Army Hospital. My father told me that Reverend Ro was leading a small congregation in Song-Do, a resort town famous for its white sand beaches, ten miles east of Pusan.

I decided to pay Reverend Ro a visit and finally located his tent among hundreds filling the entire city of Song-Do. The tents were occupied by thousands of refugees from the north, as well as high school and college students. I explained to Reverend Ro my plan to go to the NCI to continue my studies in cancer research under Dr. Harold Stewart. The reverend expressed his pleasure at my determination but was afraid that my plans might be impossible because of the war and the chaos in the government.

I handed him a three-page letter I had written to Dr. Stewart and asked him to read it and punctuate it. He asked if I had discussed this with my commanding officer and my former professors at the medical school. When I told him that I was treated like an insane kid by my former teachers and the commanding officers, he said, "I don't really blame them for laughing at you, because this is an extraordinary attempt and a revolutionary idea."

After he read the letter, he commented, "Young man, this is too long and disorganized. You didn't even mention your purpose in writing until the last sentence. These men are very busy. You must get to the point at the beginning of your letter instead of beating around the bush, asking about their health and mentioning the weather in Korea." He condensed my three-page letter to half a page and advised me to at least discuss the matter with Mrs. Rhee.

There was a large two-story house at Song-Do beach occupied by the U.S. Eighth Army Counterintelligence Corps (CIC). It had all the comforts, including oil-burning stoves. The roof was festooned with high antennas. Well-fed noncoms and master sergeants were shuffling papers here. Three miles inland stood a single-story building converted to medical research laboratories by the ROK army Medical Corps. I instructed my driver and noncoms to wait for ten minutes at the front of the building.

Three elderly professors of medicine from Seoul National University were conducting research there in basic sciences in the fields of microbiology, pharmacology, and pathology. Prof. C. B. Park, a pharmacologist well known in Asia, welcomed me and offered me a cup of tea. "You almost made Paris, France. It's too bad your career has been disrupted by this war."

"Professor," I said "I think it's temporarily interrupted by this police action of the United Nations, but I expect to continue my studies in the near future."

Dr. Y. S. Kee, a professor of microbiology who had just returned from two years of microbiology research at the Rockefeller Institute in New York City, joined us. He asked me to see Lieutenant Colonel Shin, the officer in charge of the army Medical Research Unit. I had known Colonel Shin slightly before the war, as he had been a professor of pathology in Pyongyang and had done some research work in cirrhosis of the liver.

Colonel Shin asked me if I would be willing to join his team as a research officer. I thanked him for his offer but mentioned that I had my own plans, which I did not clarify.

One cannot observe elderly professors, determined to carry out their research projects under such adverse conditions, without feeling great respect for them. As I left Song-Do in the army truck, heading back to my outfit, I was more convinced than ever, after seeing those dedicated professors of medicine, that perseverance and determination are most important ingredients in medical research than fine facilities and fancy laboratory equipment.

16
Letter from Tennessee

On the completion of Operation Ratkiller, I was allowed to return to my original outfit on September 1, 1951. My new roommate, Capt. J. H. Harr, was one year ahead of me at medical school and a second-year resident in surgery at the university hospital. A tall, vibrantly energetic, and optimistic man with a great sense of humor, he had been born with a silver spoon in his mouth, but his unspoiled character invited many friends and much respect from his colleagues. Captain Harr, the son of the chairman of Seoul's largest bank, was a competent tennis player and accomplished violinist, with an insatiable appetite for classical music. We talked every night about our plans for the future after the war—his being to become a professor of surgery at Seoul National University and mine to continue experimental cancer research.

On a cold, rainy day in September I visited my old professor at his office overlooking Pusan Harbor and asked his opinion of my intention to go to the National Cancer Institute. There was irritation in his voice as he told me to forget the idea. "It's an impossible task," he said. "You must have a letter of sponsorship from the institution, first of all. You also have to file an affidavit guaranteeing your return passage with the Department of Education of the Korean government." Then he raised three other conditions that I could not meet.

Anger flashed in my eyes, but I was able to manage a smile. I was aware that his two sons and two daughters were working in the chapel of the U.S. Fifth Air Force Headquarters in Taegu as members of the choir, trying to receive donations from the GIs for their travel expenses to the United States. I left his office with deep disappointment but with more determination than ever to achieve my goal, saying to myself, *You just wait and see. I'll pull this off alone.*

Five days later Captain Harr received an order for transfer to the Fifth Division, and I was distressed to see him go. He invited Gene Kim and me to his home for a farewell dinner the next evening. I gasped at the opulence of the captain's home, with its ornate chandeliers hanging from the high, vaulted ceilings and the luxurious carpets that covered the floors. He had everything that anyone could hope for, with a brilliant future ahead of him. But none of us could see the cloud that was looming ominously on the horizon. When he reported for duty at the division headquarters, he was assigned to the battalion unit. The ROK Fifth Division soon disintegrated, and his outfit was completely isolated. Captain Harr took two of his combat-experienced corpsmen with him to withdraw to the south, but he made a wrong turn, heading toward the north. Within five minutes, twenty to thirty NKPA soldiers appeared from nowhere and ordered them to stop with their hands above their heads. In panic Captain Harr turned and ran, without hearing a warning shot. He was killed instantly, shot in the back with five bullets. His two corpsmen were captured but were exchanged for Communist prisoners after the armistice.

Bad news always travels fast. At Pusan Hospital, three days following Captain Harr's death, Gene and I were sipping tea when we heard the shocking news. "My God, how terrible!" I exclaimed. "I could be next!"

Overwhelmed with anxiety, I visited M. S. Kim, a highly respected professor of physiology at Severance Union Medical College, who always encouraged me to continue my cancer research. He agreed with me that I had to begin sending letters to various institutions in the States. He gave me two names of professors at Northwestern University and the Medical College of Virginia. The next day I sent a letter to Dr. Harold Stewart asking him to find a position for me in his section.

Three days later I was ordered to inspect the condition of the enlisted men and the sanitation in a regiment stationed at Masan. Before I could express my unwillingness to go, the commanding officer said with a tone of authority, "Captain, this will take only a week to ten days. It will give you some time to rest. I would suggest you gather your gear and set off immediately and redeem yourself, because your military record is not in the best shape."

I worked diligently examining the enlisted men and their sanitation conditions without complaining about the treatment or accommodations. On the last day of duty the commanding officer took me to a new winery, which had been producing a substantial amount of wine for approximately two months. At the end of the tour the manager of the winery presented me with six bottles of wine.

On the way back to Pusan an idea struck me. I had never bribed anyone in my life, and I simply did not know the opportune time to do it. However, the circumstances forced me to present four bottles of wine to Captain Kim, the colonel's adjutant, and his administrative officer, Lieutenant Park. The effect was amazing! The following day they began smiling at me when we passed in the corridors of the hospital, and I felt a tinge of friendliness toward them in return.

A bloody battle continued on the various hills—Heartbreak Ridge, Bloody Ridge, and countless others between our troops and the NKPA. We were receiving hundreds of wounded daily, most of them disfigured, with their limbs missing.

A letter from B. L. saying that he had been assigned to a Mobile Army Surgical Hospital (MASH) on the eastern coast and a recent visit to T.J. greatly depressed me. Gene Kim and I had become very good friends, and I shared with him the news about T.J. and his family. My youngest sister graduated from high school and was accepted by Ewha Women's University in the premedical course. My mother was spending most of her time at a Presbyterian church in Pusan, caring for orphans and war refugees. My father found a position at Soukwang University as a professor of literature, his lifetime desire.

On Saturday morning, November 26, 1951, I was drinking coffee with Gene following the general inspection by the commanding officer. A soldier from the mail room brought me a letter. It was from Dr. Harold Stewart, at the NCI!

Dear Lieutenant Song:
At the present time I do not have a vacancy in my section in which you would be interested. However, I have written to Professor Douglas H. Sprunt, Institute of Pathology, University of Tennessee, 858 Madison Avenue, Memphis 3, Tennessee, recommending you on the basis of your letters to me and of your enthusiasm for research and of your past training with Professor Yun.

Professor Douglas H. Sprunt has a very fine Institute of Pathology, is himself an outstanding research man and teacher in this country, and will give you every opportunity possible to participate in teaching, the routine work of the pathology department, and research. I feel that this is a real opportunity and I hope it will be possible for you to take advantage of it. I suggest you write Doctor Sprunt at your earliest convenience.
With best wishes.

Very sincerely yours,
Harold L. Stewart, Chief
Pathology Section

HLS:kob

99

Gene and I composed a short letter describing my experience in pathology training and cancer research, and I typed it and mailed to Dr. Douglas H. Sprunt, in Memphis, Tennessee.

On December 10 a letter finally arrived from Dr. Sprunt, offering me a position as an instructor and resident with remuneration of $2,800 a year:

Dear Doctor Song:

Doctor Harold Stewart of the National Cancer Institute has written me that you might be interested in coming here as a member of our staff. We have a position open as an instructor and resident which would pay $2,800 a year. The person would have about one-third of his time free for investigative work.

Please let me know promptly your training, experience, etc. if you are interested.

Sincerely yours,
Douglas H. Sprunt, M.D.

DHS: ja

P.S. The University could purchase your ticket to be repaid over a period of months.

DHS

"I finally got it!" I shouted as I jumped up and down and then rushed to the office of the commanding officer, demanding to see General Kim. After listening to my explanation, he understood and gave me a thin smile.

"This war is in a stalemate," General Kim said. "Neither side can win, nor do they have any appetite for general attack. For the sake of your own future, I think you should go to the University of Tennessee and study. Who can tell our future at this darkest period of our nation's history? But at least we can hope that you can continue your cancer research for our country." He shook my hand and embraced me.

Deeply touched, I thanked General Kim in a choking voice.

I experienced an overwhelming sense of contentment and wrote long letters to my friends—T.J., still depressed but recuperating from his amputation; Charles, with the UN Reconstruction Team as a civilian physician; and B.L., assigned to the Third MASH—telling them that I had received an appointment from the University of Tennessee and probably would be leaving within two months.

With my letter from Dr. Sprunt, I went to the surgeon general's office at ROK army headquarters in Taegu. Master Sergeant Lim, in

100

the Personnel Section, was waiting to help me complete paperwork for discharge.

"Captain," he said, "this will probably take three to four weeks, and we'll call you when the final paper has been approved." Neither of us was able to foresee the complicated paperwork and army red tape that would last for several more months.

Four weeks later I received a note from Sergeant Lim saying that my discharge request had been denied by the army brass because it would set a bad precedent. However, they suggested that I put in a request to change my status from active duty to Reserve Corps, which would again take three to four weeks to circulate and complete.

On my second visit to Taegu I could not hide my frustration and irritation, although I signed the papers to roll back to the reserve unit. When I said to Sergeant Lim that I was unable to understand why they had not suggested that in the first place, he replied, "Captain, you know the army. This happens all the time. Just be patient. We'll get your papers through."

When I arrived back at Pusan, there was a cablegram from the University of Tennessee asking me how soon I could come. Dr. Sprunt also requested specific instructions that he would have to follow to facilitate my leaving the ROK army.

By March 26, 1952, I had finally received permission for a leave of absence from the ROK army to carry out my study in cancer research at the University of Tennessee, and I was issued a special passport on April 5. I was summoned to see the surgeon general of the ROK army, Maj. Gen. C. W. Yun, a graduate of Edinburgh University and a specialist in obstetrics and gynecology for thirty years. General Yun was especially kind and told me to meet him at the American embassy in Pusan on April 7, at 4:00 P.M. He took me to Colonel Anderson, a military attaché, who in turn introduced me to Dale Green, the American consul, who took me to his associate Michael Olenik. Mr. Olenik, a very conscientious young man who had been in the foreign service for three years, assisted me in filling out the visa application to enter the United States. When all the papers were finished and typed, Mr. Green scrutinized them with nit-picking thoroughness and told me that there was only one thing missing—security clearance by the U.S. Army CIC. Mr. Olenik explained to me, "That may take some time because of the backlog the CIC people are handling." However, he said that to expedite the security clearance I should go to the ROK army G-2 Section in Taegu and receive an endorsement from the section head, Maj. Gen. H. C. Kim.

On my third trip to Taegu, I was introduced to 1st Lt. Charles Baker, who immediately signed the security clearance paper and told me to see Col. Gordon Douglas, who was assigned to the G-2 Section of the ROK army headquarters. With Colonel Douglas's endorsement, General Kim signed his name and gave me his blessing.

I then visited the headquarters of the U.S. Army CIC, which was located in Song-Do, near Pusan. There I met Captain Reinhardt, an officer in charge of the CIC, who was very sympathetic. He ordered his noncom, Master Sergeant Drew, to expedite the paperwork. On my second visit there, ten days later, Sergeant Drew signed the security clearance papers and wired them to the U.S. consulate in Pusan, where I finally received an entry visa to the United States on June 1, 1952.

In the meantime, Dr. Sprunt canceled my steamship reservation from Yokohama to San Francisco and reserved a seat for me with Pan American Airways from Tokyo to Los Angeles and from Los Angeles to Memphis via American Airlines. Dr. Sprunt told me later that he had to see his senator to facilitate my release from the Korean army, for which I was deeply grateful.

First Lt. Kenneth Lucas, from Missouri, was acting as a liaison officer between the Eighth Army and the surgeon general's office of the ROK army. Lucas was able to secure a seat for me on the DC-9 cargo plane that was to take me from Pusan to Tokyo. I owed so much to so many people, and I thanked God for providing me with so many guardian angels to help me along my way.

At a farewell dinner given in my honor by my friends from the Fifth Army Hospital and the University of Seoul, along with my parents and Professor Yun, B.L. stood up and gave a speech, which I still remember. He said something to the effect that when I returned to the homeland, they might not be alive because of the wholesale destruction and continuous fighting, but I had to carry on—single-handedly, if necessary—in reestablishing cancer research in our country.

The next day, the fourth of June, I visited Rev. J. B. Koh, secretary to Pres. Syngman Rhee, and Mrs. Rhee, to say good-bye. Mrs. Rhee was very thoughtful, asking if I had enough travel money to reach Memphis. When I hesitated in answering, she told Mr. Koh to arrange for me to exchange $500, loaned me by my friend C. H. Paik, a deacon of the Pusan Presbyterian church, at the official rate. This was almost impossible for common people. The ROK government was determined to preserve as much foreign currency as they could and was refusing to exchange at the official rate for outgoing students or businessmen. They made an exception for me.

I received a note from Pres. Syngman Rhee, which he himself had written with a brush in Chinese characters, saying: "Persistent work with perseverance can even move a mountain ten feet."

A telephone call came from General Paik, former commanding officer of the Fifth Army Hospital, then assistant surgeon general at ROK army headquarters. He expressed his congratulations and good wishes for my future.

"As you must know," he said, "you were a damn nuisance as far as this army is concerned. I had not expected the uncharacteristic boldness with which you refused to accept orders when you were supposed to obey. But, anyway, you have a determination and a will to endure suffering and handicaps. I'm sure you will succeed."

General Paik subsequently retired from the army and opened up a family practice in Taejon. When I visited Korea in 1966, he had died. It was ironic that most of those who had helped me were gone when I finally became financially secure and able to repay their kindness in some way.

On the evening of June 21, my mother prepared a sumptuous dinner for the family and my friends B.L. and Charles before my departure. We thanked God that so many distinguished people had reached out to help me, and we asked His blessing upon them and my family.

I gave $350 to my parents and kept $150. Then I started packing. My self-sacrificing mother, kindhearted, good-natured, and an extremely zealous person, began sobbing, telling me, "Son, I'm ashamed of myself because we were unable to give you financial aid."

"Mother," I said, "I owe my life to you! When I reach Memphis, I'll make sure that you will lead a comfortable life."

My father, with misty eyes, looked the other way. That night I could not sleep a wink, fantasizing on my future with feelings of apprehension.

At the Pusan airport my parents, my sister In Duck, and my friend B.L. shook my hand in a final farewell. In my ROK army Medical Corps uniform I boarded the DC-9, which was carrying many American servicemen to Japan for their vacations. As the plane circled above the city of Pusan and I looked down at the mass of straw huts and the pitiful surroundings, my heart ached as I realized what a poor country this was. I promised myself that I would do my best to make a contribution to my people and my country.

At Tachikawa Airport I met a kind, helpful U.S. Army captain, Glen Baker, who was in charge of the reception area. He asked if I needed hotel accommodations in Tokyo. When I told him that I was supposed to stay with my friend's uncle, Sun-Whan Oh, president of the Korean Import and Export Company, Captain Baker provided me with transportation to the city of Tokyo.

Mr. Oh, an entrepreneur and philanthropist, was a man of determination and perseverance who had made a significant contribution to the Korean business world and education. He went back to Yonsei University and obtained a Ph.D. degree in education and business education in 1970.

While I was waiting at the airport for a military vehicle, a nicely dressed, good-looking young stewardess approached me and asked if I was going to the United States. When I explained my intention and my family situation, she said that she had been a classmate of my sister at the Pusan high school. She was going back to Pusan on a small two-engine plane with the words *Korean Airlines* painted on the side. The plane was so small that I asked her if that was the largest aircraft they had. "Yes, for now," she said, "but we expect to grow rapidly in the future."

A Japanese policeman asked me if I could speak Japanese. I answered him in English, saying, "No." He was perplexed, wanting to say a few words, but turned and walked away. I had an intense hatred toward the Japanese people at the height of the Korean War.

When I visited my father's friend Dr. L. W. Chang, former president of Seoul National University, who was a consultant to GHQ in Tokyo, he gave me the name and address of his friends in Los Angeles and asked me to look them up when I arrived there.

I then paid a visit, bringing a bouquet of flowers, to the President of Park Industries in Seoul, President H. S. Park, also founder and chairman of the Hung Han Foundation, who so faithfully supported our research project to the end, and I thanked him from the bottom of my heart as I shared lunch with him.

Waving good-bye to Mr. Oh, I left Haneda Airport on the Pan American Clipper at 9:00 A.M. on June 25, headed for Wake Island.

17
Cease-Fire

Over the vigorous objections of the Korean people and Pres. Syngman Rhee to armistice negotiations with the Communists, the first meeting was held at 11:00 A.M. on July 10, 1951, at Kaesong. The hopeful UN delegates were headed by Vice Admiral Joy. It soon became obvious that the Communists' purpose in having negotiations was to earn more time for them to gain several more pieces of real estate during the talks.

The UN delegation excluded representatives of the Korean government and armed forces, with Lieutenant Commander Underwood acting as interpreter for the negotiations. The son of a Presbyterian missionary, Underwood had been in Korea born and raised there until he went to the States for his higher education. He had no penetrating knowledge or ability to understand the Korean language and was unable to interpret the conversations correctly. Lieutenant General Nam, of the NKPA, accused the UN delegates of insincerity and called the translator incompetent, demanding several more able translators before proceeding.

The stumbling block for the truce talks was the prisoner exchanges. The NKPA demanded the return of all prisoners from the North and South, including civilian volunteers, which was refused by the UN delegates.

Lt. Gen. James Van Fleet returned to the States and retired from the army in February 1953 in frustration and anger. General Van Fleet stated in his memoirs that General Ridgway had prevented him from driving on to total victory, and many Korean people concurred with Van Fleet's view.

Pres. Syngman Rhee reluctantly agreed to go along with the truce talks after being persuaded by Gen. Mark Clark and Ambassador Bliss. To break the deadlock, they reached a secret agreement with the NKPA delegates that all the NKPA prisoners would be exchanged upon completion of the peace negotiations, and the civilians would be

105

interrogated by the Red Cross and Indian soldiers, who would persuade the unwilling prisoners to return to North Korea.

President Rhee called an emergency cabinet meeting on June 10, 1953, and ordered the release of all anti-Communist NKPA prisoners and the civilians who did not wish to return to Communist North Korea. On June 18, 1953, twenty-seven thousand anti-Communist prisoners were released. This triggered an outcry of anger and protest among the American politicians in Washington and the staff of Gen. Mark Clark. Clark flew from Tokyo to Seoul to protest to President Rhee with anger and dismay, "Mr. President, you are trying to wreck this peace—"

President Rhee raised his hand without letting Clark complete his sentence, saying, "Calm down, General. Let me tell you what I think."

General Clark continued, "Mr. President, at least you could have discussed this with me prior to the action."

"If you were in my shoes, would you do that?"

Clark could not answer President Rhee's question. "But this is Washington's policy, Mr. President."

"To hell with Washington's policy and your Joint Chiefs of Staff! You anticipated the war, and you had no intention of completing your task. Your government and your military staff failed to see the military importance of the Korean peninsula." Then President Rhee motioned to General Clark that the interview was over.

Washington sent Assistant Secretary of State Robertson to Korea. He stayed for eighteen days to persuade the stubborn old politician to go along with the peace negotiations. Finally Syngman Rhee agreed, provided that an American-Korean defense pact be signed, with economic aid to rebuild the country, military aid to increase the armed forces to twenty divisions, and the strengthening of the Korean navy and air force. He further demanded and obtained an agreement from Washington that high-ranking American-Korean military and government officials would hold regular meetings to see to the reconstruction of the nation, and that should begin ninety days after the cease-fire.

I was in Memphis when I received detailed information in letters from B.L. regarding the peace talks and President Rhee's action, and I told Dr. Sprunt that I could not agree more with Syngman Rhee. Both Dr. Sprunt and Dr. Stewart later told me that they did not blame the old man. They would have done exactly the same. Furthermore, they both said that there should not have been any cease-fire talks.

I explained to Dr. Sprunt and my colleagues at the University of Tennessee that the Korean people were extremely disappointed and heartbroken over the cease-fire action, because we had gained nothing but wholesale destruction and so many casualties. A total of 415,000 ROK soldiers were killed, and 428,568 were reported missing in action. The dead and wounded and missing in action for the U.S. armed forces were reported as 157,530. Korean civilians received the heaviest casualties, with dead and wounded numbering 1,390,968. The war created 2,394,916 refugees. There were 900,000 NKPA dead and wounded, while the Chinese volunteers counted 520,000 casualties.

With such staggering casualty figures, no nation should be satisfied without accomplishing something to unify the country. My colleagues and professors at the University of Tennessee agreed with my view.

After the cease-fire, B.L. returned to the Department of Surgery at Seoul University Hospital. T. J. Park stayed in the hospital for physical rehabilitation programs. Charles Kim secured a job as a civilian consultant at the UN administrative office in Pusan. I was suffering from the heat and humidity in Memphis, Tennessee.

18
Pathology Residency Training

John Gaston Hospital, a 300-bed city-operated teaching institution for the University of Tennessee Medical College, was the only hospital to which the black people of Memphis and Shelby County could be admitted for treatment. There were about six private rooms and several large ones, fifty-five by forty-five feet, similar to those of the army hospitals in South Korea. Visiting hours were on Sunday afternoon.

It was quite a sight, as I watched from my eighth-floor quarters, to see the black people emerging from the back door of a city bus every fifteen minutes, colorfully dressed in red, green, and yellow, walking toward the entrance of the hospital. The scene reminded me of motion pictures depicting pre–Civil War conditions in the South.

The daily routine in the Pathology Department began at 8:00 A.M. with a morning gross conference for the second- and third-year medical students, conducted by the senior members. Classroom teaching followed, from 9:00 to 11:30, with a lunch period of approximately forty minutes. My afternoons were also regimented to perform at least two adult autopsies and one stillborn examination.

I had never seen so many stillborns for postmortem examination. Black people were very prolific, I was told, and many of the babies were dead in utero. A stillborn autopsy was to be completed within seventy-two hours after the consent was signed. Because of our teaching duties and adult autopsies, we residents always waited until the last minute to do the stillborn examinations. When the secretary checked as to whether I had performed a particular autopsy, I hurried down to the basement morgue. The stillborns were kept in the cooler, each one wrapped in brown paper, tied with string at each end, with a name tag attached. After a seventy-two-hour waiting period, the particular baby to be autopsied was always at the bottom of the pile and took several minutes to locate. During the search process some of the name tags became detached, and it was sometimes impossible to identify the baby.

108

The autopsy service was extremely heavy, requiring the student prosectors to complete 1,000 autopsies a year. I became quite friendly with some of the prosectors—Andy Warner, Bob Rainey, Jerry Berkley, Jerry Little, Joe Campbell, and Max Goodman. Joe and his wife, Anne, invited me to dinner several times a month, sparing me from eating the food at John Gaston Hospital.

One Saturday afternoon during the latter part of July, Bob Matthews, a fellow resident, and his wife took me to the banks of the Mississippi River to observe battle scenes recreating the Civil War, with five hundred to six hundred soldiers. On the south side of the Memphis–Arkansas Bridge there was a large, flat area of land, approximately fifteen acres. Several hundred Confederate soldiers, in gray uniforms, were in a trench in the northern sector of the area. Five hundred yards north of that trench were several hundred Union soldiers, known as "blue bellies," waiting for the attack by the Confederate troops. After they exchanged fire, with white smoke billowing from the cannons, a loud bugle call came from the Confederate troops, followed by charges against the Union soldiers. About an hour later most of the Union troops had been killed, and a few of them had fled or were captured. Thousands of spectators cheered the Confederate soldiers, who were achieving victory, waving their flags and loudly singing "Dixie."

It was a fantastic scene, but I did not understand its meaning until Bob explained to me, "We will never accept the defeat. We won many, many battles. We would have won the War between the States, had we had more industrial resources."

"But the Civil War was almost a hundred years ago," I said. "Can't you let it go and forget about it?"

"We never called it the Civil War," Bob replied. "We always called it the War between the States, and don't you forget it."

I learned how strong southerners' emotions were, with debilitating hatred in their blood for the Union soldiers. Stimulated but confused by such an expensive re-recreation of the Civil War battle scenes, I began studying the history of the American Civil War with interest and absorbed a great deal of information. Several months later I exchanged my views with Bob, saying, "It was a tragic mistake to cause such a mass-scale destruction, both North and South, with more than half a million men dead for the issue of slavery."

Matthews protested angrily, saying that the South had to fight to preserve their economy, based on their slavery.

"I had enough of the bloody war in Korea," I said. "I'm against any kind of war. The slavery issue and economic differences could have been settled through a series of negotiations by the North and South and in staged changes in ten years." I also brought up the fact that history cannot be changed. "You knew this was coming, anyway."

I had much admiration for Gen. Robert E. Lee, who felt for the Union side as a matter of principle but had to join the Confederacy by virtue of his birth in Virginia. After the surrender they took his citizenship away and never restored it until much later. Somehow I sympathized with the Southerners, who made heroic sacrifices for their cause.

Continually plagued by the inedible food at the hospital and the extremely heavy teaching duties, combined with my inability to understand the southern accent and to express myself, I became very, very homesick.

Most of the evenings I spent in my office, trying to finish my autopsy reports. Two young freshman nursing students from Decatur, Alabama, frequently visited me—Betty Adams, a beautiful blonde with musical talent, and Joyce Sanders, Betty's roommate. They stopped at my office two or three times a week for friendly conversation, followed by bottles of beer at a neighborhood café.

Trying to overcome the language barrier, I was frustrated with my slow improvement. Martha Dixon, a fellow resident, suggested that I watch television and go to movies to improve my understanding and speaking of English. I enjoyed seeing Western movies with Betty and Joyce and afterward drinking beer.

Some of the medical students must have seen us several times, as news of a new disease entity, "Song syndrome," began spreading like wildfire. Mort Gubin probably initiated this. He would ask the students, "Do you know what Song syndrome is?" Then he proceeded to explain. "Song syndrome is: first, a blond-haired girl; second, cowboy movies; third, beer drinking. If you know these three cardinal facts, you will be able to get by his lab test."

I usually took an after-dinner stroll to the small park dedicated to Lt. Gen. Nathan Forrest and sat on a bench with Betty and Joyce for conversation. They took me on a visit to Decatur, Alabama, in Betty's car. On our way we saw many black men and women working in the cotton fields, picking cotton. It was from this, I learned, that the expression *take your cotton-pickin' hands off* originated.

As soon as I arrived in Memphis, I was approached by Reverend Soltau, an Evangelical church minister who had been a Presbyterian missionary in North Korea. Whenever I was free to do so, I attended the Sunday services at his church, except when I was on first call during the weekend.

110

There was a large white building with the appearance of a church within walking distance of the Institute of Pathology, next to the student center. One Sunday morning, after completing the first autopsy, I decided to attend the church service there. After a brief prayer, I looked around to find a fairly large congregation assembled. During the next fifteen minutes, however, I noticed that there was no sermon. A man and woman on the platform read to each other from what I supposed to be their Bibles. On my way back to my room I had a strange feeling about the whole service.

The following morning I told Martha Dixon about it. She burst into laughter and told me, "Joe, you went to a Christian Science meeting! They don't believe in modern scientific medicine. Don't you know that?"

About three days later Dr. Sprunt told me, with a big grin, "Don't feel bad, Joe. Of course you didn't know that the Christian Science building was next to the student center. The dean of a medical school in one of our southern states is a Christian Scientist, so you never know."

Dr. Sprunt emphasized that autopsy is the nucleus of pathology. He had done rather extensive research in virus infections and brucellosis at the Rockefeller Institute. He held the view that postmortem examination must be done before autolysis, the degeneration of tissue following death, sets in. I felt that he was a real slave driver, forcing three residents to perform autopsies during the midnight hour or early in the morning.

Most of the autopsies on patients who died at John Gaston Hospital and several affiliated institutions were characterized by severe atherosclerosis (hardening of the arteries) due to excessive intake of cholesterol and fat. When the atherosclerotic disease process involved both kidney arteries, it would tend to cause high blood pressure, or hypertension, resulting in enlargement of the heart. An enlarged heart cannot pump a sufficient amount of blood to bring the venous blood into circulation, and most of the patients die of congestive heart failure with a terminal complication of pneumonia. In most cases the abdominal aorta was the site of severe atherosclerosis with calcification, with a very few exceptions in children and newborn infants. A high-cholesterol, high-fat diet, combined with the humid weather, may have enhanced the formation of atherosclerosis in both white and black people. In the black population there were many aneurysms (saclike dilatations) of the thoracic aorta, caused by the destruction of the elastic

111

fibers, due to syphilis. When the spirochetes penetrate the middle portion of the aorta, where an abundance of elastic fibers is normally seen, most of the fibers lose their elasticity and are destroyed completely. The thoracic aorta then is unable to stretch and contract as the aortic blood flows down to the abdominal area.

For the first time I learned the meaning of *bad blood* in terms of the cause of thoracic aortic aneurysms among black people. To me the ordinary meaning of *bad blood* was antagonism between two people who were unable to get along, but the definition of *bad blood* in medicine was the indication of syphilitic disease processes in patients.

Most of the autopsies at Seoul National University had revealed pulmonary tuberculosis, cancer of the colon, or cancer of the stomach and liver, and a large number of patients died of intracerebral hemorrhage, known as stroke.

There were many cases of coronary atherosclerosis with thrombosis, resulting in myocardial infarction, among white people, but I had never seen a significant degree of coronary atherosclerosis, inviting myocardial infarct, in black people in Memphis. When the blacks were infected with pulmonary tuberculosis, most of them developed a so-called galloping tuberculosis and died of tuberculous pneumonia, due to lack of racial immunity against pulmonary tuberculosis. Black people were never exposed to tuberculosis until they were brought into this country and thus had no time to develop an immunity against tuberculous infection, whereas Oriental people, belonging to the oldest race of human beings, seemed to have considerable racial immunity against tuberculosis.

The traditional method of performing an autopsy was to examine the body, organ by organ, removing them and laying them on the examining table. Our chief resident, Dr. Helen Proctor, demonstrated a so-called Rokitansky method, taking all the organs, from the windpipe to the rectum, in one large block and then turning it over on the table to examine the distribution of the venous system, condition of the aorta and renal arteries, and any anatomical abnormalities. Fascinated by Helen's technique, which allowed completion of the autopsy within an hour, I began copying her method. The variety of autopsy pathology at John Gaston Hospital maintained my scientific curiosity and interest, resulting in publication of many case reports.

All the residents hated to go to Oakville Sanatorium to perform autopsies on patients who had died of tuberculosis, particularly those black patients who had galloping tuberculosis with necrotizing pneumonia. I received an idea from one of the most interesting autopsy cases and began to accumulate similar cases for future publication of a book on sickle-cell disease. Autopsy pathology was indeed the nucleus of medicine, as Dr. Sprunt maintained, and I was fortunate to have been exposed to such interesting aspects of the science.

We residents were so thinly spread with teaching and performing such a tremendous number of autopsies that we fell far behind in completing our reports for the final diagnosis. Dr. Sprunt sent memorandum after memorandum urging us to finish the autopsy reports within six months. When that method failed, he came up with a new idea that produced excellent results.

"Those who have not completed their autopsies within six months," he said, "will not receive a paycheck at the end of the month. The checks will be held until the autopsy is completed."

We intensely disliked this policy, but it did work to clean up the outstanding autopsy reports, many of which were two years old.

A newcomer, Dr. J. Robert Tetraut, who was a forensic pathologist, raised the point that forensic pathology is different from general pathology and he should be exempt from that regulation. Tetraut did not receive his paycheck for five months, and he had to borrow money from the bank for his living expenses.

When the microscopic slides were prepared from the organs examined at autopsy, it was our duty to review the case with the students who performed the autopsy with us. As we went over the slides of the lesions seen on the table, long-lasting personal relationships developed between instructor and student. During evening hours, as I studied slides in my office, students and their spouses often stopped to say hello on their way home from movies or social functions. This continued until the students graduated from medical school, and I always enjoyed seeing them during off-duty hours and at parties.

Up to the early 1950s, two major types of cancer—breast cancer and cancer of the cervix—caused more deaths in women than any other type. In my native country more women died of cervical than breast cancer.

During the mid-1920s, a Greek physician and anatomy teacher, George Papanicolau, published an article showing cellular changes in a rabbit's cervix during the hormonal cycles. Papanicolau collected a large number of cells from rabbit's vagina and streaked them on a glass slide, using his own staining technique to illustrate the appearance of the cytoplasm and the nucleus of the cells.

In the early 1940s, Dr. Herbert Traut adapted the Papanicolau technique in studying cells collected from the cervix of women, to see whether early cervical cancer would create any cellular changes. This method is now widely known as the Pap smear test, used for early detection of cervical cancer.

In the middle of August 1952, I received a telephone call from Dr. Fred Chang, a biochemist at the Cancer Research Laboratory, asking me to pay him a visit. We met the next day on the third floor of the Cancer Research Laboratory, just across from the Pathology Institute. Dr. Chang had been born in Ohio and received his Ph.D. degree in chemistry from Ohio State University. He was a third-generation Chinese-American, working for Dr. Sprunt on a project to develop a new diagnostic test for cancer by comparing nucleic acid of tumor cells and that of normal cells. Dr. Chang took me down to the cytology laboratory, on the second floor, and introduced me to Dr. Edwin Schwartz, who was in charge of the U.S. Public Health Service and the Cancer Detection Project. There I also found six students in the cytotechnology school, four Pap-smear screeners, and an instructor.

The entire building was air-conditioned—a heavenly place to escape from the suffocating heat and 95 percent humidity. I soon found myself going to the cytology lab three or four times a week to attend lectures and practice screening Pap smears with the students and the instructor. Dr. Schwartz's assistant, Dr. John Sterling, from Youngstown, Ohio, and a guest physician from California, Dr. Robert Stone, also attended class with me. This field was something entirely new, a field of pathology that I had never been exposed to prior to coming to Memphis.

The principle of the cellular changes detected by the Papanicolau smear technique is based on the physiological changes involving human skin. If a portion of skin is placed under the microscope, one will see many layers of flat, square cells, known as squamous cells. When the cells reach the very top of the skin, known as the surface epithelium, they detach themselves from the epithelial structures. The detached cells are continually replaced by new cells reaching the surface area.

In the ordinary cervical segment, which is located between the vagina and endometrium (uterine corpus), the cervical epithelial structures are composed of many tall, picket-fence-type cells, known as columnar epithelial cells, which would be replaced by square, flat cells. The surface cells are detached from the underlying main structure and accumulate in the vaginal pool. If a vaginal aspiration is streaked on a glass slide and stained with the Papanicolau method, a large number of surface cells and some flat, square epithelial cells will be seen. If

114

cancer develops in that area, there will be a large number of cancer cells on the smears.

When cancer is limited to the epithelium, women have no symptoms, or are said to be asymptomatic. When the cancer cells break through the thin barrier dividing the epithelium and the underlying stroma, reach the blood vessels or the lymphatics, and are carried through the general circulation and lymphatic drainage, the cancer is known as invasive uterine cervical cancer.

Most of the cancer cells involve many lymph glands, particularly around the ureter, below the kidney. They become hard, round masses, later choking the ureter and causing ureteral obstruction. Unable to pass through the ureter, urine accumulates above the obstructed point. When this occurs, harmful waste products do not drain out but accumulate in the general blood circulation, causing uremia, which results in death. When I was a medical student in Seoul, I saw many cases of invasive cervical cancer. During a hysterectomy the instructor would show us a large cauliflowerlike tumor mass obstructing both ureters, for which nothing could be done.

The U.S. Public Health Service had established a mass screening survey for early detection of cervical cancer at the Cancer Research Laboratory in Memphis. Only a few physicians, mostly pathologists, understood the ramifications of the survey. They had been trained by a group of pioneers, headed by Dr. Joe Vincent Meigs and his able assistant, Ruth Graham, at Massachusetts Memorial Hospital.

Smears were taken from hundreds of asymptomatic women at the Gailor Clinic of the University of Tennessee. There were approximately five thousand cells on each smear, and it was the technician's task to examine the slides from corner to corner to detect abnormal cells representing early cervical cancer. I became fascinated with the early detection method, to be followed by limited surgery to remove a focus of early cancer from the uterine cervix. This procedure saved the lives of thousands of women who would otherwise have died several years later.

One of the technologists trained by Ruth Graham was Eileen Webb, the supervisor of the Cytology Department. She gave me reference material to study and provided me with samples of negative, suspicious, and positive Pap smears. Because of the possible application of this new method in my native country, I spent much time in the lab and studied a great number of slides. For my thesis for my master's degree in pathology and microbiology, I selected a topic in the field of cytological diagnosis of early uterine cancer.

In the cytology lab I met a honey-blonde named Betsy Long. She was from Oxford, Mississippi, the daughter of a dentist. We soon became friends and began dating. Betsy lived in Goodwin House, a block south of the Cancer Research Laboratory. It was very convenient for me to walk over there to see her and then to Forrest Park.

Several weeks later Martha Dixon mentioned my dating Betsy and inquired about her personality and background. I told Martha, "Betsy wishes to have an air-conditioned Buick, a mink coat, and a small mansion to live in. I think those are very tall orders. I don't think I'll be able to provide her with such luxuries."

Martha laughed, saying, "Joe, just stay as good friends, and be careful!"

Later that year Betsy invited me to the cytology department's Christmas party. She picked me up at 7:00 P.M. in her car. We arrived at the Cow Palace, in the western section of Memphis, where the party was to be held, and I escorted her through the entrance. I immediately noticed Edwin Schwartz and his wife. Momentarily forgetting Betsy, I walked toward Ed to shake his hand. A sharp pain in my elbow caused me to wince. I turned around to face an angry Betsy. "You're supposed to take my coat off, buster!" She remained furious for some time.

Driving me back to the institute later, Betsy said, "Joe, you don't understand women at all, do you? You have a long way to go."

"Betsy," I apologized, "I just don't have time to do anything but study pathology. If I offended you, I want you to forgive me." With that remark I returned to pathology and cytology and stopped seeing her. Many years later Bob Matthews told me that Betsy had married a Jewish fellow and moved to New York City.

In the early 1940s, Dr. Von Haam, at Ohio State University Medical School, created early cervical cancer in mice by applying a carcinogenic hydrocarbon and studying the cell structures by means of the Papanicolau method. Dr. Von Haam's was one of the most significant pieces of experimental work in the field of early detection of cervical cancer. When Dr. Von Haam was visiting in Memphis in 1954, I met him and was greatly impressed by his academic attitude. During a cytology meeting in 1955 in Cleveland, when I presented my first paper, Dr. Von Haam shook my hand and asked if I would be interested in joining him at the Ohio State University Department of Pathology.

I was saddened to hear, in October of 1955, that Dr. Schwartz was leaving Memphis to join a group of pathologists at St. Mary's Hospital in Cleveland. He had been instrumental in initiating the successful mass screening survey for Memphis and Shelby County and had published several articles concerning the usefulness of the Papanicolau smear in detection of early cervical cancer.

Because of the success of the mass screening survey, The U.S. Public Health Service decided to expand and establish several pilot projects. One of the sites selected was Providence, Rhode Island. I had no idea that I would eventually end up there to establish a mass screening survey.

One of the most important functions of a pathology department is to provide excellent surgical pathology service for the clinicians. When a specimen is removed from a patient on the operating table, the surgeon sends it to the Pathology Department for a description of the specimen and a diagnosis of the disease, either to confirm his impression or to receive guidelines for future treatment. One of the rapid diagnostic methods, called a frozen section, is utilized to render a diagnosis of benign or cancer within ten minutes following removal of a small piece of tissue.

When John Gaston Hospital staff members performed a breast biopsy or a lung biopsy, they would send a small piece of tissue, in gauze, through the pneumatic tube system to the Department of Surgical Pathology of the University of Tennessee Medical School. Usually the specimen reached us in half a minute or so. But one morning a specimen never arrived from the operating room for a frozen-section diagnosis. The hospital's maintenance crew spent all day locating a tube that was stuck in the system between the operating room and the Department of Pathology.

Dr. Anderson always urged us to take a microscope with us to the operating room and discuss the findings with the surgeons and surgical residents, to evaluate the whole situation and understand the ramifications of the disease processes. I still believe that he was absolutely right.

An interesting case representing amoebic infection of the skin occurred in a forty-year-old black male who had suffered amoebic dysentery two weeks prior to admission. A widespread skin destruction occurred in the perianal region, and he had to come to John Gaston Hospital for diagnosis and treatment. When I made a diagnosis of amoebic infection of the skin, many staff members did not agree. My diagnosis was confirmed, and I decided to submit a paper titled "Cutaneous Amoebiasis," to be published in the *Annals of Internal Medicine*.

When I informed three other residents at lunch in the cafeteria that my paper had been accepted for publication, their faces went pale.

117

One said, "We can't let this North Korean kid publish all the papers here." At that comment I left the table and went up to my office. I had to learn with difficulty at a later date how destructive professional jealousy is.

At one of the Thursday evening microscopic conferences someone touched on the subject of the scholarly activities of the Institute of Pathology. Dr. Sprunt suddenly stood, turned around, and said, "If we don't count Joe Song's publications for this department, we have to use only one hand to count the number of publications you fellows have put out." The atmosphere was chilly for the rest of the evening.

Max Goodman asked me to buy him a bottle of beer and a pizza at the Pig's Place after the meeting. He said, "It was nice of the old man to make such a comment to praise your achievement."

Three blocks south of the Institute of Pathology was a brand-new children's hospital, built a year or two before I arrived in Memphis. We received a small number of surgical specimens removed from children for the diagnosis of the tumor or different and difficult inflammatory processes. When I called Anne Phillips, chief laboratory technologist at the children's hospital, asking for clinical information, she replied, "I'd like to give it to you, but I can't just now. We're having a rat race!"

Not being familiar with the expression, I said, "Hold on! Wait for me! I'd like to see the race." I thought the race with rats was for the entertainment of the sick children.

There was a pause, and then Miss Phillips said, "Do you mean to tell me that you've never heard that expression?"

"No, but I wouldn't miss the race. I'll be on my way."

"Wait a minute! This isn't what you think. It's just an expression meaning that we're so busy that I can't give you the information you want."

With that conversation I added one more American slang expression to my vocabulary. About twenty minutes later Dr. Coy Anderson walked into my office with a big grin on his face. "So you would like to see a rat race, huh?"

Two weeks after that, at a clinical pathologic conference in the auditorium, I presented a case and everyone seemed to enjoy it thoroughly. Afterward Ben Leming said to me, "You brought the house down!"

"What house?" I asked.

Dr. J. Walter Scott, overhearing the conversation, laughed and said, "Joe, that's just an expression meaning that you did a fantastic job and they really enjoyed your presentation."

In those days, when the diagnosis of breast cancer was established and transmitted to the general surgeon he then would proceed with a radical mastectomy, removing the entire breast, the underlying muscle and fat, and all the lymph glands in the axilla. This did not always cure patients with breast cancer, because most of them would have to return to the hospital with recurrent cancer and later would die. Once the cancer cells invade the bone and the liver, the bone system and the liver are literally eaten up by the multiplying cancer cells.

I often wondered, when I was a resident, how much benefit the so-called radical mastectomy brought to the patient. Now surgeons perform a procedure called modified radical mastectomy, leaving the muscles intact but removing the entire breast and all the lymph glands, so that the patients are able to raise their arms after the operation. Radical mastectomy is a mutilating procedure, incapacitating many patients. I believe that a simple mastectomy would bring about the same results.

Every Monday evening there was a pathology conference at Campbell's Clinic to discuss the various types of bone tumors and bone diseases. Dr. Scott conducted a discussion session, through which I learned a great deal of surgical and bone pathology.

I believe that Dr. Sprunt was right in emphasizing that autopsy pathology is the nucleus of medicine. I developed more ideas for publication of papers and books from the autopsy material than from surgical specimens.

A fifteen-year-old black boy who died suddenly was brought to John Gaston Hospital for autopsy. We discovered that the boy had suffered from sickle-cell anemia since birth, producing a peculiar type of liver cirrhosis. This case gave me more information for future publication of a book titled *Pathology of Sickle-Cell Disease*. Another book was also suggested by autopsy pathology, and I began accumulating material for a monograph, *The Human Uterus*, which was published in 1964.

Numerous types of fungus infections in man I had ever known to exist were prevalent in Memphis. Such fungi could not survive in North Korea's cold weather, but the subtropical climate of Memphis, combined with the high humidity, must have enhanced the growth of fungi everywhere, resulting in many different types of fungus diseases. Among them a fatal histoplasmosis was always my main concern, because I had never been exposed to such a fungus disease. Blastomycosis was also a serious malady, as far as I was concerned.

119

19
Academic Achievement

One must be willing to spend several evenings a week and occasional weekends carrying out systematic projects in medicine and cancer research in order to publish creditable papers and books. This applies to both academic physicians and those in private practice.

A strong desire for performing investigative work and publishing scientific reports must be initiated from within the individual, according to Dr. Sprunt. In fact, he never suggested or even hinted at research work to the residents and senior staff members of the Institute of Pathology. This was left entirely to the individual.

I could not suppress my burning desire to resume experimental cancer research utilizing a large number of mice and rats. Through contact with Dr. John Wood, chairman of the Department of Biochemistry, and his graduate student Matthew Crone, we launched a small-scale investigative project. This was supported in part by a grant from John Wood. I was to induce squamous-cell skin cancer in several strains of mice by application of a 0.6 percent solution of 20–methylcholanthrene once a week. This carcinogenic solution was powerful enough to induce a squamous papilloma on the skin of a mouse after one week. The squamous papilloma would then become squamous-cell carcinoma approximately one month later. Matthew Crone gave the experimental groups of mice a subcutaneous injection of cystine, an unimportant amino acid, so that we could study its influence on the rate of tumor growth. After nine months of experiments, I found no difference between the two groups of mice as far as the tumor growth rate was concerned. All the mice finally died of metastatic carcinoma involving both lungs and liver.

As I received good grades in so many of my graduate school courses in pathology and microbiology, I had to write a thesis as a partial requirement for my Ph.D. degree, but I was unable to select a subject. One of my several case reports from 1955 dealt with the cytological diagnosis of adenocarcinoma of the fallopian tube, which gave me an idea for my thesis. I mentioned my topic selection to Dr. Sprunt, who had on several occasions questioned me about it. "I think I will make a comparison, in various cancer patients, of the histological pattern of the tissue cells and the appearance of the tumor cells seen on the Pap smears."

"Well, that's a splendid idea, Joe," he remarked. "You should go ahead full-speed."

I collected 161 cases of cancer patients with various types of malignant tumors and made paraffin tissue sections to be stained with hematoxylin eosin and examined under the microscope. At the same time I made touch preparations on the tumor, to be stained by the Papanicolau method, to compare the cell types of the cancer. It took me about two years to complete this study and another seven months for publication.

Many of my colleagues mentioned to me from time to time that they would like to do research, but they simply did not have the time because of family obligations. I said to them, "If you really want to do research, you'll find the time. Look at Dr. Russell Jones, who has eleven children but is able to produce several papers a year."

I was tremendously stimulated by Dr. Jones, assistant professor of pathology and a pathologist at West Tennessee Tuberculosis Sanitarium. He was extremely productive, continually publishing papers, yet carrying out his teaching duties and routine service pathology. "You must be born with such a desire," he explained.

Whenever my medical friends saw my publications in medical journals, they would ask, "When do you find the time?" My answer was always: "You make the time if you are really interested." There was plenty of material available, yet very few pathologists utilized it.

To become a specialist in medicine, one must take intensive training in a chosen field, such as internal medicine, general surgery, pediatrics, radiology, or pathology. Each specialty requires one year of rotating internship, followed by two to four years of residency. Upon completion of residency training in the selected field, one must pass the examinations given by the specialty boards, such as the American Board of Internal Medicine, American Board of Surgery, and American Board of Pathology.

The pathology board required one year of rotating internship, followed by four years of pathology training, or five years of straight pathology training. Dr. Sprunt wrote to the secretary of the American Board of Pathology, Dr. William B. Wartman, at Northwestern University School of Medicine, about my eligibility for board examinations. Dr. Wartman informed me that I would be eligible for examinations in both anatomic and clinical pathology in July 1955, three years after I had arrived in Memphis. He took into consideration the fact that I had done cancer research at the University of Seoul School of Medicine and had also completed two years of graduate study toward a master's degree in pathology and microbiology.

I was a bit apprehensive on receiving the news, because many of the residents from the Institute of Pathology had to repeat the examinations. In fact, our chief resident, Dr. Helen Proctor, had taken the examinations in 1954 and did not pass. This gave me a tremendous fear of the pathology board examinations.

When I expressed these fears to Dr. Sprunt, he said, "Don't worry, Joe. You'll pass. But I want you to join two pathology groups. One is the American Association of Pathologists and Bacteriologists, and the other is the American Society of Experimental Pathologists."

I really felt that Dr. Sprunt was overly confident of my ability but thanked him for his comment.

The American Association of Pathologists and Bacteriologists was, of course, an academic society for pathologists and bacteriologists. To become a member, one had to prove his or her ability by performing and publishing research work in pathology or microbiology. The association rejected outright the applications of Dr. Albert Smith and Dr. Bob Tetraut, both assistant professors at the University of Tennessee, because of lack of academic accomplishment, but they tabled my application for one year. According to Dr. Sprunt, they felt that I was a potential academic pathologist because of my publications of case reports, but I had to do original research in pathology.

When Al and Bob learned that their applications were rejected but mine was tabled, they were furious. Furthermore, they disagreed with Dr. Wartman's decision qualifying me for the board examinations.

I was assigned to the hematology laboratory for a three-month rotation to gain experience in clinical hematology. The department head was Dr. L. W. Diggs, a graduate of Johns Hopkins University Medical School. In his section I was assisted by a resident in medicine, Dr. Jeff Gordon, supervisor Ann Bell, and able technologists Helen Goodman and Julia Burke, to whom I owe a great deal.

Red blood cells, which carry oxygen to all the tissues, and white blood cells, which protect the body against bacterial infection and secrete antibodies, are produced in the bone marrow. There is constant production of a mature type of blood cells from primitive cells, but only mature forms are released into the general circulation. Immature forms remain within the marrow space of the bony structures. In a patient with leukemia (cancer of the blood) the mechanism of production of mature cells is impaired for unknown reasons, stimulating the proliferation of immature forms. When a patient is suspected of having leukemia, it is necessary to examine the bone marrow by drawing about 10 cc. of marrow blood by means of a needle. To ease the pain of the needle's penetration, the cortex (hard part) of the bone is anesthetized.

Dr. Gordon asked me to perform my first bone marrow examination, on a black woman. I injected 5 to 10 cc. of novocaine onto the bony cortex of the patient and in a few minutes proceeded with the aspiration, using a fairly large, straight needle. I pushed the needle with such force that it penetrated the marrow and stuck to the other side of the bony cortex. As a result, nothing could be aspirated. When I tried to repeat the procedure, the patient screamed, and the nurses came running in. With the patient cursing, I quickly left the room and Dr. Gordon took over. Back in the lab I was teased by Ann, Helen, and Julia, who said that this was the first time this had happened since the opening of the hematology department.

After rotation through the hematology lab, I was assigned to the clinical chemistry laboratory, under the direction of James Morrison, Ph.D. He was always eager to show me the instruments used to measure the chemical elements in the body. The alterations of chemical components, such as blood urea nitrogen, phosphorus, enzymes, and blood sugar, are reflected by different diseases, and measurements of the various components indicate the severity of disease, giving guidelines for treatment. In spite of the sophisticated instruments and complicated procedures, I never developed a taste for clinical chemistry and left that department, after three months, with a feeling of relief.

My next assignment was the blood bank of John Gaston Hospital, to study blood types, antibodies, antigens, and methods of crossmatching blood for transfusions. After two weeks I became so bored that I began visiting the cytology lab for more training there. Jean Span, head of the blood bank and a broad-minded person, ignored my frequent absences from her department. A dedicated Southern Baptist, she said to me one day, "I'll make a deal with you, Dr. Song. Since I have to sign your paper to certify your completion of rotation, you show slides of your native country to my Baptist church group, and then I'll let you go." I gladly accepted her offer, borrowed some slides of Korea from the chaplain at the air force base, and received her signature for the blood bank course.

Next was the microbiology laboratory, headed by Dr. Israel David

Michelson, an associate professor of pathology and head of the Jewish medical fraternity at the university. Dr. Michelson was a graduate of Johns Hopkins University Medical School and a true academic microbiologist, spending his entire life in the study of bacterial mutation. He asked me if there were any Jews in Korea.

"I remember seeing a small number of White Russians in Pyongyang," I said, "but I'm not sure whether they were Jewish or refugees from Joseph Stalin."

From the members of the Jewish medical fraternity I heard that the university had a quota system in admitting Jewish students to medical school, and I expressed my displeasure to Dr. Michelson, saying, "I always hated the quota system under the Japanese government. It's a discriminatory regime." I recalled being the object of discrimination in Seoul, during my school days, because of my northern accent and my way of thinking.

Dr. Michelson replied, "You'll learn in the future all about the anti-Semitism and bigotry of the southern people."

A new assistant professor became my superior in the fourth-quarter teaching during the summer of 1953. The students consulted me quite frequently, saying that they could not understand my associate's lectures because of his stammering, and when they asked questions he became angry. They went to Dean Hyman's office and complained about their teacher's methods, his stuttering, and his temper. They realized that he was a well-trained pathologist, but he was unable to communicate because of his speech problem.

On November 19, 1954, the American Board of Pathology generously allowed me sufficient credit to take the examinations in both clinical and anatomical pathology, following completion of my training at the University of Tennessee on June 30, 1955. This of course would not have been possible without Dr. Sprunt's help. Once I was declared eligible for the board examination, I became very worried and began to doubt my ability to pass.

An assistant professor was saying to everyone that the North Korean kid would never pass and he would bet anyone $100 against my success. His negative reaction did not deter me. I was encouraged by comments from J. Walter Scott and Bob Tetraut, who argued with him that the "North Korean kid" had eyeballs for making a diagnosis on the slides, and they predicted that I would be the only one to pass, the first time, from the Institute of Pathology.

Martha Dixon patted me on the back, saying, "Joe, do the best you can, but don't feel bad if you fail, because a lot of people don't pass the first time."

In April 1955, I visited Dr. Joe Young, chief pathologist at the VA hospital in Memphis, to review his vast slide collection of various fungal diseases affecting human subjects. At the end of the day Dr. Young offered me a lift from the hospital to the Institute of Pathology. He said, "Joe, I have no doubt that you will pass the examination, and I mean it from the bottom of my heart."

"Dr. Young, I appreciate your confidence in me," I replied, "but I just don't feel that I have enough background."

As I passed through the hallways at the Institute of Pathology, many professional and clerical people expressed their confidence in me, but their remarks were of a superficial nature, and I paid little attention to such gestures. Nonetheless, I began concentrating my efforts on the forthcoming examinations, which were to be given in October 1955 at Northwestern University Medical School, in Chicago.

In the middle of May I telephoned Dr. Helen Proctor, who had passed the examinations successfully in April and secured a job as associate pathologist at Methodist Hospital in Memphis. I asked her to help me in preparing for the examinations. Helen showed me samples of all types of questions, including multiple-choice, true-false, exclusion-of-answers, etc. The more I studied the samples, the more discouraged I became, but I continued to study books and slides.

The weather in June was hot and humid. I was able to study in the air-conditioned histology tissue lab, with the kind consent of Jean Wells, supervisor of that section. With the help of my officemate, Dr. Edwin Herring, I bought a secondhand 1950 Chevrolet.

Dr. H. T. Lee, a Korean physician, arrived for training at West Tennessee Tuberculosis Hospital. He was a gourmet Korean cook, and my frequent visits to his apartment solved my chronic problem of hunger and indigestion.

Early on the morning of October 1, I left Memphis, with a microscope and microscope lamp in the trunk of my car, headed for Chicago. I planned to stop in Saint Louis to visit Andy Borg, who had been a commanding officer at the Field Laboratory of the U.S. Eighth Army in Pusan.

Twenty miles south of St. Louis on a two-lane highway, I was trying to pass a slow-moving vehicle when I noticed an oncoming car and was forced to stop suddenly on the wet pavement. Spinning 360 degrees, my car ended up in the ditch with steam pouring from the radiator. I must have passed out for a few moments. Someone opened the door and asked if I was all right. I was sure that this was the end as far as the board examinations were concerned.

A Good Samaritan appeared in a Ford two-ton pickup, pulled the car out of the ditch, and took me to a Western Auto store to buy a new radiator hose. I looked into the trunk and found that the microscope and lamp were intact, and I felt then that I would pass the examinations. On the evening of October 3, I reached Chicago, checked into the St. Claire Hotel, and collapsed on the bed.

The morning of October 4 was devoted to a written test, comprised of 360 questions. When I was about halfway through, Dr. Wartman walked into the room and told us that if our answer was right, we would gain one point, but we would lose one point on a wrong answer. "If you're not positive about your answer to any particular question, you had better leave it alone; otherwise you will lose a point," he said. Human nature being as it is, we took chances, answering all 360 questions.

We spent the entire afternoon on the practical examinations, with fifty Kodachrome slides projected on the screen, and examining thirty gross specimens for pathological diagnosis. When the examination was over, around five o'clock, everybody was exhausted.

The following morning we had fifty glass slides representing various human diseases for diagnosis, and I finished them all around 11:30 A.M. On my way home to Memphis, I made an overnight stop at Indianapolis to visit an old friend, Dr. Oh, who was studying virology at the University of Indiana.

When I arrived safely back in Memphis, I was bombarded with questions from the residents and senior staff members. Two agonizing weeks passed before I received the results from the board, as I did not know that Dr. Sprunt had found out the results the very next day.

I had gone through Moore's *Textbook of Pathology* to find that many answers I had given were wrong and begun drinking more beer at the Pig's Place.

Finally Dr. Sprunt told me that I had passed. When I asked him what the written test score was, he said that many of the candidates scored -56 or -70 points. "Joe, you didn't miss a single slide or a single specimen. You are now a diplomate of the American Board of Pathology.

My friend Eugene Kim, at that time a radiology resident in Hartford, Connecticut, wired me to congratulate me on my passing the board examinations. I then sent a cablegram to Charles Kim, a resident surgeon at the university hospital in Seoul. Charles later told me that when he gave the news to S. S. Lee, assistant professor of pathology, saying, "Joe is the first Korean ever to pass the American Board of Pathology examinations," Lee's face went pale. Dr. Lee had been three years ahead of me in medical school. He spent eighteen months at Cornell University Medical School, in New York, and then returned to Korea during the war.

I became very homesick and wrote a long letter to my former chief of pathology, Professor Yang, asking him to find a suitable job for me, as I was ready to return to my native country. Six weeks later I received a letter from him informing me that the position of assistant professor of pathology was available, but there would be no professional remuneration because of a recent budget cut. I made further inquiry regarding the possibility of drawing a salary one year later. His reply was not promising. He said that it might take three years to receive approval from the Ministry of Education to receive a standard assistant professor's salary.

When I showed the letter to Dr. Sprunt, he laughed. "Joe, how can you make a living without professional remuneration for three years? You'd better stay with us in Memphis."

I felt that I should gain more experience in other parts of the country and expressed my desire to relocate on the East Coast.

"I'll find a suitable position for you," he said.

On the afternoon of January 2, 1956, an overseas telephone call came from my two good friends Charles and B.L., who had tried to secure a position for me in the Department of Pathology at Seoul University School of Medicine. They told me that as long as Dr. S. S. Lee, assistant professor of pathology, was regarded as the rising sun, I would have no chance of obtaining an appointment there. B.L. said "Joe, it seems to me that you're the victim of professional jealousy." They both advised me to stay in the States.

Encouraged by Dr. Sprunt, I continued to study for my Ph.D. in pathology and microbiology. I had earned enough credits and passed the preliminary examination toward a Ph.D., but there was one big problem—satisfying the requirement for two foreign languages. I was able to pass German but had no knowledge of French. I argued with the university officials, saying that as far as I was concerned, English was a foreign language, so I should be exempt from this requirement.

"You have a point there, but rules are rules," I was told by the officials. "You must pass one more foreign language."

Dr. Wood suggested that I go to the University of Chicago to take a Japanese-language examination, and they would accept the university's certificate in fulfillment of the foreign language requirement. I was not eager to make a trip to Chicago. The Japanese language presented no problem, but I still harbored feelings of hatred toward that nation.

My courses in immunology, hematology, and microbiology added a tremendous dimension to my knowledge of pathology and medicine. I finally settled for a master of science degree in pathology and microbiology, although I learned later the M.S. degree means absolutely nothing as far as professional promotion or achievement is concerned. Nonetheless, I had to submit a thesis to the university and have an oral defense for my thesis. I shall never forget the kindness of Louise Dunagan, who prepared my manuscript of 180 pages and thirty-six illustrations, *The Cytopathology of Human Uterine Cervical Cancer*. Miss Dunagan did not charge for her typing, and I presented her with a gift of a Korean jewelry box, sent to me by my sister.

On the evening of March 26, 1956, I received my degree, along with 250 other graduates, in the auditorium of the University of Tennessee. There was a reception afterward with Miss Dunagan and Dr. T. P. Nash, who told me that I was the only resident who had pursued my graduate study to the end. Four other residents who began the course had faded away or dropped out.

It was difficult and occasionally impossible to understand Dr. Sprunt's thinking in terms of staff assignments for various teaching duties. He assigned a first-year pathology resident to be in charge of the class teaching for the fourth-quarter medical students, and I was to be his assistant. This made very little sense. The resident, a former navy man during World War II, was eccentric, crucifying medical students with strange questions and unorthodox methods of testing their knowledge. He spent three solid days lecturing on the pathology of tetanus with his tape recorder playing his lecture over and over. According to the textbooks, there are no identifiable tissue changes produced by tetanus bacilli in human subjects. He ridiculed a former navy man, who had dropped out of the U.S. Naval Academy, by asking such absurd questions that he had to walk out of the class. The students went to Dean Hyman's office, complaining about the resident's eccentric behavior and poor teaching methods.

I told the resident that I would have to concentrate on my research papers, so I would not be able to assist him. Two days later he informed me that I had to obtain permission from Dr. Sprunt to be exempted from the teaching duties. That was nonsense, I felt. I decided not to attend his classes at all.

One afternoon I was summoned to Dr. Sprunt's office. "You've done a lousy job here, Song!" he screamed at the top of his voice his face turning red.

I remained calm, saying, "Dr. Sprunt, I don't know what you're talking about."

"You know damn well what I'm talking about!"

"Dr. Sprunt, I finish my autopsies on time and got all the reports out on surgical pathology faster than anybody else here."

"I ain't talkin' about the autopsies or your research papers! If you think you're better than [here he named the resident] you're a cockeyed meatball!"

This gray-haired, stocky figure, with his red face, acting so childish, was a somewhat unusual and humorous sight. I grinned and that made him even angrier.

"What are you grinning about? Get out of my sight!"

Three weeks later I was called to his office for a second conversation which was conducted calmly with a mature attitude. *The Sprunt storm is over*, I thought: *Now it's smooth sailing.*

"Joe, I've found a job for you. There's a new project in Providence, Rhode Island, for the early detection of cervical cancer by means of a mass screening survey with Pap smears. Would you be interested?"

"I would," I said.

"I'll send a wire to the pathologist in charge of this project." Then he explained to me that Rep. John Fogarty, chairman of the House Appropriations Committee, had received sufficient funds to set up the pilot project in Providence.

At Dr. Sprunt's suggestion, I made a trip to Providence, on March 16, for a job interview. There I met with Dr. Henry Murphy, director of the state cancer control division; Dr. Jack McCormick, director of the state health department; and Dr. Jerome Hager, pathologist in charge at Providence General Hospital. Dr. Murphy introduced me to John Fogarty, the Democratic congressman from Rhode Island. I also met George Kelly, his Providence office manager, and William Lynch, his Washington office representative.

John Fogarty and the state health department officials were eager to set up the mass screening survey for detection of early uterine cancer. He had secured an $80,000 grant from the U.S. Public Health Service for operation of the survey for one year, with the understanding that the grant would be renewed for two additional years.

129

The laboratory was to be located in Unit H of Providence General Hospital's old wing. There would be extensive remodeling and renovation, as it had not been used for five years. We walked through the unit and found several dead pigeons on the floor.

Rhode Island, the smallest state of the Union, was densely populated. There were people of Italian, Irish, and Portuguese descent, a small fraction of black people, and so-called Yankees, representing Anglo-Saxon descendants. The goal of the project was to screen a minimum of 200,000 asymptomatic women to discover as many cases of early cervical cancer as possible in three years. I was to be the pathologist in charge of the project. I would train cytotechnicians and form the Central Task Force Committee, absorbing local pathologists, gynecologists, general surgeons, and general practitioners. An advisory committee was to be established, including two laypeople, a media representative, a journalist, physicians, and hospital administrators. I was very encouraged by the enthusiasm and support of the people I met.

From Providence I went on to New Haven, Connecticut, to visit Eugene Kim. We had not seen each other since I left Korea. Gene warned me that there would be political chaos in Korea because of opposition to Pres. Syngman Rhee and his regime and advised me to stay in the States for at least five years, concentrating on cancer research and more publications.

Two days later I visited Dr. H. Hahn, another of my army colleagues, who was an anesthesiology resident in New York City. He felt that I should stay in this country for good. Understanding my desire to return to Seoul for a teaching appointment and to care for my aging parents, he said, "I know how you feel. But you wouldn't be able to find suitable employment there because of the political turmoil and the professional jealousy."

I returned to Memphis to prepare for presentation of a paper titled "Pathology of Liver in Sickle-Cell Anemia" at the forthcoming meeting of the American Association of Pathologists and Bacteriologists in Cincinnati, Ohio.

Within three days I received an offer from Providence to be pathologist in charge of the mass screening survey, with an initial yearly compensation of $12,000. I discussed this with my parents and my sisters over the telephone, and they agreed that I should accept the offer. A letter from Representative Fogarty's office indicated that they would sponsor a bill to change my immigration status, enabling me to stay as a permanent resident.

During the next few months I prepared a sufficient number of Kodachrome slides to train technicians for screening a vast number of

130

Pap smears and completed a manuscript for publication in the *American Journal of Pathology*.

At one of the Thursday evening conferences, Dr. Sprunt and I had a fierce argument over a case that I was presenting. It was ovarian cancer, with components of bone, cartilage, brain tissue, and skin within the tumor. Dr. Sprunt asked me whether this represented a teratoma or the different components of cancer. We argued for several minutes concerning the definition of teratoma. I would not budge to accept his explanation.

"That's what the textbooks describe," he insisted.

"But, Dr. Sprunt, the textbook is not always right," I replied. Everyone laughed.

I appealed to Dr. Anderson. "I need your help."

He looked at me from his seat, five rows back. "I couldn't do any better than what you're doing."

All the staff members later told me that they enjoyed my going against the old man's opinion. It was a historic event for the department, according to Dr. Bill Check.

My stay in Memphis was a period of hard work and training programs, but I still believe it was the golden age of my life.

In my 1950 Chevrolet, loaded with my suitcases and stereo equipment, I arrived in Providence on July 5. I was advised to stay at the YMCA for a few days. During the night I became terribly homesick and severely depressed. Later I found a small apartment on the East Side and finally settled down for the job.

All my life I had been handicapped by my baby face and small figure. Many salesmen and physicians thought I was a seventeen-year-old kid who had just arrived from Korea. My secretary in Providence, Gloria Abbey, suggested that I take up pipe smoking to give the impression that I was a board-certified pathologist, ready for the job. It was the wrong advice. To this date I regret having acquired such a nasty habit.

I worked diligently sixteen to eighteen hours a day, talking with state government representatives and the medical staff of Providence Hospital and becoming acquainted with the local pathologists. It was my good fortune to meet Dr. Gary Romeo, a pathologist at Memorial Hospital, who became my close friend. Romeo told me that approximately 40 percent of the state's residents were of Italian descent and that there was a fierce undercurrent of antagonism among the Italians, Jews, and Irish. This became only too obvious to me during the next three years.

20
Project in Providence

To succeed in the statewide cancer detection project it was necessary to form a task force, composed of several committees. Dr. Henry Murphy became the program director. He worked closely with Robert Murphy, director of the Rhode Island Division of the American Cancer Society, and me. We organized a Publicity Committee, composed of Robert Murphy; Harry McKenna, a Providence radio commentator; Betty Adams, a TV columnist; and George Kenney, representing the state public relations office. The Medical Advisory Committee included Gustav Motto, representing the general practitioners; Henry McBride, a well-known gynecologist; Henry Gothier, a general surgeon; and Gary Romeo, representing the Rhode Island Society of Pathologists. Henry Murphy served as chairman of the committee. I decided to stay behind the scene, maintaining a low profile, and try to give much credit to Dr. Murphy and Dr. George Waterson, an emeritus of the Department of Gynecology at Providence General Hospital.

The laboratory director, Dr. Jerome Hager, hired an experienced cytotechnologist from Roosevelt Hospital, in New York City. She became the source of continual problems, antagonizing not only the physicians but also members of the media and employees of the hospital's housekeeping department. It was the unanimous decision that she be dismissed.

When my attempt to obtain trained cytotechnologists from Memphis failed, it became obvious that we needed to recruit students and teach them to read Pap smears and discover tumor cells among the normal cervical epithelial cells.

Operating the project required my concentrated efforts. Setting up the laboratory was a great challenge for me. I worked fifteen hours a day, negotiating with the state comptroller's office for budget changes and dealing with laypeople as well as physicians to coordinate the committees. In fact, the project gave me considerable experience in dealing with people with a certain degree of administrative skill, which became invaluable to me in my future career.

One day in August, I was invited to have lunch with a prominent physician. As we conversed at his country club, he criticized Dr. George Waterson severely for rejection of his staff-membership application at Providence General Hospital. "George Waterson is an old New England Yankee who hates Irish people," he said. "My great-grandfather was unable to get a job in the Boston area because no one wanted an Irishman, so he had to change his name and pretend to be Scottish to obtain a menial job."

"Most of the policemen in the Boston area are Irish, aren't they?" I asked.

"Now you have to be Irish to get a job as a cop. George Waterson hates me because I'm Irish," he replied.

"But Henry McBride, his associate, is of Irish descent, isn't he?"

He grimaced but did not answer.

A week later I played golf with Dr. Stanley Cohen, a general surgeon and gynecologist at Miriam Hospital. He told me that they had to build their own Jewish hospital because they were denied staff membership at Providence General Hospital. He was extremely bitter at not being able to get onto the staff of the largest private hospital in Providence.

I emphasized the fact that our aim was to screen 200,000 women, regardless of their nationality or race, and all the physicians who participated in the project would be treated fairly and equally. It was disheartening to see the undercurrent of fighting among the different nationalities in the medical profession.

For the next three months I taught four students, using a condensed program covering the histology of the female genital tract, biology of the cells, and characteristics of cancer involving the uterus and cervix. This enabled the students to screen a large number of Pap smears mailed in from various parts of the state.

We were advised to include Drs. Wilson and Ellis, from Brown University, as a team of consultants. Through Dr. Ellis I was exposed to the field of electron microscopy and was able to use his RCA electron microscope. Two years later we published a joint paper on the study of the basement membrane of the normal and diseased human uterine cervix and subsequently presented it in Dallas, Texas, at the American Society of Clinical Pathologists meeting.

The first inspection by the NCI of the National Institutes of Health (NIH) was held on September 20 by a team comprised of Drs. I. N. Hon, George Williams, and Douglas Sprunt. Dr. Sprunt was very happy to see me and to observe the progress that I had made. He urged me to get married and settle down in Providence.

A fatherly figure, Dr. Sprunt had won the reputation of being the bull of mid-South. He had fought to build his department and had gained world renown in the fields of pathology and bacteriology. Much later all of Dr. Sprunt's disciples contributed to having his portrait hung in the hallway of the Institute of Pathology when he was ready to retire. One month before he was scheduled to leave, he changed his mind and decided to stay on as chairman of the institute for the rest of his life, receiving one dollar a year from the university. I was saddened to hear that they removed Dr. Sprunt's portrait from the building and forced him to retire. He sued the university and the board of trustees to remain in his position. Fierce legal battles followed.

My friend Nathan Kaufmann later told me, at a meeting in San Francisco, that it was undignified for Dr. Sprunt to sue the university, even being willing to go to the U.S. Supreme Court if necessary. Dr. Anderson, Sprunt's right-hand man and second in command, was also sued by him. These events that took place at the University of Tennessee caused rapid deterioration in the quality of pathology teaching and practice at that institution.

Dr. Sprunt died in 1984 after losing his legal battles and his friends. That taught me the lesson that there is a time to live and a time to die—and a time to retire.

A letter from my old friend Eloise Jones, a pathology resident in Memphis, informed me of Dr. Sprunt's report after his inspection in Providence. He told them at the Thursday evening conference, "My boy is spreading his name throughout the New England states and has done an excellent job in organizing the cancer project in Providence."

She also mentioned that a certain doctor had been dismissed from the university but was able to secure a job as a pathologist at a hospital. Several dental students had complained of his teaching methods to Dean Hyman, who had advised Dr. Sprunt to relieve him of his duties. Eloise also expressed her fears about a doctor who had been drinking heavily for the past ten months.

Dr. Bob Tetraut was appointed county medical examiner, based on his formal training in forensic pathology at the Armed Forces Institute of Pathology (AFIP). Bob said in a letter to me that my job was well done in establishing the state screening survey and all of my friends were proud of my achievement.

On September 10, 1956, Dr. Henry Murphy informed me that three visitors would be coming on the following day to inspect our lab. Dr. Bill McLaughlin, director of the Massachusetts Division of the American

Cancer Society; Dr. William Meissner, a well-known Massachusetts pathologist, of the New England Deaconess Hospital; and his secretary, Jean Conklin, arrived at 10:00 A.M. to spend all day with us, discussing methods for launching a mass screening survey in Massachusetts for detection of early uterine cancer.

Dr. Meissner's dignified manner and penetrating observations impressed me. A week later I received a telephone call from him asking me to be the moderator of a seminar on uterine cancer cytology for the Massachusetts Society of Pathologists. The seminar was to be held on a Saturday and Sunday in mid-October at Harvard Medical School, with thirty pathologists attending. I was overwhelmed! I told Dr. Meissner that I would be happy to do so but was afraid to take such an assignment because of my being young and inexperienced in conducting seminars for academic and practicing pathologists. Dr. Meissner insisted that I accept the invitation, and I felt honored.

When I arrived at Building D of Harvard Medical School at eight o'clock on Saturday morning, I was surprised to see twenty-eight pathologists already at their microscopes. Most of them were experienced academic pathologists or practicing pathologists, and some of them were older than my own father. I froze momentarily but then began showing my Kodachrome slides to describe normal Pap smears, abnormal smears, and positive smears containing many tumor cells.

I met so many famous pathologists that weekend: Drs. Phil LeCompte, Sam Burgess, Merle Legg, John McKay, and other truly academic scientists. Their enthusiasm and willingness to listen to a young pathologist encouraged me. Dr. Meissner, a gentleman and a genuine scholar, gained my highest and lifelong admiration. A letter of appreciation and a check for $385 arrived three days later from Dr. McLaughlin. I asked Jerry Hager if I could endorse the check over to my sister, a freshman in medical school in Korea.

Representative Fogarty, through his assistant, George Kelly, introduced a private bill, H.R. 3441, in Congress. This bill gave me the status of permanent resident of this country without going through all the red tape and hearings outlined by the U.S. Immigration and Naturalization office in Washington. Congressman Fogarty enjoyed receiving periodic reports of the screening project from Dr. Henry Murphy and asked for more detailed information from me at monthly luncheon meetings.

By the end of December 1956, we had recruited 360 physicians and ten clinics and were receiving 240 Pap smears daily. A full staff of four screeners and one supervisor examined the voluminous number of Pap smears mailed in from various parts of the state.

During one of our weekly conferences, as an associate and I discussed a positive Pap smear containing twenty or more cancer cells, my associate asked me who the physician was. When I said that it was Dr. Gene Croce, pronouncing it "cross," he corrected my pronunciation, saying, "It's *Croche*, because he is a dago." This was a new term to me, and when I said that I did not understand, he replied, "He's an Italian, a wop."

A week later, during a luncheon meeting, I asked a well-known gynecologist, of Irish extraction, about the nationality of the associate who had used the disparaging terms. This doctor said, "He's a sheeney, a real kike, and he tries to pass as a German." I recalled a word Dr. Sprunt had used for Irish people—*hobs*. Hearing every day new expressions and derogatory remarks concerning the different nationalities in this small state, I told myself that I was learning the real facts of life.

Dr. Murphy drove me to Newport one evening for a dinner meeting of the Newport Hospital staff. He told me that the state health department was composed of pure Irish people, including Jack McLaughlin, William Lynch, and Tom Casey, and no one had been selected from the Yankees. I questioned why there was so much prejudice, since this is such a great nation, a melting pot for different cultures and nationalities.

Dr. Murphy asked me, "Aren't you prejudiced against the Japanese and some other nationalities?" I could not answer his question.

Nevertheless, we had screened 25,000 women and found that 86 percent of the Pap smears were negative, or normal, 11 percent represented atypical findings, due to inflammatory reactions or pregnancy results, and the remaining 3 percent were suspicious. Of 3 percent of 25,000 women, we discovered by tissue examination 148 cases of early cervical cancer, 28 cases of invasive squamous-cell carcinoma of the cervix, and 19 patients with adenocarcinoma of the uterine fundus. None of the 148 patients had been suspected of having early uterine cancer, and most of them were completely cured.

Representative Fogarty insisted that there be a second project-site visit for more realistic evaluation as to the size of the budget and the length of federal support. On November 15, 1956, I again met Drs. Sprunt, Williams, and Hon at the Providence airport and proceeded to a luncheon at the Brown University Clubhouse.

At the end of the meal Dr. Sprunt whispered to me that he was ready to recommend the extension of the federal support for two more years, with an increased budget, from $80,000 to $100,000 annually.

"But," he went on, "you must understand, Joe, that your project should not exceed the size of the Memphis project."

During our staff meeting the next day I persuaded Henry Murphy and Jerry Hager to accept Sprunt's recommendation and seek no further help from Congressman Fogarty's office.

Jerry said, "I agree with Joe, because I talked with Charlie Branch, a retired chairman of pathology at Boston University, now living in Maine. He told me that those three physicians intensely dislike receiving political pressure from Fogarty's office."

The project would continue through the end of December 1959, with an annual budget of $100,000. We discovered more unsuspected cases of uterine cervical cancer, as the Central Cytology Lab, consisting of four screeners, one senior cytologist, and the clerical staff, was receiving two hundred smears a day. The whole project was running smoothly with routine procedures.

"You're making general surgeons and gynecologists very rich," said Murphy and Hager in unison. Hager continued, "There are plenty of crooks among the general surgeons and gynecologists who would do a hysterectomy for even a slight abnormal finding on the Pap smear."

My parents kept sending me photographs of prospective brides, as I was approaching the age of thirty-one, which in my country was quite late to settle down. I returned the photographs each time with a note saying that I could not marry a girl based on a picture alone.

I had met a charming young woman, a physician who was taking residency training in internal medicine at the University of Illinois Research Hospital, in Chicago, in October of 1956. We had been corresponding ever since. She was born in North Korea, but her family had moved to Seoul when she was five years old. She spoke perfect Korean, without a northern accent like mine. On April 12, 1958, we were married at a Methodist church in Chicago. Three days later I brought my bride back to Providence. As we settled in East Providence, we began contemplating our future life together following the termination of the project in 1959.

A letter from Dr. William Meadows, medical director of the United Mineworkers Association, in Washington, D.C., invited me to inspect their hospitals in Harlan, Kentucky, and Beckley, West Virginia. They needed a pathologist, and he had learned through Dr. Harold Stewart that I would be available for a position when the project in Providence came to an end.

I visited the two hospitals in September. Never having been exposed to such dire poverty among white people as in these parts of

Kentucky and West Virginia, I was shocked to see that most of the miners' children were barefoot. As I drove along the winding roads of the two states, where mountains and high hills prevented an extension of the railroad system from Pittsburgh, Pennsylvania, I saw shacks with no indoor plumbing, and many of the children appeared to be malnourished.

Before returning to Providence, I made two more stops in West Virginia for interviews at the Fairmont General Hospital, and the University of West Virginia Medical School in Morgantown. My final stop was in Philadelphia to investigate a position at the Women's Medical College. Failing to see any challenge for my future career, I returned to Providence bitterly disappointed.

A few days later Dr. Tom Maher walked into my office with a disgusted expression on his face.

"Is something the matter, Tom?" I asked.

"Joe, I've been asked by my chief to teach surgical pathology to four general surgeons so they can pass their surgical board examinations, and I have to give at least six slide sessions for twenty-five dollars."

"Twenty-five dollars per session?"

"No, for all six sessions."

"Tom, they're not going to have a slide examination," I said. "Why don't you just go ahead and teach them the microscopic pathology? You have to put up with them, and you have only six months to go."

Later Tom told me, "You know, those four surgeons were fairly decent guys. At the end of the session they gave me a hundred dollars."

I told Tom what I had seen in Kentucky and West Virginia, and he said, "Oh, Joe, you can't be boxed into that hillbilly country. There'll be no way out. Why don't you look into a possibility at Our Lady of Fatima Hospital, in North Providence? They may have something for you."

"I doubt that very much, because that hospital has only 126 beds. I need to produce more research papers, and that can be done only in a university setting or other academic atmosphere."

"Nevertheless, Joe, you should talk to George Coleman, who's a member of the board of that hospital."

A plastic surgeon from New York City, Dr. Coleman advised me to obtain a medical license in the state of Rhode Island. He said, "Joe, you're a good man. You should stay around here, and it wouldn't harm you to get a medical license."

I sat through two full days of written examinations in various subjects. A week later Tom Casey, director of the licensing board, informed me that I had passed all the subjects.

21
Part-Time State Medical Examiner

In November 1956, I met Dr. Alan O'Dea, the 260-pound medical examiner of the state of Rhode Island, to discuss my temporary coverage for him on weekends and vacations. The scope of pathology at the state medical examiner's office was extremely varied, adding a greater dimension to my pathology experience. I examined the bodies of eighty highway fatalities, plus homicides, babies who had succumbed to sudden infant death syndrome, drowning victims, and suicides. There were also several cases of gangland killing; which exposed me to the dark side of life. An elderly pharmacist had drunk vinegar before he took a bottle of potassium cyanide. He left a note saying that a small amount of vinegar would accelerate the action of the potassium cyanide, bringing instant death.

In the summer of 1957, two hit men from Boston, in gray suits and black ties, walked into a small restaurant in Cranston, Rhode Island, and killed a man who was eating his lunch. There were at least half dozen people also eating there, but as usual, no one heard anything and no one saw anything. The victim was a large Italian man who refused to obey the Boston Mafia's orders to stop a crap game that he was hosting every night in different places in Providence. The restaurant owner told the police that he heard six shots, but when he raised his head, the two gunmen were already gone, leaving the body on the floor.

During the autopsy I recovered four bullets from the body and handed them to Henry Cruise, an agent of the medical examiner's office, to save for the state criminal investigation unit for ballistic studies. Later that day, about 4:30, two plainclothes detectives approached Henry, flashing their IDs, saying that they were from the FBI and needed the four bullets to study in connection with previous murder cases. We later learned that those alleged FBI officers were disguised gangsters from Boston. I had to go back to the restaurant with criminal division technicians to dig a bullet out from the floor.

139

A well-known gambler from upstate New York was reported missing from the Newport area during the month of August. His body was later discovered in a lake and brought to the central morgue. He had been seen by the neighbors entering a private home for a high-stakes poker game. A thorough search failed to turn up any identification or money from the dead man's pockets, and his body was so badly decomposed that there was no significant finding to explain the nature of his death. But examination of the skull revealed a depressed skull fracture caused by a dull object, indicating a homicide.

Two weeks after that, the exhumed body of a middle-aged black man was sent from Wakefield, Rhode Island, for postmortem examination. Dr. Joe Palumbo, the medical examiner in Cranston, signed the death certificate as suicide, causing political chaos among the black people. For political reasons they had to exhume his body, and I performed the autopsy. I discovered no significant findings to indicate one way or the other. Palumbo would not change his report, prolonging a political feud between the NAACP and the state of Rhode Island.

State law dictated that all highway fatalities had to be examined by the state medical examiner to rule out possible alcoholic intoxication or drug effects. Whenever I performed an autopsy on the disfigured or mutilated body of an automobile accident victim, I was strongly convinced that I was not fit to be a medical examiner.

About fifteen cases of sudden infant death syndrome were interesting, because there were no significant pathological changes that would substantiate such death. During a meeting in Boston, I mentioned this to Dr. Louis Legg, a well-known hematologist in that area. He suggested that we investigate the nature of the hemoglobin in the dead babies, but we found no conclusive evidence that abnormal hemoglobin might have caused the sudden death. Nonetheless, the wide variety of pathology findings stimulated me to look into several areas of hemoglobin abnormalities for future publication of a book.

A few years later, in Little Rock, Arkansas, I was shocked to read an article in *Time* concerning Louis Patralco, the Mafia boss in Rhode Island. He had been my landlord during my bachelor days in Providence. A docile old man, sitting in a rocking chair at the front of his Laundromat, he was always seeking a companion for conversation. Every evening when I was going up to my room on the second floor of the apartment building, he would call out, "Hey, Doc, what's new in the cancer field? Take some Italian cookies with you." I had no idea that he was one of the Mafia.

During the annual dinner meeting of the Rhode Island Society of Pathologists, I gave a brief progress report on the cancer screening

survey and was asked several sarcastic questions by a certain pathologist. He kept mentioning the name of Jerry Hager as being the backbone of the project. This irritated me slightly. After the meeting, Tom
Maher brought me a cocktail to relax. "Tom, how come this guy is
trying to give more credit to Jerry Hager in this project." I asked.

"Joe, don't you know that they were classmates? They stick together. Don't trust any of them."

"Seven out of fifteen members of the Rhode Island Society of Pathologists are graduates of Boston Medical School," I said. "You can't
mean that they stick together for anything?"

"Oh, Joe, you're so naive. You'll learn your lesson the hard way."
Then he turned and walked away.

22
Private Practice of Pathology

In the middle of June 1959, I was approached by an internist to join him in private laboratory practice at a newly constructed medical building in Cranston, Rhode Island. He, a graduate of Tufts Medical School, had complete his residency training in internal medicine and wanted to join the medical staff at Providence General Hospital. He had never been accepted by the hospital board and was unable to understand why his application was rejected. In fact, he had never received a satisfactory explanation as to why his application was turned down. He showed me the large medical building and said, "We need a laboratory in this building. Why don't you join us and have a private practice of laboratory medicine for fifteen physicians here?"

I asked him if they would support the lab within the professional building.

"Of course we would," he replied. "Otherwise I wouldn't be talking to you now."

A few days later I took Gary Romeo to show him the space allocated for a medical laboratory. Gary said, "It looks all right, Joe, but make sure that they will support the lab."

"Well, he assured me that they would."

"But, Joe, you can never trust them unless they put something in writing." Gary advised me to get out of the cancer screening survey project, because that was a dead end. Furthermore, he emphasized that there were plenty of cutthroats in the medical profession, especially among some circles.

I discussed this with my Irish friend Walter Dunkel, who said, "Joe, you should get out of that circle, because none of them can be trusted.

"Let me tell you something about that group," Walter continued. "They fight each other, trying to cut each other's throats, but then when they turn around to face their foes, they stick together like glue."

At a later date I learned this lesson at a high price, when I discovered that some highly confidential information given to one of this group leaked out the very next day to his associate. Indeed, Gary and Walter were so right.

I secured a $15,000 commercial loan from the Rhode Island Hospital Trust Company to finance the laboratory operation. All the equipment and instruments to set up a seven-room laboratory were purchased from Max Bukansky, of the Eastern Scientific Company, in Providence. I signed a lease, following consultation with my lawyer and friend Ned Handy. He advised me to rent two units in a new building, which were converted into laboratory facilities by a carpenter from East Providence. Two medical technologists, a cytotechnologist, and a secretary were ready to provide complete laboratory service for patients from the fifteen physicians in the building.

A general staff meeting was held following the open house for the new building, at eight o'clock on the evening of September 1, with the building's owner attending. During the latter part of the evening, the physicians were called to attend a special meeting.

The head physician said to me, "Joe, we've been sending our patients to a certain laboratory for complete blood count and blood urea nitrogen. The owner of the laboratory, a technician, collects twenty dollars from the patients and returns ten dollars to me."

I was unable to comprehend at first what he was saying. "You mean to tell me that you're getting 50 percent back from this guy on the lab tests done on your patients? Each one of them?"

"That's correct. And I expect you to do the same."

I was stunned. I looked around at the fourteen other physicians. They remained passive, as though he was their spokesman. I raised my voice. "You gentlemen expect the same deal, a 50 percent kickback from me and my laboratory?" They nodded.

Appalled at such an unethical request and such unprofessional conduct, I displayed my anger. "You know very well that this is an unethical request, and we're forbidden by the American College of Pathologists to give kickbacks! First of all, how do you expect me to run the lab with three technicians and a secretary if I have to give 50 percent of the collection back to you?" I continued to raise my voice. "Why didn't you tell me at first, before I opened up the lab here? I though you people were going to support the laboratory."

"We would if you decided to play ball with us," he replied.

Most of the patients referred by my fellow physicians in the professional building were their spouses, their children, Catholic nuns and priests, and Protestant ministers—nonpaying patients. This is because, as a rule, physicians extend their courtesies, not charging professional fees to their colleagues, families, or clergy.

143

To maintain the laboratory with two full-time medical technologists, a cytotechnologist, and a secretary, I was forced to take a position as associate pathologist at Providence Lying-In Hospital, a 200-bed maternity hospital in North Providence, with a yearly compensation of $12,000. I also performed most of the state medical examiner's autopsies, with a regular fee of $200 per case and $400 for homicide examinations.

During the latter part of December 1959, due to lack of patients, I was unable to engage a professional housekeeping service for the laboratory. My wife, Kumsan, an aggressive and courageous woman, volunteered to clean each room of the laboratory and scrub the floors, in spite of her pregnancy. My anger toward the fifteen physicians in that building turned into despair and depression, as I was experiencing a taste of life in the cold business world.

Providence Lying-In Hospital had approximately four thousand deliveries and three thousand surgery cases a year. The director of laboratories, Dr. Wilbur Wilson, from Saint Paul, Minnesota, was a trained obstetrician but not a board-certified pathologist. He had acquired some experience in pathology when he was assigned to AFIP for a brief period during World War II.

Dr. Wilson had served under Dr. Eastman, at the Johns Hopkins Medical School Department of Obstetrics, and had done useful research in obstetrics. He was quite capable in reading specimens of uterine scrapings, hysterectomies, and tumors of the ovary as a result of his experience at Johns Hopkins Medical School, and he taught me a great deal of gynecologic pathology. His only problem was that he wasted a great deal of time in conversation with anyone he could catch. He was a lonely man, spending most of his time in his laboratory and the hospital library.

Developing a keen interest in gynecologic pathology, especially in the histogenesis of the uterine cervix, based on the large number of fetal specimens I examined, I collected a significant number of cases for future publication of a book.

Dr. Wilson said to me, "Joe, you belong to academic medicine. Why don't you close your laboratory and go back to medical school?"

He was right. I could not foresee my future in maintaining a crippled laboratory with four people on the payroll. I shall never forget the true friendship of Dr. Andy Burgess, a Quaker, who supported my laboratory to the end by sending his patients for their laboratory procedures. Another surgeon, Dr. Jerry Rock, and many gynecologists also sent their Pap smears to the laboratory.

144

There were, however, many unethical physicians who took advantage of my difficulties and my slumping business. One busy practitioner in the field of gynecology approached me and offered three hundred Pap smears a week if I would split the profits with him. Another gynecologist came to my laboratory and said, "Joe, you're not supposed to have your technicians sitting around doing nothing. I could send you three hundred patients a month for various laboratory tests to help you out. I should like you to send me a full bill, and I'll send you a check representing half of the charges."

"Bill, how could I explain that to the IRS if they decided to audit me?"

"Well, that's your problem. I'm just saying that you should keep your technicians busy."

I thanked him politely but refused to go along with his scheme.

Most of the medical staff of Providence Lying-In Hospital were board-certified in the field of obstetrics and gynecology, but many of them did not possess the skills to perform satisfactory surgical procedures. Board certification in obstetrics and gynecology is a minimum guarantee, signifying that the physician has passed written and oral examinations, but it does not assure his skills as a surgeon.

A physician who was twice unable to pass the board examinations with the help of another doctor in both obstetrics and pathology was able to receive a certificate from the American Board of Obstetrics and Gynecology. Basically, this doctor had no surgical skills at all in either field. Several malpractice lawsuits were brought against him by his patients for his misjudgment and unsuccessful surgical procedures. When he scheduled surgery to remove a placental polyp from the uterine fundus of a thirty-three-year-old woman who had delivered a baby several days previously, medical staff members were deeply concerned about the outcome. One of them offered his help. This made him angry. "Look," he said, I'm a board man, too. If I need your help, I'll ask for it!"

During the surgery, as he was trying to remove the placental polyp, he ruptured the uterine wall and brought the intestine down through the uterus to the vaginal orifice. A skilled surgeon stepped in, removing the uterus and saving the woman's life, giving her twenty-seven units of blood. There was a big hole, approximately the size of a quarter, at the uterine fundus.

A week later, on Friday afternoon, this physician performed a tubal ligation, removing a segment of the tube from each side. Then he left town for a golf tournament. When I examined the slide under the microscope, I was appalled to see a portion of left ureter instead

145

of the left fallopian tube. The man who had performed the surgery could not be reached; consequently, they had to remove the left kidney from the young woman, who brought a huge malpractice suit against him.

The happiest time during such a depressing period was the birth of our daughter, Patricia, on April 10, 1960, at Providence Lying-In Hospital. This gave me a tremendous boost. Our eldest son, Michael, was born at the same hospital, in 1961, and our youngest child, Jeff, was delivered at St. Vincent Hospital in Little Rock, Arkansas, in 1963. Children are indeed the most precious gifts from God.

The decision was made to close down the laboratory, and the technologists were very understanding. They had told me many times that I was "digging my own grave." Gloria, my efficient secretary, stayed until the last minute without receiving her weekly compensation for three months. She refused a paycheck, saying, "Dr. Song, I feel as if I'm eating your flesh and sucking your blood. I know you're in a desperate situation." Fifteen years later, I mailed a check for $1,000 to her in the hope that this would make up for her loss during my struggling, unsuccessful, private-practice days.

The decision to return to the academic circle was initiated by my wife. Convinced that I did not belong in the business world, I investigated several positions at medical schools. During December of 1960, I received a telephone call from my former fellow resident, Dr. Ted Richman, who was going to be appointed chairman of the Pathology Department at the University of Arkansas Medical School, in Little Rock. He was wondering if I would be willing to join him and help him build the department.

My parents during the Korean War in Pusan, 1951.

President Rhee with Mrs. Francesca Rhee. She helped and supported me during the dismal days of the Korean War.

The late Dr. Myron M. Lee. The Korean ambassador to Great Britain, 1951. Dr. Lee, through the Hung Han Foundation, generously supported our cancer research programs.

The late Dr. Il-Sun Yun. My mentor during the school years, 1946–50.

Medical School graduation in Seoul, Korea, May 10, 1950.

My family in 1966. From left: Mike, age five; Jeff, age three; Kumsan; and Pat, age six.

Dr. Chong-Hwee Chun, a very energetic
and much respected professor of medicine.

My best friend for fifty years, Dr. Charles
Kim. A wise counselor and great surgeon.

My mother visiting my sister, Hyun-Duk, in Kansas City, 1968.

The late Dr. Jae-Koo Lee. A widely respected pathologist and dean of the medical school in Seoul, Korea.

The late Dr. Young-Suk Koo. The first minister of health of the Republic of Korea, 1948–51. Dr. Koo introduced me to Mrs. Francesca Rhee in April 1950.

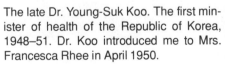

Dr. Harold L. Stewart of the National Cancer Institute in Bethesda, Maryland. A most sincere and truly modest cancer researcher, who opened the door for me in 1951.

The late Dr. Douglas Sprunt, my chief at the University of Tennessee in Memphis, 1952–56.

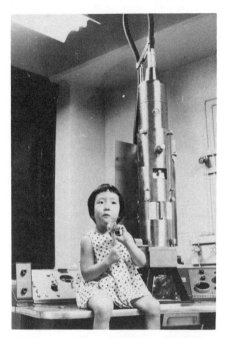

My daughter, Pat, sitting on RCA-electron
microscope, 1963.

My mother holding my daughter, Pat, 1962.

My sisters in Korea, 1964. From left: youngest sister and physician, In-Duk; younger sister, Hyun-Duk; and older sister, Al-Duk.

Mr. and Mrs. Louis B. Kang in Los Angeles. Devoted members of the Seventh-Day Adventists, who helped many Korean students with their love and generosity.

Dr. William Meissner, a gentleman-scholar and superb pathologist of the United States.

Another gigantic figure in American pathology, Dr. Charles Dunlap of Tulane University.

The late Dr. Sung-Jin Kim, a well-known surgeon in Korea. I hid in his clinic during the first month of the Korean War.

Korea's entrepreneur, educator, and philanthropist, Dr. Sun-Whan Oh, who helped many struggling scientists, teachers, and students.

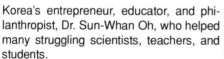

Myself following the publication of my first book, in Little Rock, Arkansas, 1964.

Myself twenty-five years later in my private practice of pathology at Community Hospital, tired and disgruntled.

23
Return to University Circle

Ted Richman met me at the Little Rock airport on the afternoon of March 1, 1961. We proceeded to the Sam Peck Hotel. The view of the medical center building from West Markham Street was impressive.
"You know, Ted," I said, "I almost came to this place in 1956."
"Oh, I didn't know that."
"You see, I was approached by Dr. Ned Anderson, the chairman of the Pathology Department at that time, for the position of assistant professor, with $8,000 annual remuneration. They had just broken ground for the new medical center." I told Ted about meeting the dean of the medical school, Douglas Lawson, who was called provost for medical affairs at the University of Arkansas, and having a discussion with Dr. Leo Miller, head of the OB-GYN Department, about setting up a cytology screening project for detection of early cervical cancer.
"But Ned Anderson was abruptly removed from the chairmanship by Doug Lawson, in April of 1956," Ted said.
"What happened then?"
"They had three court hearings because of a lawsuit filed by Ned, but he lost and finally took a position at a private clinic."
"Is Leo Miller still active?" I asked.
"Oh, yes, he's very much alive. He has the biggest clinical department at the medical center. Leo would be thrilled to have you if you should decide to accept the position here."
Leo Miller his chief associate, Dr. Jim Nelson, and I had a long discussion. Both of them were enthusiastic about having me down there for their cervical cancer project. I was much impressed with Jim Nelson, who was to become my lifelong friend.
I presented a scientific session concerning viral myocarditis for the pathology staff members and met several of the pathology residents, including Dick Young, Steve Wilson, Neil Patterson, and Gil Baker. We then discussed the academic rank for me, professional remuneration, and the scope of the research project that I would undertake.

163

I emphasized the need of an electron microscope for any future projects and research studies of tumor cells. An electron microscope is a very powerful instrument, allowing magnification of the simple cells to 100,000 times, whereas a conventional microscope, utilizing an ordinary light bulb as the light source, can achieve maximum magnification of only 1,000 times.

With a bona fide offer for the position of associate professor of pathology, at a salary of $15,000 a year, I returned to Providence to discuss the matter with my wife and Dr. Wilbur Wilson. After three weeks of consideration, encouraged by my wife and Dr. Wilson, I accepted the position of associate professor of pathology at the University of Arkansas Medical School, to begin my new duties in September 1961.

My attorney, Ned Handy, skillfully negotiated with the owner of the building where I had my lab to terminate the lease. The owner turned out to be a very tough businessman. He insisted that I continue to pay rent until the end of October but finally agreed to terminate the lease upon receipt of a certified check covering the rental payment until October 1.

Max Bukansky was very considerate and took back all the instruments and equipment. "Dr. Song," he said, "you belong to the academic atmosphere. I'm sorry you were taken in, but take as long as you need to pay me back the balance of $6,000.

Dr. Richard Ellis, a young biology professor at Brown University and an expert in electron microscopy, showed me how to align the various lenses of the electron microscope, clean the vacuum system, and take photographs of the cells subject with the RCA 3-F electron microscope.

Dr. Elizabeth Leduc, a biology teacher with numerous publications in the field of electron microscopy and tumor cells, taught me how to prepare a section with a diamond knife to study the cell subjects under the electron microscope. It was fascinating to see the images on the screen that were magnified 100,000 times. Many of the viral particles were vividly demonstrated under the electron microscope, and a mysterious figure, like the basement membrane of the cells, was also visualized.

We tried to dispose of our house before September, but the housing market was extremely slow. The realtor was unable to close any deal on the new split-level house to which my wife had become very attached.

Early on the morning of September 1, as I held my seventeen-month-old daughter, Pat, my wife prepared sandwiches and coffee for me before I left. My 1956 Hillman, a British compact car, ran beautifully all day, and I stopped for the night at a motel in Knoxville, Maryland. I spoke to my wife on the telephone that evening.

The following day I proceeded to Beckley, West Virginia, to visit Dr. H. T. Lee, a resident physician at Beckley Tuberculosis Sanitarium. The winding roads through the hills of West Virginia reminded me of the battlefields on the rugged mountains of Korea's eastern coast. My little Hillman, loaded with suitcases, barely made it up the hills, but I finally arrived at the Beckley around five o'clock on the evening of September 2. Dr. Lee had been a resident physician at West Tennessee Tuberculosis Hospital while I was in Memphis, and that evening we reminisced about the old days until late, when his son David finally fell asleep on the couch.

Early in the morning I started out again and drove all day through the East Tennessee mountains, arriving at the medical center of the University of Arkansas at 5:00 P.M. on September 3.

The people of Arkansas were extremely proud of their new medical center, situated on top of a hill on West Markham Street. The physical facilities were modern and excellent, far superior to those of Tufts Medical School, Boston University School of Medicine, and Harvard Medical School.

The Department of Pathology had been organized well by its former chairman, Dr. Heintz Schlumberger, who had been the victim of a tragic automobile accident on December 25, 1959. Dr. Schlumberger and his two daughters were thrown out of their car when it was struck by an oncoming two-ton pickup. The driver of the truck turned out to be the young nephew of Dr. Richard Hollman, a close friend of Dr. Schlumberger. Dr. Hollman was the chairman of the Department of Pathology at Louisiana State University when the accident occurred.

Although his daughters received only minor cuts and superficial lacerations, Dr. Schlumberger later developed signs and symptoms of intracerebral hemorrhage. When they rushed him to the medical school Emergency Department, only interns and first-year surgery and neurosurgery residents were available, as senior staff members were either out of town or unavailable because of the holiday. Treatment was delayed, and when they sent Dr. Schlumberger to Washington University Hospital, in Saint Louis, there was nothing that could be done. It was impossible to evacuate a large amount of clotted blood from the space called the lateral ventricle of the right hemisphere of the brain. He was sent back to the university hospital in Little Rock, where he remained in a coma. Eventually he was transferred to Little Rock Veterans Administration Hospital, and he lived on as a vegetable for several years.

Though a borderline genius and a highly academic person, Dr. Schlumberger had never carried a sufficient amount of life insurance. A small policy, taken out when he was in the service during World War II, was of no help, because the company would not pay the face amount as long as he was alive. The University of Arkansas curtailed his pay three months following the accident, which was standard procedure. This alienated many of his friends. Through an appeal by Mrs. Schlumberger, Dr. Ted Hill, chairman of the Department of Pathology of the University of Cincinnati Medical School, initiated a drive for funds among Schlumberger's friends most of whom were the chairmen of pathology departments at various medical centers and medical schools. I was told that because of their animosity toward the University of Arkansas, Schlumberger's friends who served on study sections of the National Institutes of Health would not approve any research grant applications submitted by members of the faculty of the University of Arkansas Medical School.

Through a tremendous effort by Dr. Douglas Lawson, dean of the university medical school, and the search committee, they finally selected Dr. Fred Davis, from a state university in the south, for the position of chairman of the Department of Pathology. They also told me that Dr. Coy Anderson, of the University of Tennessee, was interviewed twice but turned down the appointment.

When I became a consultant in pathology at the Little Rock Veterans Administration Hospital, I took Dr. William Hunter, a first-year resident, with me up to see Dr. Schlumberger on the fifth floor of the hospital. We were saddened to see one of the greatest academic pathologists receiving tube feeding and remaining in a comatose state. He finally died six years later. Due to lack of funds, his three children were sent to San Antonio and New Jersey to live with their uncles and aunts. Mrs. Schlumberger enrolled at the University of Arkansas to receive a teacher's certificate.

The university was expecting to have Dr. Fred Davis as their new chairman of the Department of Pathology, but he changed his mind and decided not to come to Little Rock. The dean of the medical school, Dr. Lawson, who was about to leave to take a position as medical director in research with a large pharmaceutical company in New Jersey, was compelled to fill the vacancy. He finally approached Ted Richman to come back as the department chairman.

Dr. Lawson called five pathology residents to his office and informed them of his decision to appoint Ted Richman chairman. Dr. Rudy Pearson voiced his objections, based on Richman's lack of administrative skills.

The sophomore pathology teaching course began on September 9, 1961, with eighty-nine students enrolled. I was curious to learn the whereabouts of the residents I had met during my interview in March. I asked Rudy Pearson, "Where are those bright residents—Gill Baker, Allan Rose, and Sid Beattie—who impressed me so much when I was visiting here for a job interview?"

"They went to the University of Missouri to complete their last two years of pathology training."

"Why did they go there?" I persisted.

"You'd better ask them. I don't know," he replied.

Later I discussed the lack of residents with a senior resident, Dr. Dick Young, and his answer was equally evasive. "But don't worry, Dr. Song," he said. "We have two straight interns, David Packard and Bob Coleman, and we expect two more next July." On August 1 a new resident, William Hunter, arrived to begin his training in pathology.

During the reception for new faculty members, held at the Jeff Banks Building, I met the new dean of the school, Dr. Winston Short, and the new vice president for medical affairs, Stan Whaley, and their wives. Stan Whaley had been a radio commentator at John Brown University, in Hebrew Springs, Arkansas, and was a distinguished-looking gentleman with a voice like that of an opera singer. Winston Short had been associate dean of the medical school at the University of Miami, and his wife, Jean, was a retired internist.

Another faculty member whom I met at that reception was Dr. Ron Hoke, an assistant professor of pathology, who had come with Ted Richman from Tulane University. Ron had finished his residency at the end of June 1961 and joined Richman instead of going back to his home state of North Dakota. I liked Ron very much because of his unassuming manner. He introduced me to Dr. Jim Dakin, who had been an assistant professor before Ted Richam came and was currently a practicing pathologist with a large private laboratory. Jim took me to a corner of the reception hall and whispered, "I hope you made the right choice to join Ted Richman in the Pathology Department."

"I hope so, too. Is there anything the matter?"

"Well, Ted was not their choice as the new chairman," he said. "He put tremendous pressure on the search committee. When they

167

refused to consider him as a serious candidate, he left for Tulane University to join Dr. Charles Dunlap."

"I know Dr. Dunlap very well," I said. "He's a gigantic figure in American pathology and most respected by all the students and faculty members at Tulane."

Jim went on, "I understand that he advised Ted not to take the chairmanship at Arkansas University."

Walking away from Jim Dakin, I began to mingle with the other people and met a hospital administrator, Dave Johnson, who seemed to be carrying a chip on his shoulder, like many hospital administrators. I later found out that he took a dim view of the University's future plans after Dean Douglas Lawson left the medical center. He supposedly took a position at the American University in Beirut, Lebanon.

The sophomore class of 1961 was rather unusual in that so many of the students were older, in their midforties, with colorful backgrounds and interesting professional careers before they came to medical school.

Alfred Rader was a former manager of the Pet Milk Company, in Alabama. His charming wife, Ellen, was earning a living by developing films at the local photo shop. A former football coach at Oklahoma College, Rex Morgan, was a warm person with a radiant personality. Another interesting student, a former U.S. Air Force fighter pilot named John Kendall, was very friendly to everyone. Walter Guyer, an undertaker for more than twenty years, was studying to become a general practitioner.

I was pleased to see three black students in the class, reflecting the progress of the people of Arkansas and the university on behalf of their black people. One of the students, Jim Robertson, asked me if I knew Dr. Leon Gottlieb, of the Boston University Pathology Department.

"I know Leon very well," I replied.

"My mother is working for him. She's a technician in his electron microscopy laboratory."

"How interesting! Are you from Boston?" I asked.

"No, we're natives of Arkansas, but she found a challenging job at Boston University. I plan to go to Boston when I finish medical school."

"That's an exceptionally good idea, Jim, but you must complete medical school here."

When Jim did not show up in class for three days, the dean of the medical school came up to the classroom to inquire about him. I learned that Dean Short had called Jim at his home and urged him to attend class. When I saw Jim later, I asked what had happened.

"I was sad and depressed for three whole days because of something that happened during the lab exercise in pathology."

"What was that?"

"One of my group shouted at me at the end of the lab session, 'Hey, nigger, pick up those instruments and clean them!' I had an urge to punch him in the nose and knock him down, but I restrained myself and walked out. Another student, Harvey Graham, a Jew from Boston, cleaned the instruments for me."

"I didn't know Harvey was from Boston, and a Jew."

"Well, Harvey was in the junior class at Boston University Medical School. He had a fight with a resident in internal medicine and grabbed him by the neck and punched him. Harvey was expelled, but he was able to find a spot in the sophomore class here."

"I'd like to meet Harvey," I said, "because I know some of the Boston University medical faculty members."

When Harvey came to my office, I was saddened to hear his story—of getting in a fight because he was called a "Jew boy." I told Harvey, "You'll find anti-Semitism wherever you go. Just don't pay any attention to it. Do your work and finish medical school. Why don't you join a Jewish medical fraternity at this university?"

"There's no Jewish fraternity here, and there's only one other Jew in my class—Jerry Guttman, from Hot Springs. In fact, he's only half-Jewish, but he doesn't try to pass as a Gentile."

"The University of Tennessee Medical College had a Jewish fraternity. I think perhaps you should start your own fraternity here," I suggested.

I recalled a microscopic session with four Jewish students at the University of Tennessee. I asked them the size of their Jewish medical fraternity. Ronald Scheinberg, a blond, blue-eyed Jew, told me that they had forty-eight students and several Jewish faculty members and the head of the fraternity was Dr. Israel David Michelson.

I also recalled my friend Dr. Edwin Schwartz, the head of the cytology laboratory in Memphis, to whom I was assigned as a teaching assistant for the Fifth-quarter students. Schwartz and four students were absent during the Jewish New Year, and I had to carry out a heavy teaching assignment.

Walter Guyer was a very interesting middle-aged man. One day he walked into my office and asked me to explain the criteria of cancer cells seen on Pap smears, because he had been late in attending my

169

lecture. I went over it with him while he was telling me about his background. Walter had been a mortician for some twenty years in a little town in Arkansas where there was no family physician. Despite genuine efforts to attract a physician for the six hundred people, no one was willing to settle down there. The townspeople asked Walter to go to college and the University of Arkansas Medical School to become their family practitioner. They would carry on his undertaking business while he was gone.

John Kendall, age forty-eight, was a former professional soldier. He had been a fighter pilot with the U.S. Fifth Air Force in Korea. John and I spent many hours reminiscing about the Korean War. He said, "Maybe some of the bullets fired from my plane went over your head, Dr. Song. Don't you think that's possible?"

"It's distinctly possible, John, but you must remember that we lost many good soldiers because of the mistakes made by your Fifth Air Force planes."

"Well, it was war, you know. We didn't mean to shoot your people down."

John was flying a U-2 plane after the Korean War when they discovered that his cholesterol level was exceedingly high. He was grounded and given a desk job, which he did not like. "I never wanted to be a paper shuffler in the administration office of the Fifth Air Force. So I decided to become a physician, and after a series of examinations I was accepted by the University of Arkansas Medical School. I was the oldest student in the freshman class."

I liked John very much because of his mild manner and cordiality, and I helped him in the pathology course after class. During his senior year, while taking a bath, he died of an acute coronary thrombosis.

We all attended his funeral, held at a Lutheran church. As a faculty member, I was asked to say a few words. With choking voice, I said, "John was a courageous man who never gave up his original goal, against all odds and difficulties. We shall miss him very much."

When a pathology resident is assigned to surgical pathology service, he usually has had from three to six months of experience in autopsy pathology on patients who died at a hospital. During an autopsy the prosector removes all the organs and examines the entire system to correlate the clinical findings with the autopsy results. A large number of tissue blocks are saved, and the histology technicians make slides of them.

Dr. Jay Dixon, an intelligent and handsome first-year resident from southern Arkansas, came to surgical pathology service after six months of autopsy pathology duties. From the first day he was enthusiastic, describing the gross appearance of the tissues as to size, appearance, and consistency of the tumor, if present. He then cut a small square piece of tissue and placed it in a 10 percent formalin solution for fixation. A histology technician sent all the tissues through a Technicon machine to remove the formalin by applying a series of alcohol solutions of different concentrations. The pieces of tissue were then transferred into xylol solution to extract the alcohol, and finally they were embedded in plastic cassettes containing melted paraffin. The paraffin blocks were cooled in a refrigerator. Then the histology technician, using a microtome, cut very thin paraffin sections to be mounted on a glass slide. All the slides were stained with two basic dyes: hematoxylin solution for the nuclei of the cells and eosin preparation for the cytoplasm of the cells.

After the slides were prepared and mounted, the surgical pathology resident could examine them for a diagnosis. A senior pathology staff member would go over the resident's findings with him and check his diagnosis of certain types of tumors or inflammatory lesions. The surgeons and gynecologists were then notified of the diagnosis of the tissue, either for the patient's future treatment or the discharge from the hospital. Jay Dixon had sufficient background in medicine either to concur with the clinical diagnosis or to advise the physician of the final diagnosis.

During one surgical pathology session, Jay suddenly asked me about the quality of students at the University of Arkansas Medical School: "I know you've been around several medical schools. How would you compare the students of this school with those at the University of Tennessee or Tufts Medical School?"

"That's a good question, Jay," I said, "but I don't see any significant difference in the student quality between this school and medical schools on the East Coast."

"I understand that the students at the University of Tennessee are not as good as those at our school. I was told that they have a mass production system, turning out 320 students every year."

"Yes, they do. They have a quota system, producing over three hundred physicians annually."

"What about medical schools on the East Coast, like Tufts and Boston University?"

"Those are private schools, you know, but I failed to notice any significance in the quality of students. Some of the University of Tennessee students, I felt, didn't belong in medical school, but that's one man's observation."

Jay continued to probe. "What about the quality of the faculty members of each medical school?"

"The clinical faculty at the University of Tennessee is basically part-time, because they maintain their practice."

"Our clinical faculty here is all full-time members of the university," Jay said.

"I know. The clinical faculty at the University of Arkansas is far better, or at least they're devoting their full time to teaching and service of the patients here."

"What about your medical school in Seoul, Korea?" he asked.

"Well, that was different. The medical students of my day in my country were far superior to those of any medical schools in this country, because they were highly selected from six to seven thousand applicants. We always had two or three geniuses, and I haven't found one single genius in the medical schools here where I have taught, including the University of Tennessee, Boston University, and Tufts Medical School. But the quality of the faculty members at the University of Seoul was mediocre. Only three or four of them tried to teach new things and were able to keep up. Most of the basic science or clinical medicine professors kept teaching from their twenty-year old notebooks. Perhaps they were unable to study or prepare their lectures because of the unstable political conditions in South Korea. As you know, Jay, some of the faculty members here at Arkansas are nationally renowned in their fields."

"What about the students at Harvard Medical School?" Jay went on.

"I never had an opportunity to teach Harvard medical students, but my friend Gary Pearce, who was a graduate of this medical school, became an instructor in pathology there. The only difference he found was that the medical students at Harvard never extended their coffee breaks. When Gary said, 'We'll have a ten-minute break and then meet downstairs for a demonstration,' all the students were there one or two minutes before the deadline. But why are you so anxious to find out these things, Jay?"

"I'm just curious about the quality of students in other schools." With that we finished our surgical pathology session and went down to the cafeteria for a cup of coffee.

When my father passed away, in October 1959, I asked my mother to come to this country and live with us. After fifteen months of consideration, she finally accepted our invitation. We picked her up at the New York airport on June 20, 1961.

172

During the evening of October 11, 1961, I received a telephone call from my friend Bill Hahn, a music teacher at Barrington Bible School. He informed me that our son, Michael John, had been born at 4:02 P.M. and both mother and baby were fine. Bill also said that my mother was dancing in the streets because we finally had a son to carry on the family name.

I always had an uneasy feeling whenever someone told me that I had to have a son to carry on the family name. I never understood the significance of the tradition in my country of preserving the family name. We consumed a large amount of champagne that evening—Edwin Hale, Ron Hoke, Dick Young, Ted Richman, and I.

Two days later I rushed to Providence to be at my wife's bedside because of her postpartum complications—profuse hemorrhaging. The complications were corrected by that superb obstetrician Dr. Walter Dunkel, who told me, "Joe, your baby boy is the first one crying for milk, just like his old man."

In two days I had to return to Little Rock to attend a gynecology conference in Hot Springs, to discuss the histogenesis of the uterine cervix.

24
Resident Teaching

I always enjoyed the Wednesday morning sessions with our pathology residents and interns discussing endometrial or uterine pathology, based on tissues received from the Department of Obstetrics and Gynecology at the University of Arkansas Medical Center.

"Women most commonly see their doctors because of excessive uterine bleeding or heavy menstrual flow, or frequent or irregular menstruation," I told the group. "For the purpose of discussion, we base the menstrual cycle on a twenty-eight-day cycle. But many women do not have a 'normal' twenty-eight-day-cycle. Some have a thirty-six-day cycle or a twenty-two-to-twenty-four-day cycle.

"The tissues obtained by a gynecologist or the family physician through dilatation and curettage, known as D and C, or uterine scrapings, are sent to us for diagnosis and interpretation of the disease. In a few cases you will find a cancer in the endometrium or the uterus, or cystic hyperplasia of the endometrium, which causes excessive uterine bleeding. But many of the specimens obtained through D and C show no pathological changes, as irregular menstruation or heavy uterine bleeding can be a functional disease.

"As you know, the menstrual cycle and menstrual period are influenced by a woman's state or anxiety. During the latter part of the Korean War, three young female university students were arrested by the North Korean security police for alleged counterrevolutionary or antiwar activities against the North Korean People's Army. The young women were tried for thirty minutes and sentenced to death by hanging in six weeks. The black hair of one of them turned gray in a week's time, and menstruation ceased in all three. They were eventually rescued by UN forces, but it took a long time for them to regain their normal endometrial function."

I showed many Kodachrome slides to illustrate different types of endometrial changes caused by an excessive amount of the female hormone estrogen, or changes induced by inadequate influence by the hormone.

During our coffee break at the cafeteria, a senior pathology resident, Rudy Pearson, sat down by me. "Dr. Song, you were born in North Korea. How did you end up in Little Rock, Arkansas?"

I gave Rudy a brief history of my exodus from North Korea and my subsequent activities during the Korean War.

"Really?" Rudy's eyes widened. "You participated in underground activities against Soviet Russia?"

When I nodded, he said, "I did the same thing against the German troops in Norway. I was a thirteen-year-old boy, but I worked for the Office of Strategic Services of the U.S. Army, gathering information regarding troop movements of the German army in my country. When they closed in, the OSS smuggled me out of Norway and found me a foster home in Little Rock. I went to high school and college and became a medical technician in the blood bank of this hospital. But I found it very difficult to take orders from groups of conceited physicians, so I decided to become a doctor. Now here I am, trying to finish my pathology residency training. The Germans were good soldiers, but I didn't care for them. You probably felt the same way about the Japanese."

"Rudy, in my opinion the Japanese people are basically cruel and capable of killing innocent people, including women and children." I went on to tell him about my high school experience with the Japanese teachers. "One day during the summer of 1944, a Japanese teacher, Mr. Sasaki, told us, 'You boys have to do your best to win this war against the Americans and British. If we lose this war, the Americans, being cruel and barbaric, will come into this land and break your bones and castrate all the male population.'

"That night I woke up with a nightmare and began wandering around the house. My father came out of his bedroom and asked me if anything was wrong. I repeated Mr. Sasaki's comment. My father said, 'Don't be ridiculous! Americans are very civilized and broadminded people. My cousin is a successful businessman in Los Angeles, and my great-uncle is a well-to-do farmer in Hawaii.'

"My father despised the Japanese. He said, 'The Japanese people are basically a barbaric race. They think nothing of burying alive a thousand Chinese people, including women and children, in a so-called Nanking massacre. Don't believe what they say, and don't let them know that you are pro-American.' "

"I thought the Germans were the worst race in that regard," Rudy commented. "They killed millions of Jews during World War II."

175

Recalling the mass murder and atrocities committed by the North Korean Communists, I said, "I think there's no exception in that regard. Every race, every nationality, and every armed force in the world is capable of committing such atrocities under certain circumstances."

At that moment Rudy and I were joined by three senior residents in obstetrics and gynecology—Charlie Smith, Mose Smith, and Jimmy Halger—for an extended coffee break. They asked me to conduct a teaching session every Tuesday morning for the senior staff and house officers of the Department of Obstetrics and Gynecology.

"Why don't you people join the Wednesday morning pathology conference?" I asked. "I always show a large number of Kodachrome slides, selected to illustrate the different histological patterns of cancer of the endometrium and of the uterine cervix."

Mose said, "Well, Dr. Miller, our chairman, felt that you could teach us from the basic embryology of the female reproductive system up to the pathology of all the reproductive organs."

"I'll have to think about it and discuss it with Ted Richman," I answered.

The very next day Ted came to my office and asked me to initiate a weekly session for OB-GYN staff members on the physiopathology of the female reproductive system. "Leo Miller called me yesterday and asked me to motivate you for a teaching session for his people. If you can afford to take on another session, it would be good for the whole medical center."

"But, Ted," I protested, "I'm spread thin already, and I'd like to take some time to think it over."

Two days later Jim Nelson took me to Lake Maumel for fishing. The serene beauty of the lake, with its abundance of fish, reminded me of my boyhood in Pyongyang, Korea.

Jim explained to me the history of the OB-GYN Department and their achievements in the field of cancer control. This led to the question of whether I would be willing to undertake another mass screening survey for cervical cancer in Little Rock and surrounding Pulaski County.

I interrupted him. "Jim, I had the project in Providence, and I'm not about to jump into another one. Do you know how much work is involved in setting up such a project? It takes at least a year for the groundwork and enormous effort to form several committees, before the project starts, and establish a training school for cytotechnologists. It would take at least seven years of my life, and I'm not going to get involved in that again."

In a telephone conversation with Dr. William Meissner, a few days later, regarding a thyroid tumor, I mentioned their desire to involve me in the screening project.

"Joe, I understand your reluctance," he said, "but you must realize that you are an expert in this field."

"But I'm trying to get into experimental cancer research. I want to get away from a cytology project of this kind."

"I understand, but there are only three or four people in the country who have some kind of experience in setting up such a mass screening survey, and you're one of them."

I thanked Dr. Meissner for his flattering comment, but I decided not to get involved.

"Uncle Joe" was the nickname given me by the residents and interns of the Pathology and OB-GYN Departments. I liked it, as I thought it carried a certain degree of affection.

One Saturday afternoon during the latter part of October 1961, Rudy Pearson took me to his home in South Little Rock to meet his mother, visiting from Norway, and his wife, Glenda. The house was well built but not pretentious. In his study was an impressive collection of books on war history, including World War II, the Nazi occupation of Norway, and several volumes on the Korean War.

Glenda brought us coffee and homemade doughnuts. As we visited, I said to Rudy, "I understand your interest in World War II and the German occupation of Norway, but why are you reading books on the Korean War? In fact, it was never a declared war. They always called it a UN police action."

Rudy replied with a cynical gesture, "It was a hell of a police action, with forty thousand American soldiers killed in Korea. I thought you were a pacifist, Uncle Joe, but I saw several books on the American Civil War in your office. You must be interested in war history, too."

"I am a pacifist, Rudy. I'm opposed to any kind of war, either local or on a worldwide scale. I would hope that all disputes could be settled by a series of negotiations, because I've seen enough human misery and suffering. But I think I'm a naive fool, because the history of mankind proves otherwise. For example, the American Civil War, which was based on economic issues, became an extremely emotional one. It was such a devastating war, with more than half a million soldiers killed on both sides. It could have been settled in a long-range plan to change the Southern economy, which was dependent on the slaves, to a more industrial system. As you know, the Southerners never called it a civil war. They always referred to it as the War between the States. Southerners have told me that if they had had more industry, they would have won the war."

Rudy changed the subject. "What about the Pacific war, which was launched by the Japanese naval forces by attacking Pearl Harbor?"

"That was engineered by Yamamoto, their most able admiral, who knew that they could never win a war against the United States if it lasted more than two years. He spent several years in Washington as a Japanese naval attaché but was foolish enough to believe that if the Japanese could knock off the entire Pacific fleet, the Americans might seek peace by negotiating with them."

"That shows how shallow the Japanese mentality was, Uncle Joe. He should have known the industrial capacity of this country and the spirit of the American people."

"I believe he was opposed to a hopeless war," I said, "but he was forced by many Japanese army officers to open fire. His position reminded me of that of Gen. Robert E. Lee, who was against the Civil War but felt obliged to join the Confederate army because he had been born in Virginia."

"Did they really think that the Americans would come to the negotiation table with the complete destruction of the Pacific fleet?"

"My father never thought so. In fact, he was quite happy when the Japanese attacked Pearl Harbor. He told us, 'Now there will be hope for the Korean people, because Japan is holding a tiger by the tail. Within three years the tiger will land in Japan. There will be indescribable hardship and countless war casualties, but in the end we will gain our independence.' "

"You never had a chance to gain independence from Japan because the nation was divided into two countries, decided by Stalin and Roosevelt."

"That's right. It was a tragic mistake on FDR's part."

"I'm convinced that he was really sick when he agreed to the partition of the Korean peninsula," Rudy said.

"I don't believe it was his intention to divide the country permanently. He was taken in by the Russians."

"What do you think of Harry Truman's giving the order to drop an atomic bomb on Hiroshima?" Rudy persisted.

"I can never condone such an action, causing seventy thousand civilian casualties. But my father never had any sympathy for the Japanese who died in Hiroshima. He told me that the Japanese had it coming because they had killed millions of innocent people in Korea, Manchuria, and China. He said it was punishment from God."

178

"He hated the Japanese that much?"

"Oh, yes, he was anti-Japanese to the core. As a matter of fact," I went on, "he was convinced that Japanese soldiers dug many underground tunnels or graves to execute Korean intellectuals, professors, physicians, and engineers before they surrendered to the U.S. forces."

"Was that a fact?"

"I don't know. But we saw many tunnels and fields containing drums of gasoline and airplane parts, for what purpose it's difficult to say."

"But they never had a chance to commit such atrocities."

"No, their emperor accepted the terms of surrender on August 15, 1945."

"Was the emperor really the ruler?" Rudy asked.

"No, I think he was just a figurehead of the Japanese government. He was constantly manipulated by hot-headed army officers of field grade—majors and colonels and a few general officers who led Japan into such defeat."

"But Japan is rising fast as a powerful economic nation."

"Unfortunately, it looks that way," I said with distaste.

"Is your father still alive?"

"No, he passed away in 1959."

"But you all survived the Korean War, which I think was induced by this country."

I was taken aback to hear such a bold statement. "Do you really think so? The Korean War was induced by this country? For what reason?"

"To cause the slumping economy of this country in the early 1950s to recover."

"Do you have any evidence to prove that?" I asked.

"Well, many things point in that direction." Rudy went on to explain. "First of all, the speech by Dean Acheson before the National Press Club was a direct invitation for the North Koreans to invade. We used to have an engineer at the University of Arkansas by the name of D. Scott who was a chief petty officer in the U.S. Navy in Hawaii during the Korean War. Scott told me that the island of Hawaii was saturated with surplus weapons and unused ammunition and they were seriously discussing dumping all of it into the Pacific Ocean, so that the wheels of the military industry would turn again."

"Rudy, I can't buy this story, because forty-five thousand American soldiers were killed during the Korean police action."

"Well, about fifty thousand people are killed on this country's highways annually. That doesn't make too much difference. And more than half a million soldiers were killed during the American Civil War."

"Was the American economy resurrected during the Korean War?" I asked.

"Many people think so, Uncle Joe. I believe the war was probably induced by this country to consume all the surplus weapons and ammunition."

Engineer Scott or Rudy may indeed have had a point. I recalled that all the ammunition for the M-1 rifles and machine guns used in the Korean War had been made in 1943 or 1944.

That night I was unable to sleep, going over and over our conversation. My thoughts went back to the summer of 1950, to the Korean hills, where so many young soldiers, civilians, and high school volunteers died senselessly.

The American Cancer Society made a substantial grant to the University of Arkansas Medical Center to encourage its faculty members to perform cancer research, citing the fact that no significant cancer research results had been published by the university's medical school. The grant was divided by several departments for cancer research in either clinical or applied areas.

Our chairman, Ted Richman, suggested that I apply for an institutional cancer grant, since I was the only cancer researcher in the department. A sum of $5,000 was awarded for my study regarding the development of the human uterine cervix, based on tissue studies of the uterine cervixes of fetuses, infants, and children. Ted told me that Dr. Papas, chairman of the Department of Pediatrics, showed a keen interest in my study. I accumulated a large number of specimens obtained from autopsies and surgical material by three pathology residents—Jay Dixon, Bill Hunter, and Leo Davis.

With the help of a prominent businessman and realtor, Ed Gibson, I was able to rent a house so that I could move my family down from Providence. Several students assisted me with moving my personal effects, and in April 1962 I brought my wife, six-month-old Michael, seventeen-month-old Patricia, and my mother to Arkansas.

Jim Nelson asked me to present a paper at the annual meeting of the Central Association of Obstetrics and Gynecologists, held in Hot Springs. It was a full day's seminar, attended by a large number of gynecologists from Arkansas and the neighboring states.

I met the secretary of the association, Dr. Henry Gardner, from Houston, Texas, who was a well-known gynecologist in that state. Gardner and I had a heated argument regarding the nature of cervical and endometrial polyps. He asked me after my presentation, "Is it a tumor or is it something else?"

"Based on my observation," I answered, "endocervical and endometrial polyps are not tumors, but they represent nonneoplastic growths, because of either inflammation or an excessive amount of hormones."

Gardner raised his voice slightly. "Do you have proof?"

"The polyps can be found in fetuses' and infants' uteri," I said.

"Is that a fact? How interesting! You should write a full manuscript for publication."

At a cocktail reception later, Dr. Gardner said, "I didn't mean to be unkind, but this was something new to me."

About the same time, the governor of Arkansas received a letter from a widow in Harrison, Arkansas, who had a large peach farm. She blamed the death of her husband, her brother-in-law, and her nephew on two pesticides, Aldrin and Dieldrin, which they had used to spray their peach trees. She stated that all three died of a highly malignant brain tumor, glioblastoma multiforme, in less than three years. She urged the governor to investigate the possible role of the pesticides in their deaths.

Being a busy politician, the governor either overlooked her letter or ignored her request. Three months later he received a second letter, much stronger in tone than the first, urging him to take immediate action or face the loss of a significant number of votes in the forthcoming election.

The letter, with the governor's note, was sent to the president of the University of Arkansas, in Fayetteville, who referred the matter to the dean of the medical school, in Little Rock. Dean Short then asked Dr. Ted Richman to investigate the matter.

When Ted approached me with the letters, I told him that I was fully occupied with a manuscript that I was preparing for publication. Dr. Ron Hoke, who was studying for his board examinations, politely declined the invitation to get involved in the pesticide issue, referring the matter to Dr. Dick Young. Dick was preparing a surgical pathology manual for our residents. He suggested that Ted give the assignment to a chief resident, who promptly passed it on to the second-and-third-year residents. Finally Bill Hunter, a first-year resident, was asked to carry out the investigation with a sufficient research grant to conduct experimental studies. Bill was a competent family practitioner from Crosett, Arkansas. He asked me to become his adviser, since he had no experience in conducting experimental pathology on pesticides. I agreed to help him.

Bill was able to obtain a large quantity of Aldrin and Dieldrin from the Shell Oil Company, the sole manufacturer and a subsidiary of the British Oil Company. He brought to my office two buckets full of Aldrin and Dieldrin in solid rock form, emitting toxic fumes.

"I think we'll have to break these rocks down to powder form," I said. "Then we can mix it with Purina Dog Chow to feed the rats and mice and see whether it causes a brain tumor or cancer of the organs."

Then Bill informed me that we had to buy a grinder to crush the rocks.

"Why don't you talk to Jim Tatum, the veterinarian in charge of the animal quarters, on the top floor of the medical center?" I suggested. "They must have a grinder up there."

"I just talked to Jim, and he gave me the address of the company we should approach for a new grinder."

We also had to order a large number of animals, sixty Holtzman rats and 180 mice of C3H, CBA, and C57 strains, from Jackson Memorial Laboratories, in Maine. Several weeks later the first shipment arrived at our receiving dock. It had been mistakenly delivered to the University of Kansas, in Lawrence, and left unattended for three days. Consequently, about a third of the animals were eaten by the others. This made a bloody mess, causing screams from the office girls in the receiving area when the shipment was finally delivered to our medical center.

When the second air-cargo shipment, containing the same number of rats and mice, arrived at our laboratory, we divided them into several groups. The control group received ordinary Purina Dog Chow, containing no pesticides, while the experimental groups received Purina Dog Chow containing 0.5 percent Aldrin and Dieldrin.

The next day an urgent call came from Jim Tatum. Bill and I ran up to the top floor of the medical center and found all the animals dead. It was obvious that 0.5 percent of the pesticides mixed in the Purina Dog Chow was too toxic.

We received an additional institutional cancer grant for the third shipment of experimental animals and for hiring part-time help from the medical students. We hired a sophomore, Leon Baker, to carry out the experimental studies. Animals receiving the pesticides were sacrificed at 30, 60, 90, and 120 days and were autopsied. All the organs, including brain tissue, were fixed in a 10 percent formalin solution, and histological slides were made for observation.

In the meantime, Bill Hunter was seeking a reputable institution for completion of his last two years of residency training and was able to obtain a position at the New England Deaconess Hospital, in Boston.

"Uncle Joe," he said, "I must tell you that I'm very happy to get out of this rat race, and I'll be far away from here when you have a paper ready to be published." He and his family left during the latter part of June 1963.

Three months later Leon Baker called, with excitement in his voice. "Dr. Song, I think I found something in the liver of this mouse! You'd better come over here and see it!"

There was indeed a liver cancer, called hepatoma, in several mice of C3H strain. "Leon, we're looking for a brain tumor. Let's examine the brains of the mice," I suggested.

In all the brain tissues examined we found no evidence of the highly malignant tumor glioblastoma multiforme. But most of the mice that received Dieldrin had developed large liver cancer, while the control groups naturally had no tumor. The Holtzman rats developed no liver tumor, although there were some areas of necrosis (cell death) and tissue destruction, and regenerating nodules were apparent.

"Did you really find hepatoma in the mice?" Bill asked on the telephone when we called him.

"Yes, indeed. Many of the mice that received Dieldrin developed a large hepatoma."

"Isn't that great? We should write a paper about that."

"I hope you can find the time to write a full manuscript, Bill," I said, "because I'm trying to finish my paper on endometrial polyp."

I promised Bill that we would send all the Kodachromes and microscopic sections for him to examine and tabulate the results for publication.

Dr. Ted Richman and Dean Winston Short were satisfied with the positive results of our experimental studies on the pesticides. They were happy to have some evidence to report to the president of the university, who undoubtedly would convey the results to the governor of Arkansas. I had no notion that this investigation would create much controversy and undesirable publicity for the following two years.

The prominent Houston gynecologist Henry Gardner, whom I had met in April of 1962, had a huge practice. In spite of that, he was so energetic and academic that he produced a monograph titled *Benign Diseases of the Vulva and Vagina*, published by the C. V. Mosby Company. Gardner told Jim Nelson to remind me to finish a manuscript to be published by the Association of Obstreticians and Gynecologists. Consequently, Jim called me twice a week to urge me on. I kept saying, "I'm working on it, Jim. Give me more time."

With the help of Edwin Hill, assistant professor of pediatrics and pathology, I obtained a research grant from NIH for the sum of

$39,700, with the same amount for two additional years. I hired a technician and an assistant, Frances Stalling, who was a tremendous help in carrying out research studies concerning the changes of the liver in sickle-cell disease and the histogenesis of the uterine cervix.

25

Back to Medical School

During the early part of May 1963, the wife of a physician was reported missing. It was common knowledge that she had a long-standing psychiatric problem and had attempted suicide several times. The physician hired private detective agencies to locate his wife. After about ten days, his son told him that there was a strange, awful odor coming from the attic of their house, which led to the discovery of his wife. She apparently had taken an overdose of sleeping pills. The county medical examiner insisted that we perform an autopsy, and I was asked to be the prosector. The only positive finding was the discovery of an excessive amount of phenobarbital in her stomach contents and in her bloodstream. I was asked to sign the certificate, including the number of my Arkansas medical license, which I did not possess.

The executive committee of the medical school held a special meeting, about a month later, to discuss the problem of my not being licensed in Arkansas. The state of Arkansas did not recognize graduates of medical schools outside the United States and Canada. During the meeting an associate dean was asked to approach Joe Vaser, chairman of the Arkansas Medical Board, to make an exception in my case. Vaser replied that there was no way to waive the state regulations.

At a subsequent session of the executive committee, it was unanimously agreed that in order to obtain an Arkansas license, I had to repeat the senior medical school year to receive the M.D. degree from the University of Arkansas Medical School.

Much discussion followed. Finally Dr. William Reed, chairman of the Department of Psychiatry, came up with the idea that I could repeat the senior year by going for three months during the summer and maintaining full salary from the medical school. Bill's point was that since all the faculty appointments were based on nine months a year, I would have three months' free time to go to school in 1963, 1964, and 1965. That was perceived to be a brilliant idea, but they wondered if I would be willing to accept such an arrangement.

185

The dean, Winston Short, suggested that I pass the Part I examination of the National Board of Medical Examiners. This was opposed by Henry Marvin, Ph.D., head of the Anatomy Department, and Dr. Richard Eaton, chairman of the Department of Medicine. Dr. Masayuki Hara, a graduate of Stanford Medical School, who had an impeccable reputation as the only cardiac surgeon in the mid-South, claimed that it was an absurd idea—that a man of my caliber should be able to obtain a license without going through school again.

Jim Nelson, representing ob-gyn, said, "Dr. Joe Song is a real asset to this medical center. He's the first and only competent ob-gyn pathologist this institution ever had, and the medical school should be willing to accommodate him." I later learned that Jim made a speech lasting more than five minutes, praising my accomplishments and past academic achievements in the field of obstetrical and gynecological pathology.

The conclusion was that Ted Richman, as Pathology Department chairman, should ask me if I would be willing to go to school for the next three summers without sacrificing my salary.

"I don't know, Ted," I said. "I'll have to think about it. That would mean a dramatic change in my career, and I really hate to go back to school."

"I know how you feel, Joe, but I believe this is the only way for you to obtain an Arkansas license."

The next day I was visited by several members of the faculty, including Dr. Ben Trump, head of the Orthopedic Surgery Section, and Dr. Ben Hawk, a former navy medical officer who came to the university six months prior to my arrival. Both men literally begged me to accept the decision of the executive committee, emphasizing that nine months of schooling would pass quickly.

Another faculty member of the OB-GYN Department, Dr. Steve Fish, urged me to go through it, saying, "We would hate to lose you, Joe, because you're the backbone of the ob-gyn field in this medical center." Steve, a historian, was very much interested in medical history. He was scheduled to give a talk on how President Garfield died in the latter part of November 1963, but he canceled his speech because of the assassination of President Kennedy during that month.

My wife and I had a lengthy discussion about my going back to school. She said, "If you can swallow your professional pride and go through one year, an M.D. degree from an American medical school may come in handy in our future relocation and your career."

The next day I told Ted Richman that I would accept the decision with much reluctance and went down to see Winston Short to register

186

and pay my tuition. Winston told me to discuss it with Stan Whaley, who said, "Well, now, Joe, I think we'll just forget about your paying tuition, since you'll be the oldest student in the class." With that I officially became a senior medical student at the University of Arkansas Medical School and was assigned to the Department of Obstetrics and Gynecology as a clerk for six weeks.

I had no difficulty in delivering babies in the normal cephalic presentation, with the use of regular forceps. But my second delivery was a difficult one, a breech presentation, and I panicked and yelled for help. A second-year resident, Duane Jones, rushed in to take care of it, telling me to watch his technique. I am grateful to those residents and senior staff members of the OB-GYN Department who were so thoughtful and did their best to make me feel at home. The chairman, Leo Miller, was a very capable department head. He asked if I would be willing to take written examinations with the other students.

"Why not?" I asked. "I'm one of your students."

Later I was told by Steve Fish that I passed with no difficulty, attaining an A average. "I owe you one, Steve," I remarked, "and you know what I mean."

Dr. Gene Ackerman, assistant professor of medicine, was a very competent internist. The head of the Medicine Department, Dr. Richard Eaton, was well respected, with a national reputation as an expert in emphysema research. His associate Jim Pierce was an excellent teacher.

In June 1964, I again became a senior medical student to complete the curriculum by going through the departments of surgery, urology, psychiatry, and pediatrics. Dr. Jack Growden, professor and chairman of the Department of Surgery, asked me to review the Pap smears taken from his wife once a year. Dr. Masayuki Hara was my strong supporter. Dr. Michael Fielding, assistant professor of surgery, impressed me with his sincerity.

The head of the Urology Department, Dr. Joe Headstream, helped me through some difficult times. He allowed me to do whatever I pleased, as a senior medical student, in handling his patients. Dr. William Reed, professor and chairman of the Department of Psychiatry, gave me detailed instructions in that field. My old friend from our Memphis days, Dr. Bob Matthews, and his assistant, Dr. Bob Shannon, went out of their way to accommodate me in their psychoanalysis and group sessions.

My only difficulty during my clerkship was with an assistant professor at the clinic. However, Dr. Ronald Harding, a second-year resident in pediatrics, was extremely kind in his teaching and in handling our well babies.

One day someone grabbed me from behind. I turned to find Dr. Paul Dennis, associate dean of the medical school and a professor of pediatrics. He smiled and said, "Joe, I know how difficult it is for you to go through this. But maintain your sense of humor. This will be over in no time."

As a whole, it was a very interesting experience, going through the senior year with the medical students I had taught two years before. I learned valuable lessons in humility and friendship, which will last a lifetime.

26
Book Publication

Finally, in July of 1963, I completed my manuscript for publication. It was titled *Histogenesis of Human Cervix Uteri* and consisted of ninety-eight pages, with forty-five black-and-white illustrations. After mailing it to Dr. Henry Gardner, I picked up the telephone and called Jim Nelson. "You can get off my back now, Jim! The manuscript is on its way to Houston," I told him.

He laughed. "I didn't mean to pester you about this, but Gardner kept calling me. I'm so glad you finally finished it."

In a telephone call the next month, Dr. Gardner told me that the manuscript was so long, with so many illustrations, that the *American Journal of Obstetrics and Gynecology* could not spare the space for the entire article. "I think you should publish it as a small book, a monograph," he added.

I discussed the matter with my assistant and secretary, Fran Stalling, who also urged me to publish it as a book.

"But I don't know how to approach the publishers for this kind of book. That's something I've never done. I think they should approach me," I said.

"No, they don't know you. We should approach the publishing firms."

Fred Haskin, representing the W. B. Saunders Company, came to my office in September, asking me to give him two copies of the manuscript.

"Two copies?"

"Yes. We'll send one copy to Harvard Medical School and the other to Johns Hopkins University for their evaluation and opinion."

"But, Fred, I don't have the manuscript completed. I'm going to do it in the future."

He reiterated their desire to have two copies, and I was noncommittal.

The next day Dr. Howard Richardson, an independently wealthy pathologist at North Little Rock Veterans Administration Hospital, was in my office. Howard was a man with impeccable credentials, from Washington University to Memorial Hospital in New York City. He had made it very clear before he took the job at the VA mental hospital that he would not perform autopsies. All the autopsies, about twenty cases a year, were done by our residents. The hospital housed several thousand mental patients, who tended to fight and kill each other during the hot summer months. One of our residents, Leo Davis, after performing five autopsies one summer expressed his desire to discontinue doing autopsies on mental patients, so we assigned two new residents.

I confided to Howard my intention of publishing a book. His reaction was totally unexpected. "Joe, you'll have nothing but enemies if you publish a medical book. Let me tell you about my friend Dr. George Pack, a world-renowned general surgeon. He was chief surgeon at Memorial Hospital, in New York, and he had many friends until he published his first medical book."

"Why was that?" I asked.

"Because not many people can publish books. This was based on professional jealousy."

Dr. Bess Richardson, Howard's wife, was also a pathologist, having been appointed assistant professor at the University of Arkansas Medical School. She recalled that her friend Dr. Bernard King had lost his contract on the West Coast because of publishing a book against the wishes of his department chairman. "Bernard had to go to New York City to get a job," she said. "As you know, Joe, professional jealousy is so destructive."

In spite of the stories told by the Richardsons, I decided to inform Ted Richman of my intentions. His reaction was: "You don't have time to do a book."

"I'll find the time to do it," I said.

Two weeks after the letters went out to the publishers, I had a visit from Dr. Howard Sato, associate professor of anatomy. He took me out into the hallway and whispered, "Joe, do you have any grant money available for publication of your book? A salesman from the F. A. Davis Company came to my office yesterday and asked me to inquire about the availability of grant money to finance it."

"No," I said, "I don't have that kind of money. There's only five or six thousand dollars left in the institution cancer grant."

"Have you told Ted Richman about this?"

"I passed it by him. He was indifferent."

"I'm afraid you'll have a problem with Ted when this book is published."

"Why?" I asked. "This is supposed to be an academic institution, isn't it? This kind of activity should be encouraged."

"Well, let me tell you about Dr. Max Weinstein. Max was an assistant professor of medicine at one of the prestigious eastern medical schools when he was approached by a publisher to publish a book on blood diseases. Being an aggressive man, Max accepted the assignment and then told his department chairman, who disliked the idea of Max publishing a medical textbook. The chairman told him, 'You're too young to do a book.' In spite of such discouragement and criticism, Max went ahead and published a book on blood diseases that became a bible in that field and was translated into several languages. But he lost his job; they didn't renew his contract. Max then built his own empire on the West Coast. Joe, you're not as big as Max Weinstein, so think it over."

"I've made up my mind to do this book, no matter what happens," I said.

That evening I was with my friend Dr. Jim Dusenberry, a professor of pharmacology. I asked him why people were reacting in such a strange and small way to my attempting to write a medical book.

"Well, to be honest with you, Joe, they're very envious of your ability and the good reputation you're enjoying. But there's more to it than that. Frankly, Joe, it's because you're a Korean refugee and you're able to write better papers than they can and even attempt a textbook. Some people can't stand that, because they're natives of this country and are too busy to write books. Here you come, a foreigner, and you're able to publish several papers a year and now are willing to tackle a book. You must understand their feelings, too, because human emotions run very, very deep."

I received a contract from the Charles C. Thomas publishing company with instructions to sign both copies and return the original and they would publish my book. On the recommendation of Fran and several of my residents, I finally signed the copies and executed the contract.

About a week later Dr. Edwin Thomas, a close friend of Ted Richman, came to my office. "Joe, why don't you divide your manuscript into two sections and send it to the New York Academy of Sciences? I'm sure they would publish it in two parts in the *Annals of the New York Academy of Sciences.*"

191

"You're a little too late, Ed. I've already signed a contract with a publishing company."

Ed said nothing, but bit his lip, turned, and walked out.

In anger I went up to see Stan Whaley and asked his advice. He said, "I don't understand why they're behaving like a bunch of jealous children. Your publishing a book would be a feather in the cap of this institution. You should go ahead with your original intention. I wish more faculty members would publish books, for the institution's sake."

Fran Stalling was very excited about the publication of the book. She began an exhaustive literature search, with the help of Rose Hogan, a competent and efficient librarian at the university hospital. Paul Chase printed numerous black-and-white photographs and color plates to be used in the book. Fran told me that this would be the first book published by a faculty member of the University of Arkansas Medical Center—a very significant event.

"But, Fran," I said, "I was told that there was an excellent book, titled *Diagnostic Radiology,* published by a former radiology chairman, Dr. David Gould."

"Oh, yes, I forgot about that. He was the best radiologist at the medical center."

"What happened to him?" I asked.

"He went to Denver during the racial problems created by the Hall High School incidents."

"Tell me about that, Fran."

"Well, when Hall High School refused to admit a couple of black students, Eisenhower sent federal troops to escort them to school, and there was a bloody riot."

"But why would Dr. Gould leave Little Rock?"

"He was a Jewish man," Fran went on, "and he was unable to sit back and see such riots in the city. He was an advocate of racial injustice being discontinued immediately and Hall High School admitting black students. This upset many people on the main campus of the university. Several young radiologists followed Dr. Gould to Denver, but one of them is back in Little Rock, working at Arkansas Baptist Hospital. Dr. Gould died suddenly of a heart attack."

Much later we had dinner with Dr. Jack Lane, the radiologist whom Fran had mentioned. He recited a Japanese poem in his thick, heavy southern accent, and it was very funny indeed.

The book was progressing slowly but steadily. It required my working at the office several weekends and late in the evenings in addition to performing my routine service duties and teaching.

In the middle of October 1963, Braxton Dallam Mitchell, of Williams and Wilkins, a reputable medical book publishing company, visited me. He brought me a complimentary copy of *The Human Embryology Textbook* and asked me to show him my manuscript.

"Mr. Mitchell, I haven't completed the manuscript," I explained. I'm still working on it, and it will probably be another six months before it's finished."

"Dr. Song, we should have sent you a contract for your signature, but I think we missed the boat. You know, we used to go to England to seek authors for medical books."

"Why England?" I asked. "There are plenty of professors in this country who could publish better books than the English."

"It may surprise you, but we just haven't been able to recruit competent authors for medical books. Many of the energetic and competent physicians at the Ivy League medical schools won't accept an assignment because of fear of going against the will of their professors or chairmen and being dismissed." He cited several examples of such instances at eastern medical schools.

"Are the English any better than the Americans in writing medical books?" I inquired.

"They seem to be broad-minded people, and if one of them accepts a book assignment, the rest of them will help him in getting all the materials he might need. We have never had any problems with British authors. They are a very cultured people."

"I can't understand this, Mr. Mitchell. Surely there are competent professors here who could publish better books," I reiterated.

"Well, that's the way it has been."

I read an article concerning the Nobel Prize in the fields of physiology and medicine. The Swedish Academy of Science and Medicine had decided to expand the nominating committee by adding three American physicians. Yet when they accepted the invitation, the Americans shipped volumes of their own published books and papers, along with letters stating that they should be nominated to receive the Nobel Prize. Appalled and disgusted by these actions, the Swedish Academy politely declined the self-nominations and threw away all the books and papers. The Americans were never again asked to serve on the nominating committee, I was told.

Were these American physicians just so naive and/or so conceited that they had to nominate themselves for the prize when they had been asked only to serve as members of the nominating committee? Many European physicians wrote sarcastic articles saying that

America has a long way to go to create its own culture and learn humility and modesty in the fields of science and literature.

I had a different interpretation. It is my belief that the American physicians were not ignorant slobs, as they were pictured by the European articles, but were highly intelligent and academic scholars who offered an honest, uninhibited revelation of their true feelings. Most of the medical textbooks published now are authored by American physicians and are readily accepted throughout the world as significant publications.

Trying to complete the second chapter of my book, I was deep in thought when Ted Richman shouted at me, "Look, Joe! Look who's here!"

At that outburst I turned to see a distinguished-looking gentleman standing in the doorway. "My God—Bob Hardy! It's been a long time." I went over to shake his hand.

"It has been a long time, Joe. Perhaps six or seven years since you left Memphis?"

"That's right. How is your wife, and my former chief, Dr. Sprunt?"

"Ann is fine, and our two children are growing up fast. And Dr. Sprunt is doing very well."

"What brings you here, Bob?" I asked.

Ted interrupted. "Bob has been approached to take over the administrative job at the university medical school hospital."

"Really? That's wonderful news!"

About the time I came to Memphis from the Korean front lines, Robert Hardy had arrived to begin his duties as administrator of John Gaston Hospital. I was invited to the Hardy home on two or three occasions. Ann was a very intelligent woman with a kind heart and refined manners. Bob was the best general hospital administrator I have ever known. I have met many hospital administrators, but I have never found anyone like him. He exhibited genuine humility and treated the house staff, interns, and residents with respect.

I asked Bob Hardy to come into my office, and we had a pleasant conversation, reminiscing about the good old days in Memphis. "Joe," he said, "you always know where Dr. Sprunt stands, because he's so straight and honest, unlike many southern gentlemen."

"Yes, indeed. He never played games with anyone, which was unusual for a southerner."

Many of the southern-born physicians whom I dealt with were very kind, but their actions on some occasions were extremely controversial. This puzzled me. When I mentioned it to Tom Maher one time, he said,

"They're bigoted." I believe there were exceptions, though, such as Dr. Sprunt, who was always direct in expressing his thoughts and desires.

"Bob, I think it would be wonderful if you would take over the position of administrator of the university hospital," I said.

"Well, I'll have to think about it and discuss it with my wife."

"By the way," I commented, "I was on the same plane as Dr. Howard Wilson, your neighbor. He has very high regard for you and Ann."

"When was that?"

"About six weeks ago, when I went to Miami to take the examinations."

"But I thought you were through with examinations and schooling. What examination was that?"

"I had to take the clinical pathology examination to be certified for a future position."

As we continued to talk, Bob asked, "What have you been doing, Joe? And are you happy here at the University of Arkansas?"

"Yes, indeed, I've been happy, and I'm now preparing a monograph to be published in the near future."

"Really? What is it about?"

I explained to him the events leading to the publication of the book including various complications.

"Well, Dr. Sprunt told me several times that you could produce under any conditions. So you can do it."

With that remark we shook hands again and Bob left. He accepted the position of administrator of the university hospital. I learned much later that he moved on to the University of Oklahoma Hospital several years after I left Little Rock. It was he who advised me to take a position in Midtown Hospital rather than accept one at Doctors Hospital, in Cleveland, Ohio.

When the tumor cells are confirmed by a pathologist on the Pap smears, he recommends that a cervical biopsy be taken as a confirmatory procedure. There is a very thin and fragile structure, called the basement membrane, in the cervix uteri, which separates the surface epithelial layers from the underlying supportive structure, called the stroma. The stroma contains connective tissue, numerous small blood vessels, and lymph vessels to nourish the epithelial cells in a normal state. Cancer cells are derived from the epithelial cells and eventually destroy the basement membrane, penetrating the supportive structure to become invasive cancer of the cervix.

When the tumor cells break through the blood vessel walls and grow within the vessel lumen, one can assume that the cancer will spread through the blood and lymph vessels to the adjacent lymph glands and farther up into the kidney region. Several large lymph glands become harder around the ureter and compress it, resulting in obstruction of urinary flow from the kidneys. With the draining system impaired, the body accumulates waste material in the blood, and patients with invasive cervical cancer eventually die of a toxic syndrome called uremia.

This was the common mechanism of death in women with widespread invasive cervical cancer before the Pap smear screening method was implemented to discover early cancer of the cervix, known as carcinoma in situ. When the biopsy confirms the tumor cells in the cervix, it is up to the gynecologist to remove a small focus of preinvasive cancer by cervical conization or amputation of the cervix. Pathologists have been trained to seek the status of the basement membrane when they are asked to make a diagnosis on cervical biopsy specimens. When they confirm the intact basement membrane, the diagnosis of preinvasive cancer, or carcinoma in situ, can be delivered to the gynecologists and surgeons.

The basement membrane is very fragile, dividing the epithelial structures from the underlying stroma. Quite often the membrane is damaged due to noncancerous conditions, such as severe inflammation, called cervicitis, or in some cases pregnancy. The demonstration of the basement membrane then becomes more difficult, requiring a special procedure utilizing the electron microscope. The ordinary microscope depends on an electric light bulb as the light source and has very limited magnification capability—not more than 1,000 times—whereas the electron microscope, utilizing electron beams as the light source, enables pathologists to magnify the tissue up to a maximum of 150,000 times. The irony of electron microscopy, however, is that it takes several days to a week to confirm the light microscopy findings.

During the course of my investigation of preinvasive cancer of the cervix, I learned that there were several special staining procedures, utilizing different dyes, to demonstrate the basement membrane vividly. Among them the most effective was Heidenhein's hematoxylin eosin staining method, which brought up the basement membrane as thin, delicate, and bluish in color. Black-and-white illustrations of electron microscopy presented no problems in publishing a book, but Heidenhein's and other special stains would require color illustrations.

After several weeks of deliberation and discussion with my assistant, I decided to insert a color plate in my book and approached Payne

Thomas, my publisher. He informed me that he would include as many black-and-white illustrations as desired without any cost to me, but he would have to send out color plate illustrations; consequently, I would have to bear the cost. Thomas quoted a price of $975. When I approached Ted Richman with the idea of using $975 from my grant for this expense, he advised me to go through the institution research grant committee, the chairman of which was Dr. Henry Marvin.

When I asked for his support, Marvin said, "Well, I'll have to bring this up to the entire committee for their opinion and decision."

A week later he came to my office. "Joe, they wouldn't go for that."

"Look, Henry," I said, "I have $4,000 to $5,000 left in my institutional research grant for the purpose of studying cancer of the cervix, and this is a very relevant cause. What was their objection?"

"I can't tell you, Joe," he answered in a sympathetic tone of voice.

"Henry, you guys spend more than $975 in wining and dining visitors from the NIH and other universities. Yet you voted against a scientific publication that I think is very significant for this medical center. I'll talk to the dean of the medical school and the vice president of the university."

"Why don't you talk to Ted Papas?" Henry suggested. "He has supported your research and shown a keen interest in your study of uterine cancer."

Dr. Ted Papas, a graduate of the University of Iowa and the son of Greek parents, had mentioned that he was keenly interested in my study because this area had been neglected in the pediatric field. He had commented sometime previously that no one had studied the growth pattern of the cervix uteri and the endometrium in newborns and children. Ted was one of few supporters of my book being published.

When I finished my presentation at Ted's office, emphasizing how important it was to include this color plate in my book, he grinned. "I think you should simmer down. Let me talk to members of the committee again."

Several days later I received a call from Ted urging me to see Henry Marvin at my earliest convenience. Marvin told me that the committee had reconsidered my request and approved the expense of including a color plate. "Joe, I was all in favor of your publication, but strong opposition from Tom Mahon prevented the approval of the request?"

Mahon? You mean the new head of the ob-gyn section? You've got to be kidding. He's a strong supporter."

"Mahon thought you should ask him to contribute a chapter or two in your book," Henry explained, "but you never approached him." I raised my voice. "I don't need him as a coauthor! This was my study. It took me ten years to accumulate all the material, and Mahon has contributed nothing."

"I know that, Joe, but he has a strong influence on this medical center."

"That's true, Henry, but he's an egomaniac, and he thrives on flattery and compliments from other people, including his residents." When my book was finally published, in October of 1964, it was hailed by the residents of the OB-GYN Department as well as the junior and senior faculty, except for Mahon, who remained cold and indifferent. Again I felt the destructiveness of professional jealousy.

I soon discovered that completing my book would not be as easy as I had expected, because of my daytime duties. Teaching medical students and pathology residents and conducting several weekly conferences for residents of ob-gyn, surgery, and internal medicine took most of my time, leaving only Saturday afternoons and Sundays for working on the book. Progress became painfully slow, requiring my spending additional time on two evenings a week, besides the weekends. The deadline for completion of the manuscript was long overdue. An exhaustive search of the literature and writing in the evenings and on weekends required persistent drive and perseverance.

I had determined to complete my schoolwork as a senior medical student from March through the end of August 1964 with a meager monthly stipend of $600, paid from my research grant. It became necessary for my wife to supplement our income by working part-time as an instructor in medicine.

The attitude of the department chairman and Edwin Thomas remained cold, but I was oblivious to their sarcasm and unkind remarks.

In May 1964, in anger, I signed a contract for another book, *Pathology of Sickle-Cell Disease,* for Charles C. Thomas, Publisher, with the intention of finishing the manuscript in eighteen months. Convinced that in order to undertake another book assignment and increase my professional income I had to become my own boss, I called my good friend Edwin Schwartz, in Cleveland, Ohio, and asked him to help me find a position at a medium-sized hospital. Acting with his characteristic enthusiasm and celerity, Edwin found several hospitals in Cleveland that had openings for a pathologist.

The Doctors Hospital was rather small, with 150 beds, utilizing a converted apartment building to house the patients. "But they're going to build a new hospital in the vicinity of Shaker Heights, and it will soon become a medium-sized hospital of 400 beds," Edwin said. "I think you should investigate the possibility there."

At Edwin's suggestion, I contacted the administrator and set a date for an interview during the middle of August. The administrator and his assistant and the chief radiologist were very kind, extending every courtesy to me during my brief stay in Cleveland. The radiologist emphasized that they would like to have a pathologist with an academic background to establish pathology residency programs at their new hospital, which would be built in sixteen months.

"What would it take to have you as a pathologist?" asked the administrator during our luncheon meeting.

I explained to them why I was looking for a position, telling them about my situation at the University of Arkansas. "Gentlemen, I'm almost broke because of my becoming a senior medical student again and the curtailment of my income, which had reached a maximum of $18,000 per annum. I must have $50,000 for the first year."

The administrator almost dropped his roll when I mentioned that figure. "We are expecting to pay a new pathologist a yearly income in the neighborhood of $25,000."

"Well, if that is the situation," I said, "then I would gain only $7,000 a year, with the task of rebuilding your laboratory."

"The figure you mentioned is not really out of line," the radiologist commented.

In my hotel room later, after dinner with Ed and his wife, Sue, Ed remarked, "You must be crazy, Joe. The average compensation for a pathologist in the Cleveland area is $25,000 a year. They'll never offer you what you asked for. I don't even make that kind of money, and I've been here fifteen years."

"Well, we'll just wait and see what they come back with in their counteroffer," I continued drinking my martini.

When I showed Ed a galley proof of my forthcoming monograph, he was visibly impressed and asked me whether I would dedicate the book to my parents or to my children.

"I'm thinking of dedicating this little book to my former chief, Dr. Sprunt."

"Oh, no, Joe, you must not dedicate it to that politician. He has so many enemies throughout the country. That would be a mistake. They'll never sell this book." He continued to point out that I had been exploited by Sprunt.

"As you know, Joe," Ed went on, "he pulled some fast ones on me while I was in Memphis and stole so many papers that I had written.

They're still publishing papers based on my research and investigation."

"I know what you're talking about, Ed, but the letter from Dr. Sprunt in November 1951 saved my life during the dark days of the Korean War by offering me a spot at the University of Tennessee. I can't forget that as long as I live."

"But you worked hard. You paid him back ten times more than what he did for you. Can't you see that? It would be a big, big mistake if you decided to dedicate your monograph to Sprunt."

On my way home from Cleveland I kept mulling over what Ed had told me about Sprunt until the plane landed. Ed's suggestion to dedicate my first monograph to Dr. Harold Stewart, of the NCI, made good sense and deserved consideration. After all, it was Dr. Stewart who had approached Dr. Sprunt for me, but I felt that Dr. Stewart could wait for the next book. Ed had argued with me, saying, "You really didn't think that a letter from Sprunt actually saved your life, did you?"

"I didn't mean it literally in that sense, Ed, but the letter really saved me from going back to frontline duty, which could have been fatal."

In spite of all Dr. Sprunt's shortcomings—his being a politician, his violent temper, his tendency to exploit unfortunate people, and his dictatorial nature—I felt deeply that I should dedicate my monograph to him. When the book finally was published, he never even acknowledged the dedication or sent me a letter of thanks, whereas Dr. Harold Stewart showed his affection and great appreciation when I dedicated my second book to him.

Edwin Schwartz may have been right in feeling that I made a serious mistake in dedicating the book to Douglas Sprunt, but I have no regrets, as Dr. Sprunt was the first person to offer me a position in the United States.

In April 1964, I finally completed the manuscript, titled *The Human Uterus—Morphogenesis and Embryological Basis for Cancer*, containing 150 illustrations, and mailed it to the publisher.

27
Job Interview

I was rotating through the internal medicine, psychiatric, and pediatric departments for the final six months of my clerkship as a senior medical student. Members of the faculty and the resident physicians in the three departments were enthusiastic in their support, trying to help me get through the ordeal. To this day I am grateful to many of the faculty members.

Dr. Howard Richardson dropped into my office one day for small talk. He mentioned that I had to be certified in both anatomical and clinical pathology.

"Howard, I was certified by the American Board of Pathology in 1955," I said.

"I know that, and we're all convinced that you're a good surgical pathologist, but you must be board-certified in clinical pathology to be the director of a pathology department at a large hospital, in order to maintain their pathology residency programs. And now is the time for you to prepare to take the examinations in chemistry, microbiology, blood bank, hematology, and clinical microscopy."

"I never paid much attention to that field, because that was not my main interest, although I was eligible to take the examinations in clinical pathology in 1955."

"Well, I'm afraid you must have both boards to be the director of the lab of any sizable hospital," he insisted.

While I was busy studying and reviewing the clinical pathology fields during the hot month of July, I received a conference telephone call from Dan Conway, assistant administrator, and Sr. Mary Eileen McCain, administrator of Marymount Hospital, in Midtown. They asked me to come for an interview for the position of chief pathologist, which was still held by Dr. Fred Thompson, who had resigned several months previously.

"Dr. Song, we would like you to meet members of our board and the search committee when Dr. Thompson is out of town," said Mr. Conway.

"I would rather not do that, Mr. Conway. You see, I go by the book, and according to that I must consult with the incumbent pathologist before entering into any negotiations. So it has to be at a time when Dr. Thompson is in town."

"I understand what you are saying," Sr. Mary McCain remarked. "We will schedule you at a later date."

"Sister, I'm studying like mad to pass the examinations for the clinical pathology boards, which will be given in Miami on October 5, and I would rather wait to hear the outcome of that before I make a trip to Midtown, if that is agreeable to you."

Both Sister McCain and Dan Conway agreed that this would be a prudent way to pursue the matter.

Two days later Dr. Sprunt called me from Memphis. "Joe, I heard through the grapevine that you're looking for a suitable position to relocate."

"That's true. I'm finishing my senior medical student work at the end of August, and both the dean of the medical school and Ted Richman consented for me to take a new position as of January 1965."

"Why don't you come up to see me before you accept any position? I would like you to come back to us as a professor of pathology."

I thanked Dr. Sprunt for his consideration and agreed to meet him for lunch at the student center the following week. I decided to drive to Memphis, taking along my wife and our son Mike, who was three years old. We left Little Rock around nine o'clock in the morning. When we arrived in Memphis, all the streets were blocked by the city police. President Johnson's motorcade was passing through downtown Memphis; consequently, I was about two hours late for the appointment with Dr. Sprunt. During our afternoon conversation at his office, I did not mention the forthcoming book or that I had decided to dedicate it to him.

He said, "Joe, I would like you to come back to me as a full professor of pathology at $25,000 per annum."

I was very grateful to Dr. Sprunt for his offer but declined, saying, "I had always hoped to come back, but I'm afraid it wouldn't work out for the department."

"Why? You knew I always wanted you to come back to Memphis."

"I'm aware of that, Dr. Sprunt, but as you know, your associate Coy Anderson never liked me during my residency training and never paid attention to my work. It just wouldn't work out, although I would give my right arm to become a member of your staff."

I also emphasized the fact that I was determined to take a position as chief pathologist so that I could make my own decisions concerning books to publish and papers to present at conventions.

202

Dr. Sprunt understood but reiterated his offer, if I should change my mind. He also thanked me for my courtesy visit from Little Rock.

"Well, I couldn't refuse your desire to see me," I said. "Please extend my kindest personal regards to Mrs. Sprunt."

Two weeks later I drove to Miami to take the examinations and have a short vacation with my wife and our two oldest children. During the three days of the examinations the weather in Miami was extremely bad. The people were preparing to cope with a hurricane that was supposed to hit Miami Beach the next day. When we returned to Little Rock after four days of vacation in such miserable weather, I called Mr. Conway and set a date for my forthcoming interview in the latter part of October.

Arriving in Midtown on the afternoon of October 21, I was met at the airport by Mr. Conway. He was instantly likable because of his openness and honesty.

At seven o'clock the following morning I took a cab to Marymount Hospital. It was a cool, crisp day, and I made a survey by walking around the vicinity of the institution, which was rather small, having 297 beds.

Mr. Conway made arrangements for me to meet with Dr. Fred Thompson before talking with members of the board.

Dr. Thompson said, "You know, you're the only pathologist who has asked for me before entering into negotiations for this position."

"I had no idea that there were several pathologists who have come to investigate this position," I commented.

"Oh, yes, they have interviewed four pathologists already, and each of them was brought in while I was out of town or unavailable."

"I had the impression that they were going to wait for me. I thought I was the first candidate for interview."

"Oh, no, and they will probably interview four more after you."

I told Dr. Thompson that a position had been offered me by a hospital in Cleveland, and we discussed some of our mutual friends in Ohio.

At the noon luncheon I met members of the search committee, composed of Drs. John Baker, Leo Pearson, Paul Harding, Peter Stein, Dan Crocker, Neil Hinton, William McCormick, and Gus Schroeder. The chairman of the board, William Rankin, was also present. He was a gentle and sincere man, who would become a good friend of our family when we settled in Midtown.

The committee members asked me why I was looking into this position.

"Gentlemen," I replied, "I'm making $18,000 a year at the University of Arkansas, and I need to earn more money to have any kind of plans for my family."

"Why this hospital, Dr. Song?" questioned Dan Crocker.

"I'll be very frank with you. I don't even know what kind of hospital this is. Dr. Seger, chairman of the Department of Pharmacology at the University of Arkansas Medical School, told me to make sure that this is not an osteopathic hospital. You do have an osteopathic medical school here, don't you?"

Dr. Baker smiled and said, "Well, we deserve such a comment. Yes, indeed, we have a school here."

Dr. Crocker asked me if I was certified by both boards.

"Yes, I am. Just before I left Little Rock, the stewardess handed me a piece of paper from my secretary saying that I had passed the board examinations in clinical pathology."

They all laughed.

I was told much later by Dr. Peter Stein that the committee had a special meeting on the same evening, after I left Midtown, to discuss the outcome of my interview. They all agreed on one point, according to him. "At least he's honest about the money, and he was frank about his purpose in looking for a private practice."

From my brief visit in Midtown I had no way of knowing that Marymount Hospital was a second-class community hospital with only one internist who was certified by the American Board of Internal Medicine and there were no fellows of the American College of Physicians among the staff. Furthermore, the hospital had no board-certified obstetricians and gynecologists, most of the staff being self-trained men and ineligible for the examinations given by the American Board of Obstetrics and Gynecologists.

I was, however, very much impressed with the city and the surrounding farm communities, as well as the sincerity and friendliness of the people, who, according to my wife, are down-to-earth folks.

Dr. Bob Matthews, my old friend from the University of Tennessee, now a senior psychiatry resident at the University of Arkansas, came to see me during the first part of November, grinning and smoking a cigar.

"Joe, I heard you're going to the North." he said.

"I'd like to go to Midtown."

"But why? That's in the middle of nowhere, in the cornfields."

"I like the people," I replied.

"Joe," he continued, "I think you should investigate the opening at Providence Hospital, in Kansas City, Kansas. Bob Rainey is the chief of staff, and he told me that they're looking for a pathologist."

"I know Bob Rainey. He was a general surgeon, wasn't he?" I asked.

"He still is, but he's president of the medical staff, and he told me to let you know that there's an opening at his hospital. It's a 397-bed acute care institution. I think you should be in a bigger city than Midtown."

It had been more than three weeks since I visited Marymount Hospital, and there had been no word. So I gave a copy of my curriculum vitae to Bob, asking him to send it to Kansas City. Three days later I received a call from the administrator, Sister Marie, asking me to appear before the search committee at Providence Hospital. I agreed to go through the interview and a series of discussions with the medical staff and Sister Marie on November 15.

On November 13, Dan Conway, from Marymount Hospital, called me and informed me that the administration and the board of trustees were sending him to Little Rock to have a serious discussion with me on November 18, if that was agreeable to me.

I then called Sister Marie, in Kansas City, to tell her of the forthcoming meeting with Mr. Conway, who would be coming to Little Rock with various documents. "I believe they are serious about discussing the position in Midtown, and I feel that I must cancel our appointment."

"I appreciate your honesty in telling me about this," she said. "If it doesn't work out, please call me anytime."

I took Dan Conway to Sam Peck Hotel and then to the Embers, where we had dinner with Bob Hardy, administrator of the university hospital, and his wife. The following morning Mr. Conway came to my office with a proposed contract for the position of chief pathologist at Marymount Hospital. We spent the entire morning reviewing the contents of the contract, making several minor revisions in the wording of the document. To this date I have great respect for Dan Conway because of his administrative skill, honesty, and fairness. He informed me that my compensation would be based on House File 21 of the state code, clarifying the situation of pathologist versus the institution. He explained it to me in detail, saying that since the practice of pathology is the practice of medicine, the institution cannot hire a pathologist to practice medicine. Therefore, the compensation has to be based on a percentage of net income, or percentage of gross income. The pathologist cannot be on straight salary as an employee of the hospital.

I noticed in the contract that I was to receive $40,000 as a basic draw, plus 5 percent net income, totaling $50,000 per annum. Conway said, "But you will be alone for a while, because everybody is leaving. You may have to hire a local pathologist to help you. So we are prepared to pay you $75,000 for the first year."

"Well, Mr. Conway, I think that's very fair. It's more than I bargained for. However, I would like to take this contract to our chairman and the dean of the medical school as a professional courtesy, if you don't object."

Both Ted Richman and Dean Short reviewed the contract. They told me that they thought it was a good one and they would allow me to leave the institution at the end of December 1964 instead of June 30, 1965.

My monograph, *The Human Uterus,* was finally published by Charles C. Thomas on October 1, 1964. As the author, I received twenty free copies of the book from the publisher. About a week later ten students from the sophomore class came to my office. "We heard you're leaving the medical school," they said. "We bought copies of your book, and we'd like you to autograph them."

"But you guys shouldn't have bought them. I could have gotten them cheaper for you, had I known your intentions, because there is a 40 percent author's discount."

"Well, we already bought them, so will you please autograph them for us?"

Touched by their gesture, I signed each copy: "With deep appreciation."

On the morning of December 1, I was in the office of the vice president in charge of medical affairs for the university. "Stan, I'm supposed to receive my medical degree during the June commencement, when I'll be practicing in the north. Must I stand in line to receive my degree with the other graduates?" I asked.

"Well, Joe, I think we can waive that regulation, since this is a special case."

I expressed my deep appreciation and gratitude, saying, "Stan, I owe you and the medical center a great deal, and I hope there will be something I can do for the school."

"You have brought distinction to the medical center by publishing a book and many papers. The members of the faculty and the residents in the OB-GYN Department will miss you very much."

"As you know, Stan," I said, "I love an academic job with teaching and research. I have an inspirational desire to teach residents. But I came to the conclusion that I must have my own department in order to carry out investigational work, with complete freedom to publish books and papers."

"I fully understand how you feel, but I still believe your leaving is a loss to our medical center," he remarked.

"You have many good men here, Stan, such as Dick Eaton, Jim Goodman, and Masa Hara. They are the pillars of the medical school."

"Indeed they are, but we will miss you very much." With that we parted. When I left his office that day, I had no notion of our future meetings in Bethesda, Maryland, years later, when he became vice president in charge of communications for the NIH.

At a lavish farewell dinner party given for us by the faculty members of the medical and pharmacy schools, Ben Hawk leaned over, holding a glass of champagne. "Joe," he whispered, "I'm so glad you're going to have your own department."

Manfred Morris, a biochemist, told me to follow U.S. Highway 65 north. "It will take you to Midtown if you don't go south."

"I intend to take that highway, with one intermediate stop at Chillicothe, Missouri, to visit an old friend, Col. Ken Lucas," I said.

"Who is Ken Lucas?"

"Colonel Lucas was in Korea with the U.S. Medical Service Corps, attached to the office of the surgeon general of the ROK army. It was Colonel Lucas who obtained a seat for me on a U.S. cargo plane from Pusan to Tokyo."

So many toasts were proposed by my friends that evening that my wife had to drive me home because I was drunk.

On the morning of January 2, 1965, I kissed my mother, my wife, four-year-old Pat, three-year-old Michael, and thirteen-month-old Jeff good-bye and left in my Hillman, which was loaded with suitcases and books.

After spending the night at Springfield, Missouri, I arrived at the home of Ken Lucas, in Chillicothe, around one o'clock in the afternoon. We had a late lunch on the porch and spent the next two hours reminiscing about the rough days in Seoul and Pusan during the Korean War. Colonel Lucas had retired from the U.S. Army Medical Service Corps. He had his own insurance agency and was quite content with the business.

Crossing the Missouri state line, I saw a vast area of farmland. My Hillman was making barely fifty miles an hour with its load. A glow of lights in the distance brought a thrill of anticipation on that cold January evening, when my car suddenly lost power and finally stopped. I checked the gas gauge, and it registered empty. Looking around for a service station, I saw nothing but barren fields.

A few minutes later a two-ton Ford pickup stopped in front of me and an elderly farmer stepped out. "Having trouble with your car?"

"I believe I'm out of gas," I said. "Is there any gas station around here?"

"There's a Phillips 66 station thirty-five miles from here. Let me give you some of my gas to get you to that station. How much does this little car hold?"

"About eight gallons, I think."

"Young man, you need a bigger tank to drive through here, because you never find a service station when you need it."

He filled my tank with his spare gasoline, refusing the money that I offered. In the years to follow I found more such good-hearted people. Some time later, in June of 1966, when we were heading for Lake Okon for a vacation the right rear tire of our Mercury station wagon blew out. I was trying to figure out how to change the tire—something I had never done in my life. Within three minutes two cars pulled up and two men came to our rescue—a Cadillac salesman from Fort Nix and a teacher from Middlesex. They said to the children, "You kids stay in the car. We'll do the job." When they replaced the ruptured tire with the spare, they told me to have it repaired or buy a new one at the Okon station. They, too, refused the money I tried to give them. We were impressed with their kindness and helpful manner. Pat said, "Now, Dad, we'll stay here for good."

I finally arrived in Midtown late in the evening of January 3 and checked into the Hotel Commodore. Then I notified Dan Conway of my safe arrival. He and his wife, Jane Anne, invited me to dinner on the following day. A warm friendship, which was to last many years, began at that dinner table.

28
Community Hospital Practice

A 297-bed acute care facility, Marymount Hospital was one of many hospitals owned and operated by the Sisters of Allegiance, with national headquarters in Washington, D.C. The institution had been founded by nuns from Ireland and had several provinces throughout the country. Marymount Hospital belonged to the Central Province, which operated a dozen or so hospitals in the West and Midwest.

My immediate task was to maintain and develop further the training program in pathology and set up research projects related to patient care in terms of improved diagnostic methods and treatment. Rather than having a basic research project, the University of Arkansas Medical Center had consented to transfer the remaining $27,600 of the research funds from that institution to Marymount Hospital when I left Arkansas. I soon found out, from the NIH, that the state health department had to approve such a transfer.

I was introduced by the director of the state health department to Dr. Madeline Shepard, chief medical officer in charge of maternity health care. When I asked her to sign the paper approving the transfer, she refused to do so. "It's nothing personal, Dr. Song. The only reason I can't sign the paper is the fact that your hospital has no board-certified obstetricians and gynecologists. Not a single one."

"But there must be a mistake. We have five or six obstetricians and gynecologists at the hospital."

"Let me point out to you, Dr. Song, that your chief of obstetrics and gynecology, Dr. Gus Schroeder, is a self-trained man. He's not even eligible for board examinations. And Dr. Patrick McCormick has never applied for certifying examinations."

"What about Dr. Rob Cassady?" I asked. "He appears to be a very capable physician in his field."

"His application was turned down by the American Board of Obstetrics and Gynecology."

"Why was his application rejected?"

"I don't know. You'll have to find out for yourself."

"But Drs. Sinton, Hall, and King are certified specialists, aren't they?" I persisted.

"Yes, they are, but they are identified as staff members of Metropolitan Hospital," she explained. "Their practice at your hospital represents only 10 percent of their work. They must do more than 60 percent to be considered staff at your hospital. Consequently, you don't have a single physician who is certified by the American Board of Obstetrics and Gynecology."

I was soon to learn that Dr. Madeline was indeed correct. I had assumed that all the members of the medical staff here were certified. I was dismayed to find that only one internist among eleven internal medicine staff members was certified by the American Board of Internal Medicine. None of the internists were Fellows of the American College of Physicians. Deeply disturbed, I approached Dr. Patrick McCormick about his partner, whose application was rejected by the American Board of Obstetrics and Gynecology. "Pat, how come his application was turned down?"

"Well, Joe, let me tell you. He sent an application to take the examinations, but when the members of the Metropolitan Hospital staff found out, two of them torpedoed his application, saying that Rob has been doing a uterine suspension technique."

I had no idea that there was such cutthroat fighting going on among the physicians in this city, but I had to agree with the view that the uterine suspension technique is an outdated method, no longer considered to be a valid surgical procedure.

A couple of days later I was having lunch with an internist, Dr. Albert Frank. "Al, I understand you're the only board-certified internist at this hospital," I commented.

"That's right. I'm the only one who passed the examinations several years ago."

"What about the eleven other internists we have?"

"Well, most of them aren't even eligible for the examinations, because they're self-trained internists, having only one or two years of residency."

"A three-year residency is required to be eligible for board examination," I noted.

"I know," Al said, "but guys like Sam McCain failed the first time and never reapplied."

"What about his partners, Neil Smith and Joe Casey?"

"They never bothered to take the examinations," Al replied.

"Are you a member of the American College of Physicians?" I asked.

"No, but I would like to be. The only trouble is that those internists at Metropolitan Hospital hated me so much that they wouldn't sponsor my application."

"So we have no American College of Physicians members at this institution?"

"I'm afraid that's true, Joe."

"Why don't I sponsor your application to become an associate first and then to be promoted to fellow of the American College of Physicians? You would need two publications to become an associate."

"I know that, but I don't have time to write papers. Maybe you could help me by publishing a few articles with me," he suggested.

That night I recalled the previous conversation with the chief pathologist at Metropolitan Hospital, Dr. Jack Lane, who had said, "Joe, I hate to tell you, but you landed in a third-rate community hospital. Most of your staff members are general practitioners, and only a very few are really qualified specialists."

"What about Lutheran Hospital?" I asked.

"They have more board-certified specialists than you do. In our hospital 85 percent of the medical staff members are board-certified. Furthermore, Joe, it takes a man to do business."

It was not until several years later that I understood his last statement.

The next day I was in the administrator's office, discussing the matter with Sister McCain; William Rankin, chairman of the board; and Ben Kean, immediate past president of the board of trustees.

"I never doubted the qualifications of the medical staff here," I commented, "because I assumed that all of them were board-certified in their own fields. But now I find that only a few members of the staff are really qualified to practice in their chosen fields."

Bill Rankin sighed. "Well, I'm afraid that's the situation here. We all realize that we need more board-certified specialists. We hope you can help us in achieving that goal."

"I'm facing the monumental task of maintaining the pathology residency and doing some research," I said. "But to make members of the staff board-certified specialists is more than I expected."

Dan Conway expressed his hope that I could "pull some strings, at least in the field of ob-gyn."

"I do know several key people in that field, but it will take a long time and tremendous effort to stimulate and motivate members of the

211

staff to take the examinations to become board-certified specialists in obstetrics and gynecology, which is my subspecialty."

Sister McCain smiled and said, "We'll do our best to support you in this gigantic task, Dr. Song."

I felt that I was being pushed into a corner. "I can't suppress my feelings of disappointment, but since I'm here, let us all pull together."

I initiated action by calling a meeting in the administrator's office on January 21 at 10:00 A.M. William Rankin, Sister McCain, Dan Conway, Dr. Leo Pearson, chief of staff, and I met to discuss our future policy with regard to board certification for the Department of Obstetrics and Gynecology. The atmosphere was charged.

"It is unacceptable," I began, "to have our Department of Obstetrics and Gynecology staffed with non-board-certified physicians. We must do something about this—either bring in young physicians with board certification or motivate our current staff members to complete their training and take the examinations to become diplomates of the American Board of Obstetrics and Gynecology."

"Is it absolutely necessary to have board-certified men?" questioned Sister McCain.

Bill Rankin, a placid man, was keenly aware of the importance of board certification. "Sister," he explained, "it makes very little difference in the routine practice of obstetrics and gynecology whether they are board-certified or not, because most of the patients don't understand the difference. However, it is a reflection on the image of any hospital to have an insufficient number of board-certified physicians."

"Nobody ever raised the question before," said Sister McCain. "What about a man like Henry Sears, who has been practicing for over twenty-five years at this hospital?"

I interrupted her. "Sister, Henry Sears is a grand old man with superb technique, but he is self-trained, having come in on a 'grandfather clause' in general surgery and gynecology. Of course, there was no American board of ob-gyn until 1930, and he is not to be blamed for lack of board certification. The board was organized in 1930 as a determined effort to improve standards in the practice of obstetrics and gynecology. I have no doubt that there are many highly qualified gynecologists who do not possess the certificate, which was first issued in 1936. But here we are in 1965, and we must have at least several staff members who are diplomates of the American Board of Obstetrics and Gynecology."

"Joe is right, Sister," emphasized Mr. Rankin. "To maintain our standards of practice in this community, all members of the section should be certified."

Leo Pearson turned to me. "Joe, you've done a great deal of work in ob-gyn pathology, and you must know many key physicians in the field. Can you help us in that regard?"

"I know a few people, but what can they do to motivate our staff to gain eligibility and take the examinations?"

"Do we have board-certified surgeons?" asked Sister McCain.

Leo replied, "We have one or two board-certified general surgeons, but there are five or six old but experienced physicians who have been operating for years without any certification problem under the grandfather clause, and there isn't anything we can do to stop them."

"I think we should concentrate on one subject today," I continued. "To improve the standards of practice in obstetrics and gynecology. Is it possible for us to ask those board-certified men from Metropolitan Hospital to become full-time staff members of this hospital? As you know, they're doing most of their practicing over there and admit only 10 percent of their patients here."

"Well, that's a possibility," said Bill, "but how can we entice them to become full-time people here?"

Dr. Pearson had a suggestion. "There's another way to gain more certified obstetricians and gynecologists—by approaching the university hospital, Central University Medical School, and the University of North Central and importing young physicians completing their residency training programs to settle at our hospital for practice."

"Leo, I think that's a good idea. Do you mean to go to the university hospital and the two other medical schools and talk to residents who are about to start their practice?" I asked.

"I mean to ask our ob-gyn staff members to bring them in as assistants or associates or partners," he explained.

Bill looked at me. "Joe, can you talk to three or four obstetricians and gynecologists who might need an associate or partner in their practice?"

"I'll be glad to do so," I replied.

We agreed to meet again a week later at the same time for further discussion.

I approached five physicians individually about their need for a board-certified obstetrician and gynecologist as an additional staff member. Each one told me it would be four or five years before he was ready to help.

During the next meeting in Sister's office, I reported, "It appears that we will not have a full-time board-certified man for at least four or five years. But I've come up with an idea, although it's a long shot, to motivate our people here and raise their scientific standards. Why don't we plan a seminar in the field of obstetrics and gynecology? We could invite some nationally renowned professors to come here and conduct a day-long seminar. At the same time we could have our own ob-gyn staff meet them and get help."

"That's a very good idea, Joe," said Bill, "but do we have the financial resources to do that?"

"I believe the pharmaceutical companies will be more than happy to finance such a seminar, not only for our staff, but also for the physicians of our state."

"Will you undertake this project, Dr. Song?" Sister McCain asked. "I know you have too much to do in the lab, but if you could find the time, we would all be grateful."

"Sister, this is my subspecialty, and I'll be glad to explore the matter."

The idea of having a hospital medical day devoted to the field of obstetrics and gynecology, which was to continue for the next several years, originated in Sister McCain's office on that day.

I had never been exposed to a community hospital medical practice until I became chief pathologist and director of laboratories at Marymount Hospital. My brief medical career had been centered around academic circles, where dedicated scientists enjoy teaching medical students and publishing research papers. This is in sharp contrast to the business world of medical practice, where the quality of a physician is largely measured by the size of his practice and wealth built from income paid by his patients.

On January 15, Dr. Dan Crocker, a general surgeon who was a Midtown native and the son of a physician, visited me in my office. "Joe, I've heard that the state board of medical examiners issued only a temporary license for you and is demanding to review your contract before they issue a full license. Is that right?"

"That's right," I replied, "and I'm unable to understand what authority they have to review my contract with Marymount Hospital."

"I'll explain it to you, Joe. Back in 1956 we had a big lawsuit brought by the pathologists, radiologists, and anesthesiologists against the Hospital Association. It was initiated by your predecessor, Fred Thompson, who was a well-known politician in medical practice. The lawsuit was based on the belief that the practice of pathology, radiology, or anesthesiology is the practice of medicine, so therefore the physicians must be compensated by Blue Shield instead of Blue Cross."

"Dan, I'm having a difficult time comprehending the difference in the payment by Blue Shield and Blue Cross. After all, the money is the same, isn't it?"

214

"Well, as you know, Blue Cross pays hospitalization, but Blue Shield is the method of payment for physicians' services, and I think they won the suit qualifying that the institution cannot practice medicine in terms of pathology, radiology, and anesthesiology."

Dan explained to me that the city of Midtown lacked interest in medical science research and any academic activities in medicine, but it had two hundred millionaires.

"That's a very intriguing situation, Dan, but I have never dreamed of becoming a millionaire. I would just like to combine academic activities and pathology practice at this hospital to make some future plans."

"But you'll become a millionaire. Your predecessor, Fred Thompson, was a multimillionaire when he left here, although he had only a pair of old shoes when he arrived in this city in 1946."

I gave Dan a complete rundown on my battle with the state medical board, emphasizing that they had no right to demand to review my contract with Marymount Hospital, because that was purely my business. The explanation given by Rick Oates, an attorney for the state medical board, was that because of House File 21, ruled by Judge Moore, stating that the practice of pathology is the practice of medicine, the hospital could not employ pathologists on a straight salary, and the board had previously reviewed two contracts before they issued a full license.

To solve this problem, Oates suggested the names of three attorneys who might review my contract and satisfy the demands of the medical board. Of the three people suggested by him, I chose Ed Kline to act on my behalf to review the contract and send his opinion to the medical board. Oates agreed to this.

During the State Medical Society annual meeting in April, Mr. Oates suggested that the chairman of the medical board, Dr. Bill Sage, of Central City, and I have a discussion on a private basis to compromise in this issue. In the latter part of April, Dr. Sage and I met at the Hotel Savoy and had a long discussion regarding licensing problems. He said, "Young man, you have caused much trouble by refusing to allow us to review your contract."

"Well, Dr. Sage, I think that is my own business and none of the members of the board have any right to demand to review my contract."

"Let me tell you," Dr. Sage continued, "we just don't like to see any hospital get away from House File 21 by employing a pathologist on a small salary, in the range of $15,000 to $20,000 a year."

"My God, Dr. Sage! I was getting $18,000 at the University of Arkansas. Why would I come to this position for less money? They agreed to

215

pay $50,000 a year, on the basis of a 5 percent net income plus a basic draw."

He was taken aback, raising his eyebrows. "You mean to say that you're getting that much money from this hospital?"

"Of course I'm being paid generously. Why would I sacrifice my academic position to come to Midtown for a meager income?"

"Well, I didn't know that, but I'm glad to hear that at least they are not taking advantage of a young man. After all the legal troubles and battles you have had since January, I think you deserve a break. I'll send a letter to Oates to issue a full license."

I left the room with complete satisfaction and another lesson learned in dealing with the real business world of medicine. I discovered that this was the only state in the Union in which hospital-based physicians were compensated through the Blue Shield organization as practicing physicians.

When I told Dan Conway that I would be getting a full license in the near future, he said, "Do you mean to tell me that we'll be doing business in a totally legal sense when you get a license?" We finished our coffee at the snack shop and went back to our respective offices to carry on our routine work.

I soon discovered that some of the medical staff members were using outdated techniques. For example, one general practitioner was measuring a patient's red blood cell volume and the amount of hemoglobin by an old filter paper method that had been discarded long before.

One day I was visited by an internist, Dr. Peter Stein, who deplored the lack of board-certified internists at the hospital. According to him, one of our doctors had only two years of internal medicine residency when he began his practice of internal medicine. Another physician had never completed his residency in internal medicine but built a large practice in the city as an internist. I was dismayed and expressed my opinion that there should be some regulatory mechanism to select qualified and board-certified internists for this hospital.

Peter said, "They're all friends of the Sisters here." He went on to tell me that the general practitioner, Dr. Sean Cheek, had spent time in prison for income tax evasion. "Sean Cheek had another office in Western Hill and never reported his cash income to the Internal Revenue Service, but he opened several anonymous savings accounts in the banks of Kansas City, Chicago, Omaha, and Minneapolis under assumed names. When his receptionist was unsuccessful in getting a raise, she called the IRS and tipped them off to four out-of-town bank

216

accounts. After a considerable struggle with several lawyers, Cheek finally lost. He served eight months at Fort Leavenworth Federal Penitentiary." Peter stated that according to the American Medical Association's rules and regulations, those physicians convicted for income tax evasion should be denied permission to return to practice at the same institution where they were employed when they committed the crime. "But Cheek was a friend of the Sisters here, and he donated a sizable gift so they would let him come back and continue his practice."

I had numerous visitors among the medical specialists who would drop into my office to criticize their colleagues' medical practice, their personal lives, and the size of their estates. I was very careful not to repeat what they said. When they left my office and met their fellow physicians in the hallway, they would greet them with a big smile and a handshake and carry on pleasant conversation, regardless of the remarks made a few minutes earlier.

29
Tissue Committee

The cardinal function of the tissue committee at any hospital is to determine the necessity of surgical procedures. If no abnormalities are found by the pathologist who examines the tissue or organs removed from a patient in the operating room, the case is referred to the tissue committee for their scrutiny. A physician may be summoned before the committee to explain why a certain tissue or organ was removed.

There was no tissue committee activity when I was at the University of Tennessee or the University of Arkansas Medical Center, as far as I can recall. In fact, Dr. Ted Richman attempted several times to establish a tissue committee but was unsuccessful because of the opposition led by Dr. Leo Miller and Dr. Jim Nelson. Miller's argument was that they were not in private practice and thus did not remove uteri and ovaries for economic purposes; furthermore, he always emphasized, the committee could not be chaired by a pathologist, who never sees patients or takes care of their complaints and diseases.

Today, I believe, every community hospital, whether of teaching or nonteaching nature, is required by the Joint Commission for Accreditation of Hospitals to have a tissue committee as a standing committee. Most hospital tissue committees are headed by a pathologist, general surgeon, or gynecologist serving as chairperson, assisted by a pathologist as secretary.

At one hospital on the East Coast, it was strange to see a hospital administrator chairing the tissue committee, overruling the physicians' opinions. He had the title of executive director, and his five assistants were called assistants to the director. The director had very little regard for physicians, manipulating them in his own way. His assistants had an equally bad and arrogant attitude toward the physicians, treating them like children.

The tissue committee at Marymount Hospital was composed of Dr. Sam Crone, a general surgeon serving as chairman; myself as secretary; Dr. Henry Silk, a self-trained gynecologist; Dr. William Cane, a general practitioner; and Dr. Benjamin Kildare, an ear-and-throat specialist. No administrative staff member was invited to join the committee, as we dealt with medical matters and the performance of the hospital's medical staff.

The committee had been plagued with the problems of uteri being removed from women under the term of dysfunctional bleeding, as well as appendixes being removed from patients under the diagnosis of acute appendicitis, yet a thorough examination of the tissue failed to reveal any evidence of inflammation. We were facing two serious situations: (1) many uteri were being removed from women of childbearing age, in their late twenties and early thirties, under the impression that there was a uterine prolapse with cystocele; and (2) too many normal appendixes were being removed by one medical staff member.

It is distinctly possible that prolapsed uterus can cause significant pressure on the urinary bladder, causing leakage of a minute amount of urine during vigorous physical exercise or coughing, but it needs to be verified by a second physician, preferably a urologist, who would certify the necessity of vaginal hysterectomy to relieve such pressure.

It was also apparent that the committee could not tolerate so many normal appendixes being removed under the impression of chronic appendicitis or prophylactic appendectomy.

Three months later I explained to the committee that they should require a second opinion on uterine prolapse with cystocele and rectocele before vaginal hysterectomy with repair could be performed. Second, it was the responsibility of the committee to stop the unnecessary appendectomies, which were commonly performed by one particular medical staff member. I was advised to make a recommendation to be submitted to the executive committee for a final decision.

The medical staff executive committee, composed of the chief of staff, the secretary of the medical staff, and the chiefs of various services, held a special session and passed a resolution that required a second opinion, preferably by a urologist, to justify vaginal hysterectomy with anterior and posterior repair on a woman under age thirty-five.

A grim-faced gynecologist who had a large practice walked into my office the next morning. "Joe, I understand you put restrictions on vaginal hysterectomy with repair. Whose side are you on?"

Irritated by his blunt remark, I raised my voice. "I act the way my conscience dictates! If there is genuine uterine prolapse with cystocele, you don't need to worry about anything, do you?" He stalked out of my office.

219

We finally had a mechanism for controlling unnecessary vaginal hysterectomies on young women. But the bigger problem we faced was that of controlling the appendectomies. A physician from Jackson, a town of six thousand people forty miles south of Midtown, was performing one or two or more appendectomies every day, and most of the specimens were found to be normal.

We again discussed this matter at the regular monthly meeting, and I stressed that something had to be done about this unnecessary procedure. Members of the committee asked me to review all the appendectomies performed by sixteen physicians in the past five years to determine the acceptable accuracy of the preoperative diagnosis of acute appendicitis. An exhaustive study, which took three months to complete, yielded an accuracy rate in the range of 35 to 90 percent. No one had scored 100 percent. A doctor from Jackson had an accuracy of 35 percent.

At a special tissue committee meeting I said, "Gentlemen, this has got to stop! I think Henry Silk should send a letter to this physician asking him to discontinue his procedures."

"Why don't you compose the letter, Joe?" Henry suggested. "And I'll sign it."

The letter dealt essentially with the fact of the low accuracy rate on preoperative and postoperative diagnosis. I asked the doctor from Jackson to limit his appendectomies to those patients who really needed them.

Two days later, as I was told, the doctor spotted Henry Silk in the elevator and led him out to a corner of the hallway. "Henry, you and I have been friends for a long, long time. What do you mean by sending me this kind of damn letter? Doesn't our friendship mean anything to you?"

"I just signed the letter."

"Then who wrote it?" he asked.

"Joe Song composed the letter."

Five minutes later a red-faced doctor burst into my office, where I was showing a surgical pathology slide to one of my residents. "Young man," the doctor blurted out, "let me tell you, I was practicing medicine when you were still in diapers!"

I dismissed my resident, closed the office door, and explained to the doctor that there is no such entity as chronic appendicitis in most cases, and a prophylactic appendectomy could no longer be tolerated.

"I think there *is* such an entity, Joe. You will hear from my lawyer!"

I shouted back, "You can take the case to any court, even to the United States Supreme Court! I'm prepared to go all the way!"

When I reported this to the executive committee at their meeting, Dr. John Chambers laughed and said, "You got the ax, Joe, which wasn't very fair."

"I sent a slide of his last appendectomy to be reviewed by two local pathologists, Dr. Wallace Round at Lutheran Hospital and Dr. Jack Lane at Metropolitan Hospital," I continued. "They both agreed that there was no evidence of acute appendicitis. Jack, however, mentioned that judging from the engorged blood vessels on the serosa [the outer layer of the appendix], he must have massaged the appendix for a couple of minutes before it was sent to the tissue lab. Furthermore, Jack said that he was having the same problem with one of their surgeons."

After the meeting, Crone remarked, "You know, Joe, I don't believe he is a crook. He really believes that there is such an entity as chronic appendicitis, and he feels that a prophylactic appendectomy would do some good for his patients. He's just outdated, but he's not a crook."

"Where did he go to medical school? Do you know?"

"He went to the University of Minnesota School of Medicine," Crone replied, "but it was a long time ago."

Dr. Crone impressed me as the best surgeon I had ever met. I repeatedly saw him make judgments and decisions of which other physicians would not have been capable. He was indeed a gifted surgeon, a gentleman, and the best friend I had during my tenure at Marymount Hospital.

At a special executive committee meeting a resolution was passed to require consultation for any appendectomy to be performed by the aforementioned physician for a period of six months, at which time all of his cases would be reviewed.

Approximately six weeks later, as I was about to have dinner one evening, my daughter, Pat, answered the telephone and called me to talk with Dr. Crone.

"Joe, I was just told by the surgery staff that Dr. Stan Duncan is doing an appendectomy on a nine-year-old boy who presented no symptoms or signs of acute appendicitis. The only information I have is that his kid brother, a six-year-old, had acute appendicitis two days ago and his mother insisted that Duncan perform an appendectomy on her oldest son as a prophylactic measure."

"My God! Duncan is a general practitioner. How come he can perform an appendectomy?"

"Well, Joe, you know, he and four other physicians in the General Practice Section have privileges on a grandfather clause and there's nothing we can do about that. Why don't you nail him through the tissue committee?"

The next morning I verified the information that Duncan had admitted the older brother for a prophylactic appendectomy. I called a special tissue committee meeting, and we sent a strong letter stating that there was no medical judgment warranting an appendectomy on this boy.

Two days later I was confronted by a livid Dr. Duncan, who kicked my office door and shouted, "Young man, let me tell you, I was practicing medicine before you were born!"

"Dr. Duncan," I said, "there is no such entity as a prophylactic appendectomy that can be tolerated in this day and age. That boy had no symptoms of acute appendicitis. How could you perform such an operation and expect to get away with it?"

"Well, his mother insisted that I do it."

"But you should use your own judgment." I was adamant, repeating that no prophylactic appendectomy could be tolerated at this institution. As he left, I received the threat that his lawyer would call me.

A couple of days after that, in a meeting with Sister McCain, Dan Conway, and Bill Rankin, I said, "None of our general practitioners is qualified to perform an operation involving the abdominal organs or breast area. It's ridiculous that this kind of practice by five members of the general practice section is allowed to continue. It has to stop! We must revoke their grandfather clause."

Bill Rankin said, "I know how you feel, Joe, but it would take tremendous legal manipulation. I'm afraid it would be a long-drawn-out process of court procedures and legal battles. We'll just have to wait for them to die off one by one."

As I respected Mr. Rankin's judgment and Sister McCain's decision, I made no further comment. Sister McCain was a very dedicated nun, although she had not been trained to be the administrator of a large hospital. But I always valued her opinions and advice.

On the morning of October 16, 1965, I received a telephone call from Sr. Georgina O'Hara, head of the Marymount Hospital School of Nursing, requesting an appointment at 10:00 A.M. She brought with her a young hospital priest, Fr. Craig Huston. "Dr. Song," she began, "we would like to discuss the tissue report on our junior nursing student, Janice Meyers, who was operated on day before yesterday."

"Certainly, Sister," I replied. "Let's review the surgery report and the tissue diagnosis."

I discovered that this third-year nursing student had a ruptured ectopic tubal pregnancy, at nine to ten weeks. An ectopic pregnancy is nidation that occurs outside the usual locus in the uterine cavity. This includes tubal, ovarian, abdominal, and cervical pregnancy. Ectopic pregnancy is not only common, but is increasing in proportion to the incidence in the birthrate, to approximately 1 in 150. The most common ectopic pregnancy is in the fallopian tube, accounting for over 95 percent of all cases. A fertilized ovum cannot pass through the lumen of the tube to reach the usual place, the uterine fundus, to settle and grow. The right fallopian tube is affected more often than the left, in the ratio of two to one. As the pregnancy ages, the embryo, its membranes, and the placenta increase rapidly in size and remain entirely confined to the tube, with ultimate rupture, causing severe intraabdominal hemorrhage.

"We are wondering, Doctor, if you would be kind enough to destroy this report," Sister Georgina said.

"Destroy the report? As you must know, I cannot do that. This is a part of the medical record and a public document. It will have to go on the medical chart of this patient."

Sister Georgina went on to explain the situation of her student, who was unable to break her engagement to a hometown boy in Corning and had been seeing another young man in Midtown. Sister Georgina and Father Huston were trying to protect the student's reputation.

"I'm sorry," I said, "but I can't do that. Destroying the medical report could be construed as unethical on my part, and I might even face criminal charges. The only thing I can do is delay this report until the student is discharged and has gone home, but that could be for only ten days to two weeks."

Later that day I had to report the incident to our administrator, Sister McCain. She was visibly irritated by the arbitrary action of the head of the nursing school and the priest. "This is none of their business," she said. "We will just have to abide by the hospital rules and medical ethics."

"Sister," I explained, "I asked them to talk to you and get your permission to hold this report for at least five days."

"They never came to my office to discuss it with me."

After a week, when Mrs. Miller, head of the Medical Records Department, called me for the surgical pathology report, I decided to release it to her. Later I discovered that approximately ten months

223

after the incident Sr. Georgina O'Hara and Sr. Mary Murphy went to the province to report that Sister McCain was not fit to remain as administrator of the hospital.

30
Seminars in Obstetrics and Gynecology

With financial aid from the medical staff fund and several pharmaceutical companies, I, as program chairman of Marymount Medical Day for seven consecutive years, was able to attract many nationally known and world-renowned speakers for our seminars in obstetrics and gynecology. I am deeply grateful to those physicians who honored us by participating in our seminars and making our scientific activities more meaningful: Clyde Randall, of the State University of New York at Buffalo; John Brewer, of Northwestern Medical School; Leon Israel, of Philadelphia; Henry Gardner, of Houston; Henry Decker, of the Mayo Clinic; George Mitchell, of Tulane University; Roger Scott, of Case Western Reserve University; and many others who had never heard of this small hospital in Midtown. More than forty outstanding academicians made our seminars successful, their excellent reputations attracting many physicians from the neighboring states. Physicians from the rural areas of the state continued to attend the seminars year after year.

Several years later, Dr. Albert Miller of Newark, N.J. told me that the resident physicians of obstetrics and gynecology at Albert Einstein Medical Center, in New York City and Philadelphia, were urged to read my monograph because Dr. Leon Israel, a noted figure on the East Coast, gave such a fantastic review of it.

Prof. Ralph Benson, of the University of Oregon, and Dr. Keith Brown, of UCLA, suggested, during the seminars, that I publish the second edition of my monograph. Dr. Benson whispered to me, "You know, Joe, your little monograph could be a very valuable text for our residents and interns if you would revise it and eliminate some chapters for your second edition."

"I agree with Ralph's opinion of your book," Keith Brown remarked. "You should concentrate your discussions on the histogenesis of the uterine cervix in depth."

My good friend from Little Rock, Dr. Jim Nelson, took me aside during a seminar intermission and said, "Joe, I think you should present your studies in carcinoma in situ of the cervix uteri at the annual meeting of the Central Association of Obstetricians and Gynecologists."

"You really think so, Jim?" I asked.

"I certainly do. I can ask the program committee to include your paper in the September 1968 meeting in Oklahoma City."

"That's a very nice gesture, Jim. But don't you have to be a member of the association? I'm not a member, you know."

"I can sponsor your article if you wish me to do so," he offered.

"All right. Let's proceed for that meeting in Oklahoma City."

After I mailed an abstract of my paper, with Jim Nelson as second author, I called Bob Casey, an obstetrician. "Bob, I'm going to Oklahoma City for the Central meeting in September. Why don't you come along? You can meet several key members of the American Board of Obstetrics and Gynecology and discuss your problems with them."

"Okay. I have nothing to lose. I'll go with you."

"I believe you should go, not only for your admission to the board, but you will also have an opportunity to meet many academicians and gain stimulation for your future academic accomplishment."

"I don't care about academic investigation. I only want to be certified by the American Board of Obstetrics and Gynecology, not that it will help me in my practice, but as a matter of principle."

"That may be true, but it will upgrade your professional performance." I said.

I was impressed with the size and wealth of Oklahoma City, as I had never seen such a vast area of oil wells. I knew many of the obstetricians and gynecologists among the several hundred members of the Central Association gathered in the large ballroom to hear the results of investigation, research, and clinical experience in their specialty.

As I stood on the podium to deliver my speech, the electricity suddenly went out. Three minutes later, when the hotel regained its power, a slide projector lamp blew up. Dr. Jack Carter, of Shreveport, Louisiana, president of the association, pulled the microphone close to him and said, "Dr. Song, we will allocate more time for your presentation. Please don't worry about this temporary delay."

As several hundred obstetricians and gynecologists anxiously waited in dead silence, I said, "Dr. Carter, it seems to me that nothing is working well today. I suppose this is happening to me because I'm not one of you, but just a humble student in the morgue."

A thunder of laughter and applause filled the large ballroom. When I completed my presentation, they gave me a standing ovation, lasting several minutes. The presentation was evaluated and challenged by Dr. Malcolm Dockerty, chief pathologist at the Mayo Clinic, followed by questions raised by Dr. James Merrill, professor and chairman of the Department of Obstetrics and Gynecology at the University of Oklahoma.

That evening Jim Nelson took Bob Casey and me to his hotel room for drinks, and we met Drs. Dockerty and Merrill and several other university professors and chairmen. Bob was greatly impressed and later remarked, "I had never met a cadre of academicians in my life. I froze momentarily and couldn't find proper words to express my feelings."

The following day, on the plane to Wichita, Kansas, I said, "Bob, I have now paved your way to becoming a diplomat of the American Board of Obstetrics and Gynecology. It will be entirely up to you whether you pass or fail. You'll be on your own now. They told me to tell you to submit your new application as soon as possible for reconsideration."

I deplaned at Wichita to give a talk for the residents, interns, and staff physicians at St. Francis Hospital, where Dan Conway was associate administrator, having left Marymount Hospital in November of 1967. Bob came to me to the gate, where Dan was waiting for me.

"Dan, be sure to send Joe back to us," Bob said. "We need this guy. Don't try to hire him." Then Bob turned to me. "Joe, don't get any funny ideas about accepting a job at St. Francis. You're a member of the community."

The quality of questions raised by the house officers at St. Francis Hospital following my presentation was fairly impressive. An extremely intelligent Indian physician asked several penetrating questions concerning my articles.

Dr. Ray Hines, a radiologist at our hospital, had told me before I left for Oklahoma City that he had taken his rotating internship at St. Francis Hospital, where a German nun was administrator. "Sister Frances was running the hospital with an iron hand when I was on the house staff. I'm not certain whether she's still there."

Dan took me to meet the administrator, Sister Frances, who spoke with a heavy German accent. Indeed, she was the same German nun whom Dr. Hines had mentioned.

I was saddened to learn that Dan was very unhappy there. The administrator had promised many changes before Dan became associate administrator but as of yet they had not come to pass.

227

"I'm sorry to hear about your situation here, Dan," I said, "but why don't you stick around for a while until a better job and opportunity becomes available?" I tried to reason with him at the gate of the Wichita Municipal Airport just before boarding the plane for Midtown.

"I guess that's what I must do, Joe, but it's becoming increasingly difficult to deal with her." We shook hands and parted.

Back in the hospital, when I told Jim Wilkins, Dan's good friend and the hospital controller, about Dan's situation, Jim exhaled smoke and said, "Dan made a big mistake by jumping at her offer. He should have stayed here for another three years and waited for a more solid position elsewhere."

The next day I called Bill Rankin and asked him to remember Dan for a better position elsewhere.

31
New Administration

Sr. Georgina O'Hara, head of Marymount Hospital School of Nursing, was an intelligent woman but very cunning. When she gained enough support among the nuns to take over the administration of the hospital, she took several other nuns with her for a meeting with their provincial officer. All the nuns were unanimous in support of Sister Georgina's replacing Sister McCain. They reported that Sister McCain had been trying to save money and subsequently had antagonized many physicians who would like to make Marymount Hospital the best one in Midtown. "With Sister McCain staying on as administrator, we will never make any progress," someone said.

A few days prior to Sister McCain's departure for Red Bluff, California, where she had been assigned to a nursing home as administrator, I had a long visit with her and gave her a travel bag as a going-away gift. I still maintain profound admiration for this Sister, who was so sincere, so honest, and so dedicated.

Sister McCain praised my performance during the previous three years and touched upon the subject of a black diener (morgue attendant). "Dr. Song, I think you are an honorable man for trying to protect Jerry Foreman from being fired. I still remember what you said when several incidents surfaced."

"Oh, I don't recall what I said."

"Well, you said to me that if we were to fire this diener, he would end up in a black ghetto, and you felt strongly that we should give him another chance. I hope and pray to God that you will remain here for a while and keep up your good work."

"Sister, I'm glad you agreed with me on giving Jerry another chance. He's doing much better now, and I hope he will get into school to become a mortician."

"I sincerely hope so, Dr. Song." With that remark we said good-bye to each other on the morning of July 31, 1968.

Jerry Foreman was a fairly intelligent young black man with an ambition to become a mortician. However, he was caught by the security guards having a drinking party in the morgue with maids and orderlies of the hospital. A security guard also reported to Sister McCain that on his desk Jerry kept a severed human hand in a formalin jar, with a note saying: "Take your hands off." Naturally, Sister McCain advised me to dismiss this fellow, but I persuaded her to give him several more chances.

Jerry had thirteen unpaid traffic tickets. One day a police officer came to the lab to arrest Jerry, and I volunteered to pay the tickets to keep Jerry in the department. He never straightened out his problems, despite numerous chances and much help from our staff. He finally died some time later in a jail cell in Fort Collins.

When I came to Memphis, in 1952, I was shocked to see how the blacks were treated, which was the ordinary life-style in the southern states, although I had no knowledge of that before I arrived in this country.

Every Christmas I received a basket of fresh fruit from my father's friend Louis B. Kang, in Los Angeles, and I always gave it to the black orderlies at the Institute of Pathology. A black maid named Jessica Brown asked me to save my old socks, shirts, and pants for her children, because she could not afford to buy enough clothing for them. I felt sad when I saw her living conditions and was dismayed at such social injustice.

My dear friend Liz Williams, in Memphis, exhibited the true Christian spirit. When her maid developed breast cancer and went through a radical mastectomy at John Gaston Hospital, Liz visited her every day, bringing chicken soup and pie, and sat with her for hours at a time in the hospital ward, where twenty or more black women were patients. Liz and Tom Williams always felt sorry for the black people. But two relations of theirs were entirely different in their attitude. Following Christmas dinner, on December 25, 1955, we took their maid home. She lived in the middle of downtown Memphis, in a slum less than half a mile square. The area was extremely dirty, and all the houses were in deplorable condition. I said to her employer after we dropped her off, "It's a shame to have such a slum in the middle of the downtown area of this beautiful city. Why don't they clean it up? Or couldn't the city demolish the entire area and move the people somewhere else?"

He replied, "They're basically lazy and dirty people."

This man's son-in-law said, "These people should be kept low on the socioeconomic status." His remark ruined my Christmas dinner.

In November 1967, I finally obtained help in the Pathology Department. My new associate, Dr. Sam Glen, was from Bismarck, North Dakota.

In more than twenty years of association with the hospital, I have learned that there are many good and dedicated nuns, but at the same time there are some extremely bad ones in the lot. Bill Rankin once explained to me, "The nuns are also human beings. Some of them drink heavily to overcome their lonely life, and a few of them become addicted to alcohol and/or drugs. Joe, you must understand that basic fact of human life and must not maintain such a narrow view."

Our new administrator, Sister Georgina, took off for a two-week meeting in New York with nuns and administrators from the province, as well as Dr. Pete Taylor and others from our hospital. John Sams, an associate administrator who accompanied her to the meeting, later told me that he was shocked to see Sister Georgina consuming an enormous amount of liquor, particularly Jim Beam, a well-known Kentucky bourbon. A few days later the same comment was made to me by Pete. Since it was none of my business, I tried to forget it.

When Sister Georgina returned from New York, she called a general meeting and announced that there would be an out-of-town planning session involving all the department heads of the hospital, members of the advisory board, and most of the nuns. A consulting firm, from Saint Paul, would be conducting the three-day meeting. More than twenty units were reserved at the Ramada Inn, for an extensive brainstorming session. I was not impressed with this, since I had previously been involved in several so-called planning sessions. A few physicians showed intense interest in attending.

"Sam, what is the purpose of this planning session for three days?" I asked. "Can't they have a session in town at the hospital?"

"No, this is a very important session, the purpose of which is to make this hospital better than Metropolitan Hospital."

"You must be joking, Sam. An intense planning session for three days would not make this hospital any better than it is now. The quality of the medical staff will decide the grade, or excellence, of the hospital. Eighty percent of the medical staff at Metropolitan Hospital are specialists. They study the journals and attend seminars frequently and distinguish themselves as having the best community hospital in Midtown. With the medical staff we have here, we will never be able to make this a first-grade hospital. What we should do is educate our medical staff members and import specialists in every field. This three-day planning session will never bring any positive results."

Sister Georgina dramatically increased the size of the administration by having four assistant administrators, a full-time director of planning, William Moran, having been promoted from the position of director of personnel. A few days later, Sr. Mary Murphy came down to my office and confessed her mistake in supporting Sister Georgina for the administrator's position. "I had no idea, Dr. Song, that she would have an army of administrators for constant brainstorming and planning sessions involving all the personnel, including our nurses. Most of the physicians are now complaining that the nurses don't do any work for their patients."

"Yes, Sister, I've heard those complaints, too, from the internal medicine people. One of them came down yesterday and complained bitterly."

"Who was that?" she asked.

"Dr. Joe Smith. He was laughing about their wasting time having so many useless meetings. He was telling me that the nurses were having meetings on the subject: how can we provide the best nursing care for our patients? Dr. Smith said that the best way for them to provide better care for our patients was to do more work and have fewer meetings."

It was my turn to attend the planning session with the pharmacy chief, Nathan Benning; construction coordinator, George Black; chief of Nursing Service, Pam Mitchell; and consultant, Nick Cohen. After forty-five minutes of discussion, I stood up, saying, "I must get back to my office to sign my reports so that the patients can go home or receive proper treatment."

Mr. Benning told me later that I was severely criticized by Nick Cohen and Pam Mitchell for leaving the planning session before its conclusion. I said to him, "Look, Nate, why are patients being admitted here? They come to the hospital to get well, and it's our duty to provide the best treatment, based on my diagnosis. Which is more important, the patients or Nick Cohen's planning sessions? I don't care if my name is on the blacklist of the administrator. I'm just doing my job."

Nate grinned and said nothing.

Daily planning sessions were being held at the Howard Johnson motel. No administrative decisions, either trivial or major, could be made while administrative staff members, section heads, and some physicians were attending the meetings, which lasted for a week or even weeks at a time.

Bob Shelton, administrator of a Catholic hospital in Ohio, stopped to see me after visiting his son in Webster City. I asked him if they had similar planning sessions at their hospital. "We had some in the past," he said. "This is the nuns' 'big kick' right now, but it will eventually die down, probably within six months."

"You mean we have to suffer through another six months of this?" It was incredible.

"Just be patient, Joe. They'll wind down within a short time."

But more planning sessions were called as time went on. A memo to me from our administrator said that it was mandatory for me to attend the sessions, as they would go down in the history of Marymount Hospital.

I called a meeting with Bill Rankin and Sister Georgina in her office. I emphasized the fact that I was there to serve our patients with an accurate and rapid diagnosis on tissue biopsies and operations. She was very firm, requesting my presence at all the planning sessions.

"Sister, why am I here, then?" I asked.

"Well, as you know, this will make history of Marymount Hospital, and if you don't attend you are not going to be a part of it."

I said that someone had to carry on the daily routine work. Bill agreed with me and began to explain that the major function of the pathologist is to provide the best possible care for the patients. He asked her if it would be acceptable if I delegated a member of my staff to be present at the meetings.

"That's a good idea, Bill," I said. "I can ask Dr. George French our microbiologist, who had much experience in planning sessions when he was a Jesuit priest."

They were both astonished to learn that Dr. French was an ex-priest, but Sister Georgina reluctantly consented to have him represent the laboratory in the planning sessions.

The laundry manager, Will Toon, and other section chiefs complained bitterly to me that because of the many meetings their work was piling up, and they were unable to get it done. "I think you people should tell her about the conditions in your section," I said. "Don't just grumble about it to me."

Dr. French was an excellent coordinator, giving the impression as a good diplomat, that he was spending a great deal of time on the meetings. French told me, after several sessions, that he did not expect to see any significant results, and he indicated that the whole thing would wind down in about five months. He was right in his prediction, as the project was subsequently dismantled and quickly forgotten.

Several days later I was visited by the chief of the Maintenance Department, Scott Kelly. He mentioned during our conversation that his people who collected the trash from Sister Georgina's apartment recovered a large whiskey bottle every evening. He was wondering if she was drinking heavily.

"Scotty, you don't know that the bottle is hers," I said. "We have a fairly large building."

"But who else over there could afford to drink that much? There's just a bunch of nursing students living in that building."

"Yes, but you don't have any proof. I wouldn't spread that rumor around," I advised.

Much later it became common knowledge that Sister Georgina was consuming an enormous amount of liquor, and I felt very naive.

I was well aware that grants from the NIH had been steadily reduced to the point that any community hospital without university affiliation had virtually no chance of receiving a significant amount of cancer research funds, although my friend at the NIH, Dr. Dick Miller, urged me several times to submit my applications to the division of Research Grants. Dr. Harold Stewart of the NCI assured me that an application from Midtown Hospital would receive due consideration from the panel of scientists at the NIH.

Dr. Jim Sisson, of the Pathology Department at Central University Medical School, told me otherwise. "Joe, your odds of receiving a grant from the NIH are one in a million."

I decided to approach the American Cancer Society for a small grant that would enable me to set up a cancer research project with clinical significance, so I sent a copy of my curriculum vitae and a request for application forms to the state division office.

A few days later I received a call from Arnold F. Stocks, executive vice president of the American Cancer Society, State Division. "We have received your request for a grant application and your curriculum vitae," he said.

"Fine! Do I have a chance to receive a grant from you?" I asked.

"Certainly you have. But the reason I'm calling this morning is to tell you that you and I were born on the same day in the same year."

"Really? I was born in Pyongyang, North Korea, on May 11, 1927, about 7:00 A.M."

"I was born on the same day, around 9:00 A.M. What a coincidence!" he exclaimed.

"Indeed this is a coincidence. I have never met anyone who was born on the same day as I was, in the same year."

"Anyway, Dr. Song, I will send you several copies of the application forms for you to complete and mail back to me as soon as possible. I'll do my best to process them in time for our next meeting."

Our phone conversation gave me a strange feeling, but I hoped that our talk would bring positive results.

Several weeks later, members of the state division committee in awards and grants of the American Cancer Society met to evaluate my grant application. According to Dr. Henry Irwin, chief radiologist at Marymount Hospital, there were five yes votes and one no vote. A private pathology practitioner in Colton, Dr. Evans, sent a negative vote with this comment: "He has just arrived in Midtown for a hospital pathology job. He will not have time to do anything but routine pathology work. All he can do is keep his head above water." Hearing this, I barked to Dr. Irwin. "If you have a genuine interest in cancer research, you'll find the time for it. Please tell that to your friend."

Eventually I was given a $6,500 grant from the state division of the American Cancer Society, and two additional grants were approved shortly thereafter. I later learned that the opinion expressed by the pathologist in Colton was widely shared by local pathologists, who were convinced that their routine hospital laboratory work was more than a full-time job. One of them remarked to family practitioners, "Applied or basic research and investigative work should be left with university people."

I was dismayed to hear a statement by a community hospital pathologist that "unless you cut corners, you won't have time to do research or investigative projects." How untrue that was! Pathologists are by and large medical scientists and should be able to contribute something to patient care in addition to earning a living. I recalled that Dr. Sprunt always said, "There is nothing wrong in a pathologist's making as much money as general surgeons or neurosurgeons, but there should be a piece of dedication to medical science."

On receiving the grant money from the state division of the American Cancer Society, I discussed clinical research work with Dr. Milton Mann. He was a mature obstetrician and gynecologist with very keen scientific interests. Having been trained at Michael Reese Hospital, in Chicago, Milton was always looking for a research project. His associate Dr. Michael Cox was likewise research-oriented. We began studying the side effects of oral contraceptive pills on the uterus. Many investigators had previously described or suggested a considerable effect on cervical function from oral contraceptive pills. Numerous young women taking various contraceptive pills over a significant period of time showed atypical endocervical hyperplasia or endocervical polyps. It was conceivable then that the uterine mucosa and endometrium may be influenced by a variety of oral contraceptive agents.

Dr. Mann and I, with the help of Dr. Matthew Lex, analyzed 105 samples of endometrial curettings, obtained from women receiving oral contraceptives for more than seventeen months, to study possible changes of the uterine endometrium. In 26 of 105 women studied we found profound changes in the endometrium: thickened endometrial stroma, distended and increased glands, capillaries filled with blood clots, and marked atypical changes suggesting precancerous degeneration. We tabulated our results and decided to present our findings at the next annual meeting of the Central Association of Obstretricians and Gynecologists. Dr. Mann approached Dr. Henry Decker of the Mayo Clinic, the secretary of the association, and asked him to include an article. Dr. Decker very kindly held a slot for us for presentation at the thirty-seventh annual meeting, held in Memphis in October 1969.

On a clear, cool October day, with colorful autumn leaves providing a background, Dr. Martha Dixon, my friend from John Gaston Hospital, and her children took me for an afternoon picnic in a city park. Martha's son, Harry, had become an attorney and a member of a prestigious law firm in Memphis. Her daughter, Diane, was attending Southwestern at Memphis. We talked about the past, recalling Diane's ponytail and Harry's riding a small bicycle.

At noon on October 16, I completed my presentation. There was much discussion, and soon I was surrounded by many of my old friends from John Gaston Hospital. I was overwhelmed to shake their hands after such a long time, as I had left Memphis in 1956. Several young staff physicians from the University of Arkansas had come to hear my speech. Three residents from Little Rock, with outstretched hands, said, "Dr. Ben Hawk sent us here to listen to your paper." That touched me deeply.

At the front entrance of Hotel Peabody I met several hometown obstetricians. Dr. Hugh Parker put his arm around my shoulder. "Joe, your paper was even better than the one you gave in Oklahoma City."

"Thank you, Hugh," I said. "What are you people up to now?"

"We're going to ride a riverboat on the Mississippi. Care to come along?" asked Dr. Michael Cox.

I declined, saying, "I've had several occasions to ride a boat before, Mike. I took my residency training here, you know."

"So I heard. I also heard that you enjoyed drinking corn moonshine."

"That was years ago, when I was a young resident," I explained.

"They told me, too, that you took a large bottle of corn liquor with you to Midtown."

I grinned. "That must have been Mort Gubin. He likes to spread an ugly tale."

"Really, we're all very proud of you, Joe." With that remark they caught a cab and headed for the river.

236

The next morning I paid a visit to my old institution on Madison Avenue and was led to the office of Dr. Coy Anderson, associate director of the Institute of Pathology. Dr. Anderson was extremely cordial, in sharp contrast to the old days.

During lunch at the student center I mentioned this abrupt change in Coy Anderson's attitude to Dr. Bob Crocker, a former fellow resident who had subsequently assumed the position of assistant dean of the medical school.

"Bob, I was very touched with the cordiality of Coy Anderson toward me. As you know, he was always skeptical and unfriendly."

"Who can read his mind, Joe?"

"I thought he always hated me because of my ancestry," I remarked.

"Well, that may be true, but I don't think so. He treated Bengt Carson, from Sweden, and Peter Finn, from Geneva, the same way he treated you. Coy Anderson is a very difficult man to understand."

Bob Crocker finally returned to the pathology department as an assistant professor of pathology and later died prematurely at home on the morning of Christmas Day, at the age of fifty six, due to an acute coronary thrombosis.

32
Book on Sickle-Cell Disease

The normal human red blood cell, essential for the oxygen supply of every cell, tissue, and organ, has a discoid shape, with a diameter of 7.7 micron, a thickness of 2.0 micron, and a volume of 90 micron. The size of the red blood cell is variable, however, depending on underlying diseases. For example, the red cells of patients with simple anemia are considerably smaller than normal ones: diameter: 7 micron; thickness: 1.6 micron; and volume: 63 micron. On the other hand, the red cells of patients with pernicious anemia are larger than normal, possessing a diameter of 8.9 micron, thickness of 2.2 micron, and volume of 135 micron.

When a malaria-infested anopheles mosquito bites human skin and sucks the blood, a large number of minute malaria parasites are introduced into the bloodstream of the victim, where they penetrate the red blood cells and complete their life cycle. These parasites, called trophozoites, achieve their growth within the red blood cells, becoming banana-shaped macrogametocytes. When their life cycle is completed, the macrogametocytes disintegrate into millions of small pieces, destroying the red cells on such a scale that victims used to die with high fever and extensive hemolysis, causing nosebleeds and blood in the urine and feces, accounting for the name blackwater fever.

Centuries ago in the midbelt of Africa, blackwater fever, also known as malignant malaria, claimed millions of lives. To adapt to this new environment, a genetic mutation occurred that saved many people from dying of malignant malaria. The normal discoid red cells would take on a needle shape or sickle shape, which reduced their volume. Many trophozoites are continually introduced into the bloodstream, but because of lack of volume in the needle-shaped or sickle-shaped red cells, they do not grow to reach the mature forms of gametocytes, thus saving millions of victims from death. The malignant malaria problem was moderately controlled.

There are two hemoblobin chains in every normal human being—alpha and beta. The genetic mutation caused the alteration of

238

normal hemoglobin A to S hemoglobin, denoting sickle-cell hemoglobin in the beta chain. If the alpha chain also has S sickle-cell hemoglobin, the subject is known as a homozygous sickle-cell patient possessing S hemoglobin, and no normal hemoglobin A is left in the red cells. If a patient has only one S hemoglobin in the beta chain and normal hemoglobin A in the alpha chain, the patient is S-A heterozygous, or has the sickle-cell trait.

Hemoglobin S is an extremely widespread hemoglobin, because it has an evolutionary survival value, due to its protection against malignant malaria. It is found throughout tropical Africa. There is evidence that the sickling gene spread from east to west on the African continent. In Liberia sickling is less frequent in the older and longer-established populations but more frequent in those who came from the east in more recent times. Hemoglobin S is also found in India, Arabia, and southern Europe. The distribution of hemoglobin S is on a world-wide scale parallel to the distribution of malignant malaria in the African continent, southern Spain, Turkey, Italy, the Mediterranean region, India, southeast Asia, Burma, the Philippines, Indonesia, and northern Australia. Only a cold climate can prevent the distribution of the sickle-cell gene. In the world literature there was no record of S hemoglobin found in mainland China, Manchuria, Russia, Korea, or Japan.

I was never exposed to this disease until September 1954, when I performed an autopsy on a fifteen-year-old black Tennessee boy, who had died in the emergency room of John Gaston Hospital. During the autopsy I was astonished to find a peculiar type of liver cirrhosis, quite different from alcohol cirrhosis because of the size of the cirrhotic nodules and the color of the entire liver. Dr. Sprunt, who had never seen such a case, instructed me to take cultures for brucellosis from the liver and the large spleen.

To culture brucella bacteria from the specimens was a tremendous task. First of all, the brucella bacilli are anaerobic bacteria, requiring no oxygen or a very low oxygen tension for growth. To induce an anaerobic condition, we had to obtain several large pickle jars from the cafeteria and put candles in them to consume the existing oxygen. Six weeks of trial yielded nothing but contaminants.

When Dr. Israel David Michelson found out about my activities, he confronted me. "Young man, do you realize how dangerous it is to have brucella organisms growing in this area? Get them out of here fast!"

I was unsuccessful in isolating the brucella bacillus from the liver and spleen and gave up after twelve weeks.

The appearance of the cirrhotic liver was so unusual and peculiar that I began searching the literature for the explanation. In examining my slide sections from the liver, I found a large number of sickled red cells tangled together in the sinusoids of the liver, producing many areas of cell death and subsequent fibrosis. During our Thursday evening microscopic conference I tried to explain that the cause of cirrhosis in this particular case was sickle-cell disease, which no one would accept.

After reviewing the literature and preparing many slides, with photomicrographs, to demonstrate the occurrence of cirrhotic changes based on abnormal-shaped red cells, I finally persuaded Dr. Sprunt to publish the case. With some reluctance, he gave me permission to report it. Despite his highly temperamental behavior, he was a broadminded man, who allowed me to pursue many areas of scientific investigation.

An article titled "Cirrhosis of the Liver in Sickle-Cell Disease, Report of a Case with Review of the Literature," was finally published in the AMA *Archives of Pathology* in September 1955. During the pathology board examinations, held at Northwestern University Medical School, in Chicago, several candidates commented favorably. Two years later I published an original article based on a series of cases and studies, titled "Hepatic Lesions in Sickle-Cell Anemia," in the *American Journal of Pathology.* I collected more cases from the files of the University of Tennessee Institute of Pathology, the University of Arkansas School of Medicine, and the VA hospitals in Little Rock and North Little Rock and was able to analyze and tabulate the results for future publication.

When I received a cold reception from my colleagues on the publication of my first book, *The Human Uterus,* I was dismayed and disappointed. Unable to suppress my anger and frustration, I announced my intention of publishing another book. "If this is the way you people are going to treat me, you have something else coming!" I stated.

Bill Hunter asked, "What book are you going to publish, Uncle Joe?"

"Bill, you wait and see! There'll be another book!"

In May 1964, I signed a contract with Payne Thomas, of Charles C. Thomas, Publisher, for my second book, to be called *Pathology of Sickle-Cell Disease.* I informed him that the complete manuscript would be ready in eighteen months.

When the faculty at the University of Arkansas School of Medicine found out that I had signed the contract, Ron Hoke and Jim Nelson were concerned about my undertaking the job at Marymount Hospital.

"We know you're very energetic," they said, "but do you think you'll be able to publish a book besides your routine duties at a general hospital?"

"I'll have to take my time in writing the book," I admitted.

"We're confident of your ability, but as you know, service and routine pathology come before academic activities," Jim expressed.

"I'm aware of that, but I'll just have to spend my weekends and several evenings a week at the office to do the rough draft."

"Yes, I know that, Joe, but it will be difficult for you. It's too bad you won't have any residents or younger staff members to help you in the literature search. As you know, Dr. Ackerman, in Boston, uses all his residents and staff members to help him in revising his textbook."

"Well, he's a lucky man, and I'm not." With that remark I closed my office door.

Jim Nelson's prediction that I would not have time for research work or writing because of the demands of routine service duties turned out to be correct. My diagnostic service in both clinical and anatomical pathology, as well as resident teaching and administrative duties as chief pathologist at Marymount Hospital, was indeed strenuous, requiring thirteen to fourteen hours a day for approximately two and one-half years.

Dr. S. A. Gogate, a resident physician from Bombay, India, was a great help to me in my practice at the hospital. She was an intelligent young woman, neat in appearance, with mature judgment in hematology, clinical chemistry, and surgical pathology.

Most of the staff physicians were very cooperative, although a handful of "pro-Thompson" doctors were skeptical. The attitude was: "No one can fill Fred Thompson's shoes, no matter how capable he may be."

Dr. Dick Ellis had proclaimed to the members of the advisory board, before my appointment as chief pathologist, "I will never cooperate with a new incoming pathologist, no matter who he is." He was very distressed when Dr. Thompson moved to Florida. I later discovered that Dick Ellis was a man of principle and a competent general surgeon, possessing a great sense of humor. He was a rare combination of medical doctor, gentleman, and statesman. It was my good fortune to have met Dr. Ellis while he was the director of medical education at the hospital. I was deeply saddened when he died suddenly of a myocardial infarction.

Dr. Jim Smith was another decent general practitioner. When the print shop made a few errors on hematology's report form, Jim laughed and told me to be patient. He always encouraged me. "Joe," he said, "you're doing fine under the circumstances, and if you keep up your good work, you'll make many friends among the medical staff."

Dr. David Walter was honest enough to tell me that he and several other young physicians who had been trained by Fred Thompson maintained a strong loyalty to him. Walter said that all the Pap smears from their offices were still being sent to a private lab operated by Fred's associate, Dr. Charles Jenkins. "This is nothing personal," Walter explained. "We just feel that we should support Jenkins' lab because of our long association with his partner, Dr. Thompson."

"I understand," I said. "You don't need to apologize for not sending me Pap smears, because my time is very limited at this stage of the game."

A general practitioner approached me one day and asked what he could get for sending two or three hundred Pap smears a week to our laboratory.

Not understanding his intentions, I said, "You'll get faster accurate reports on the Pap smears."

"Will there be any financial reward for me in return for sending a large number of Pap smears to you?" he asked.

I flatly refused to discuss the matter any further, since the wound from my unsuccessful private practice in Rhode Island was still not completely healed. The general practitioner continued to send all the Pap smears from his patients to a private lab in another state.

At the end of 1965, I received a very nice two-page letter from Payne Thomas. It was tactfully written, commenting on the weather in the Midwest, growth patterns of the corn and soybeans in Illinois, and the political climate in Washington, D.C. In the last paragraph he mentioned that if there was anything he could do to help me in completing my manuscript on the sickle-cell disease book, he would be more than happy to do so. When I showed the letter to my secretary, Marie Peterson, she smiled and asked, "Is he checking on you to find out how much you've done on your book?"

"I suppose so," I said.

Two more letters came from him, in December of 1967 and June of 1968. I asked Marie to help me with the manuscript. When she nodded her assent, I began dictating the rough draft in July of 1968.

With the help of Mrs. Marion Jones, chief librarian of the state medical library, I was able to obtain an enormous number of reference materials for the book. I spent two nights a week and every weekend at the office dictating the manuscript. It required a tremendous amount of energy, limitless patience, and tenacity to complete such a large, comprehensive manuscript. Sickle-cell disease was virtually unknown to the public and the general medical community at this time. Only a handful of investigators who had done research in sickle-cell disease were familiar with it.

My friend from Dallas, Dr. Henry Gardner, was the speaker at one of our Marymount Medical Day seminars on obstetrics and gynecology. When he saw a portion of the draft on my desk, he asked, "Joe, are you writing this kind of book for publication?"

"I'm halfway through, Henry," I answered. "It will be published within a few years."

"But who would buy this kind of book, or read it, on a disease affecting blacks only? Once this book is published, Joe, you'll lose many of your southern friends." He was obviously unable to distinguish between racial prejudice and scientific achievement.

"But, Henry, this is a fascinating disease!"

"You're wasting your time and energy, Joe," he went on. "Why don't you revise your uterus book? That would make more sense than a sickle-cell book."

From the latter part of 1969 through early 1970, sickle-cell disease, heretofore virtually an unknown entity, suddenly became a political disease, arresting the attention of the southern politicians. When they talked to their constituents, in order to gain more black votes they would promise, "If I am elected to Congress, I will get sufficient research funds for the study and treatment of this disease."

As with most of the genetic diseases affecting human beings, there was no effective treatment in the world for patients suffering from homozygous sickle-cell disease.

My secretary spent much of her own time in typing, filing, checking reference material, editing, and proofreading. I shall never forget her dedication and assistance in making possible the publication of the book. The manuscript was completed during the summer of 1970 and mailed to the publisher. The 460-page book, including many black-and-white illustrations and over one thousand references, was finally published and distributed in July 1971. The political climate for sickle-cell disease was ripe, and I was informed that this book was much in demand. Several book reviews were published that were favorable. A few unfavorable reviews also appeared in several journals.

Prior to the publication of my book, I had decided to dedicate it to Dr. Harold L. Stewart, chief of the Laboratory Service of the NCI, and notified him on January 1, 1970. In his letter of January 8, he suggested that I dedicate the volume to a scientist who had contributed significantly to this field. Since he had never worked in the field, he felt that it would be improper for him to accept this honor.

In my reply to Dr. Stewart on January 14, I emphasized that if it had not been for his help and encouragement, I would not be here in the first place. In 1952, during the dark days of the Korean War, Dr. Stewart had opened the door for me to pursue my pathology career. I also pointed out that my first monograph, on uterine cancer, had been dedicated to Dr. Douglas H. Sprunt, my former chief. Dr. Stewart reluctantly accepted the idea of the dedication. I saw him at his Georgetown laboratory in early June of 1972, and we had a wonderful reunion.

Dr. L. W. Diggs, a 1927 graduate of Johns Hopkins University, and a professor of medicine at the University of Tennessee had done a great deal of research on sickle-cell disease. His review of my book was particularly important, giving penetrating observations:

> The essential facts are presented in a scholarly and easily read manner. The printing is excellent, the typographical and factual errors few, and the black and white illustrations sharp and well reproduced. . . . There are excellent name and subject indexes, which, together with the bibliography, make the book valuable as a reference work. It is recommended for medical libraries, for research laboratories engaged in investigations relating to sickle-cell disease, and for pathologists and hematologists. It is also recommended for laymen, administrators, and others involved in educational programs, for it places in one volume a wealth of information which is widely scattered in the world literature and hard to obtain.

I have a great deal of admiration for Dr. Diggs. When I saw him in Boston during a pathology meeting, he said, "Joe, I thought you did a good job on the book. I notice that you have an appointment as a clinical professor at Central University. Do you teach there?"

"Yes, I do, twice a month," I answered.

"How far is Central City from Midtown?"

"One-way is 130 miles, Dr. Diggs, and I drive back and forth twice a month."

"You have been very diligent since your residency days in Memphis," he continued, "and I think that is very commendable. Keep up the good work, Joe!"

Following the publication of the book, I received numerous letters of congratulation and reviews in various journals. Payne Thomas sent me copies of reviews from Western and Eastern Europe, England, South America, Africa, and Australia, which were all favorable. I treasure the review by Dr. H. Lehmann, of Cambridge, England, who wrote as follows: "Though many thousands of patients all over the world are suffering and dying from sickle-cell disease, much less attention is paid to this group of disorders than to many rare maladies. It is only in 1971 that books and monographs have begun to appear solely devoted to certain aspects of sickling, and this is the first exclusively concerned with the pathology of sickle-cell disease." In summary, Dr. Lehmann said: "This is indeed a most valuable book of reference, not only for medical practitioners and students, but also for hematologists, geneticists, and biochemists."

The book was also highly recommended by the English medical journal, *Practitioner*.

One year after the publication, another article appeared in the *Pathology Journal of Australia* with these comments: "Technically, the volume is well presented and with excellent black and white microphotographs. In Australia, where sickle-cell disease is still uncommon, this book will not find widespread use by either the clinical hematologists or the pathologists. However, as a source of itemized reference, it is a successful text and is recommended as such."

Within this country letters of congratulations came from many sources. A humorous one from my friend W. M. Christopherson, M.D., professor and chairman of the Department of Pathology of the University of Louisville, said: "Dear Joe: I had no idea that you were undertaking such a large work. When I think of you, I always think of the uterus rather than blood cells. At any rate, it will be a welcome addition to our library, since we see a great deal of this in Louisville."

One Sunday afternoon in October 1971, I was awakened from my nap by my eleven-year-old daughter, Patricia, calling, "Dad! Dad! There's a Dr. Johnson, from Philadelphia, who wants to talk to you!"

Dr. Johnson identified himself as a medical adviser to the Southern Christian Leadership Conference (SCLC). "I am pleased to inform you, Dr. Song, that you have been selected to receive the Martin Luther King, Jr., Medical Achievement Award for your outstanding contribution in the research of sickle-cell anemia."

Being a bit groggy from the sudden interruption of my sleep, I did not fully comprehend and asked Dr. Johnson to repeat his statement. He said that several scientists who had done research in sickle-cell disease were to receive medical achievement awards on April 30, 1972, at Convention Hall in Philadelphia. "Would you be able to attend the banquet to receive your award if your expenses were paid by the SCLC?"

I asked him to hold for a moment while I discussed it with my wife. After talking with my family, who wanted to go to the ceremony, I accepted his invitation.

The date and place of the banquet were subsequently changed to May 31, at the Grand Ballroom of the Sheraton Hotel, and I was informed that President Nixon, who had been scheduled to attend, might not be able to do so. When I called Johnson's office in the latter part of May, he assured me that a prepaid ticket would be waiting for me at the United Airlines ticket counter at the Midtown airport. I had previously notified him that I would be bringing my family at my own expense and asked him to reserve a room for us at the Holiday Inn, near the Sheraton Hotel.

On the afternoon of May 31, I found no prepaid ticket at the airport but used my charge card to obtain all of our tickets, confident that my expenses would be reimbursed at a later date.

At the Philadelphia airport we were met by a black chauffeur, who drove us to the Holiday Inn in a Cadillac limousine. When we arrived at the Sheraton Hotel, at 7:30 P.M., for the ceremony, we were astonished to find more than two hundred blacks blocking the entrance, demonstrating against the SCLC. They were holding placards and distributing pamphlets stating that the members of the SCLC were committing fraud, using thirteen scientists to raise funds.

At the head table I saw my old teacher Dr. L. W. Diggs, in a tuxedo and black bow tie, and several other well-known men, such as Anthony Allison, a British scientist from Nigeria, and Dr. H. Lehmann, from Cambridge, England, a world-renowned physician who had devoted his entire life to studying man's hemoglobin.

Dr. Lehmann came to me and shook my hand. "I knew you would be here, Joe, since you created such a monumental work on sickle-cell disease." He told the people around him, "I know this boy. He should be very proud of his work."

Dr. Diggs was also very complimentary and introduced me to David Hartman, the television actor. A few minutes later Muhammad Ali, the famous black boxing champion, and his two bodyguards walked into the hall. At the head table was labor leader Jimmy Hoffa, talking to some of his supporters, many of whom filled the grand ballroom of the hotel.

There was a long delay before the ceremony began. Senator Tanney, from California, was unable to wait more than two and one-half hours and finally left. Dr. Sam Johnson, coordinator for the awards banquet, followed him to the entrance, apologizing for the delay. Black photographers and TV cameramen were filming until 10:30.

We were kept waiting until 10:00 P.M., when Rev. Ralph David Abernathy, head of the SCLC, finally began the awards ceremony, which lasted about an hour. This was followed by a long speech by

246

Jimmy Hoffa, who complained about the lack of federal support for research in sickle-cell disease. Loud applause from his supporters ended the ceremony at 1:00 A.M.

On the following morning, at 10:00, there was to be a press conference, which we were all urged to attend. I found Dr. Diggs sitting alone in the pressroom in his tuxedo and bow tie. "It doesn't appear that the press conference will take place," I said.

No one from the press or television stations arrived until 10:20. The press conference was completely disorganized, and demonstrators were shouting at the door. I was dismayed to discover that we had been used by the organization to raise funds.

It was widely reported in the Midtown newspaper and the hospital newsletter that I was supposed to be one of the first recipients of the Dr. Martin Luther King, Jr., Medical Achievement Award. This invited many letters of congratulation from Washington, D.C., and from my native country, Korea.

A letter from our previous administrator, Sr. Mary Eileen McCain, arrived on May 2 congratulating me on my receiving the award. She said she liked Red Bluff, California, which was very quiet.

I had notified Dr. Harold Stewart, prior to our going to Philadelphia, about the award and expressed my desire to see him. He very kindly asked me to come to his office on Old Georgetown Road, in Bethesda, on June 2, saying in his note: "You have worked hard and intelligently since you came to this country. All of your friends are proud of your achievements."

Dr. Stewart had previously retired from the NCI but was unable to sit at home and tend his flower garden, so his disciples had created a lab for him so he could continue his cancer research. He was a sincere and truly modest scientist, respected by everyone in the field of pathology and cancer research.

A letter of congratulations came to me from Dr. Charles Dunlap, another outstanding figure in American pathology, who was serving as professor and chairman of the Department of Pathology at Tulane University. He had been at the NIH for a meeting in the middle of May when he was told by Dr. Stewart that I would be receiving an award. Dr. Dunlap had been kind to me during my residency, my tenure in Providence with the state health department, and my years at the University of Arkansas Medical Center. He followed my career with keen interest, always praising my performance during my residency to his circle of friends, the pathology department chairmen of various university medical schools.

247

I told my friends that we will never again have such giants as Charles Dunlap, William Meissner, and Henry Moon. Dr. Moon's parents came to this country from Korea and settled in the San Francisco area. He attended medical school and subsequently became the chairman of the Department of Pathology of the prestigious University of California in San Francisco. He was the first Korean physician to be appointed to such a position. I kept in close contact with Dr. Moon until he died of nasopharyngeal cancer at the age of fifty seven.

When I returned to Midtown with a large plaque from the SCLC, I received several letters asking me to become consultant for medical research institutes, which I was more than happy to do.

In spite of two letters from me to the SCLC concerning the promised expense payment, I had not received anything from the organization. In October a letter finally came from Dr. Sam Johnson, from Ghana. He apologized for the great inconvenience that the organization had caused but emphasized that it was not a matter of negligence on their part. The fact that there had been a pending legal attachment on all the funds concerning the awards banquet, and apparently he had to leave the country. We decided to forget the whole incident.

Three weeks later a telephone call from Denver, Colorado, informed me that I had been selected to receive another award. The caller identified himself as a vice president of the American Torch Club, located in Denver, which was to have an award ceremony for those who had made a significant contribution to sickle-cell anemia research. I politely declined but suggested a name for him to contact. "Dr. Ted Robinson, of Detroit, Michigan, has done a tremendous amount of work in this field," I said. "I think you should approach him for the award."

"Well, Dr. Song, he gave us your name to contact," was his comment.

When I declined the invitation over the telephone and told my wife about the second award, she could hardly stop laughing.

33
Okinawa Assignment

Several small islands known as the Ryukyu Islands are located approximately 350 miles southwest of Kyushu, Japan. The largest one, Okinawa, densely populated, with 1 million people in 1970, was a bloody battleground during World War II. Under U.S. Army occupation since April 1945, this once war-torn island was converted into a beautiful resort area with interlacing paved highways from the northern tip to the southern end. Spurs and canyons radiate from its mountain ridges, carving picturesque coves in which sailboats anchor beneath the cliffs. Its lovely bay is known to be perfect for sailing and scuba diving. Glass-bottomed boats ply the harbor, through which marine life, including coral, is studied.

Okinawa became an important strategic military base in the Pacific Ocean. Under the benevolent policies of the U.S. Occupational Force, many once poor islanders became owners of thriving businesses, and countless destitute people became self-sufficient or self-supporting.

Ryukyu University, in Naha, is a reputable teaching institute with an enrollment of five to six thousand students. As the university has no medical college, selected students go to mainland Japan for training, and most of them stay there permanently for medical practice. Consequently, there is a shortage of physicians to care for the large population. One of the most significant projects of the U.S. Occupational Army was the establishment of American-style training programs to attract medical graduates from Japan to receive residency training and settle there. A 220-bed teaching hospital was built by the U.S. Army in Gushikawa City, in the central region of the island. The army then asked the University of Hawaii Medical School to institute approved residency programs in the fields of internal medicine, anesthesiology, obstetrics and gynecology, pediatrics, radiology, and orthopedic surgery.

Dr. Neil Gault, Jr., a graduate of the University of Minnesota Medical School, was appointed the first director of the residency training programs. Taking a sabbatical from his position as associate dean of the University of Hawaii Medical School to initiate the programs, he did an excellent job, recruiting many reputable physicians from the United States for assignments lasting one or two years. With his enthusiastic approach and keen interest in training the native physicians, Dr. Gault laid the groundwork for residency programs that would last more than ten years. He was highly respected by the native physicians, the faculty members of the University of Hawaii Medical School, and the teaching staff from the United States. Dr. Gault was a friend of my mentor, Dr. J. K. Lee, professor of pathology at Seoul National University, and remained the backbone of the Okinawa projects even after returning to the University of Minnesota as dean of the medical school.

In 1970, Dr. Robert Sudrann, who succeeded Dr. Gault as program director, approached me concerning serving as a consultant in pathology for the Okinawa training programs—more specifically, training physicians and technicians to detect early uterine cervical cancer in the general population. My friend J. R. Lee, a cardiologist from Newfoundland who had previously served in Okinawa, had told Bob that I might be available for a short assignment. I accepted the offer to become a consultant in pathology and the cervical cancer detection program at the Central Hospital in Okinawa for the month of July 1970 and mailed several hundred Kodachrome slides three weeks prior to my departure.

I was told to report to Travis Air Force Base, in San Francisco, and proceed to the protocol section. At midnight the corporal took my bag and drove me approximately two hundred yards to the TWA plane that would take me, along with two hundred army personnel, to Kadena Air Force Base, in Okinawa. I asked if we should walk to the plane, but he said, "No, Doctor, you have a GS-15 rating. I have orders to drive you to the plane." Members of the crew were standing to receive me as the first one to board the plane. I was overwhelmed at such VIP treatment, as I had never before been such an important person.

During the long flight one of the servicemen became seriously ill, complaining of severe abdominal pain, radiating up to the left chest. As there was no other physician on board, I was asked to examine him. Despite the fact that I had rarely examined a live patient since the Korean War, I took his pulse and reached the conclusion that the pain was not related to his heart. I told the pilot to report to Kadena Air Force Base and have them arrange for a physician and an ambulance to meet the plain. "His pain is probably caused by intestinal obstruction or acute inflammation," I commented. The man died two days later, I was told, due to acute pancreatitis.

Bob Sudrann was waiting for me when we landed. I also met John Matthews, a very cordial retired colonel of the Medical Service Corps, then serving as an administrator of programs. I was allowed to use a 1966 Ford sedan driven by a native chauffeur. At the hospital I was introduced to members of the faculty from the United States. Dr. Bob Hutchinson, an orthopedic surgeon from Kansas City, was to remain as my friend following the completion of the Okinawa programs. Many of the American faculty members were genuinely interested in teaching and training local physicians and were eager to learn their language. Dr. Bob Benning, a cardiologist from Memphis, was a gifted physician with an aptitude for languages. To my astonishment, he mastered the Japanese language in three years, although he spoke with a heavy southern accent. Many of the faculty members, however, were opportunists, taking advantage of their GS-15 ratings and spending a great deal of time during office hours shopping at the various PXs and taking sightseeing trips to photograph the landscape and the people.

I noticed that the natives were very reluctant to authorize autopsies, and only one autopsy was performed during my stay. I was astonished to discover that so many women presented advanced stages of uterine cervical cancer, beyond any possible treatment.

A dinner party was held at the Kadena Officers' Club to celebrate the promotion of Dr. Bob Hutchinson to brigadier general of the U.S. Army Reserve Corps. I commented to his wife, Jean, who was an internist, and Bob Sudrann on the high incidence of invasive cervical cancer among the young female population here. They both thought there should be a population screening project for cervical cancer for the island and urged me to make a feasibility study.

When a civilian pathologist from Naha General Hospital came to show me a difficult and unusual case of a malignant tumor arising from the nerve trunk of the hand of a forty-seven-year-old man, I made some inquiries about the existence of any program for uterine cancer control. "It is very much needed for the purpose of cancer control for Okinawa's female population," he said, "but no one has even suggested it."

Most of the native physicians and administrative staff at the Central Hospital were very friendly. Among them the administrator, Dr. Kubota, a native of Okinawa and a graduate of Kyushu University Medical School, was very kind and appreciative of my work. I was invited for dinner at his spacious home on a hilltop overlooking the beautiful seashore. As we sat in the garden after dinner, enjoying the sunset, he told me his life story.

"I was a young surgeon at Naha Hospital when the Americans landed here in Okinawa. We were forced to evacuate to the southern tip of the island. I hid in a cave with more than one hundred civilians after I became separated from the main hospital body. We were told horrible stories about American soldiers committing atrocities against civilians and were warned never to surrender, because they would burn us to death instantly. Many of our young nurses took their own lives, jumping off the cliffs. I was the first one to respond to the American call to surrender."

"What happened to you and the other civilians?" I asked.

"We were taken to a camp and given food and clothing. They were indeed decent people, those American soldiers. What a lie our own soldiers told us!"

"You know by now that Americans are very broad-minded people, with humane feelings," I remarked.

"Yes, they are. The soldiers helped the old people walk from the caves and picked up many babies and cared for them. We should never have trusted our fanatic soldiers. My wife, an independently wealthy woman, took refuge in Taiwan with her parents and two younger sisters. They were treated in such inhuman ways and were told to kill themselves with grenades rather than surrender to the American invading forces."

Kubota continued, "You know, Dr. Song, I wanted to settle in Japan when I completed my surgical training at Kyushu University Hospital. But when they found out that I was from Okinawa, no one would give me a chance." He spent some time describing the unfair treatment and discrimination by the native Japanese. "Did you have a similar experience in the States?"

"Of course. As you know, prejudice is part of human nature. But my people suffered more discrimination from the Japanese. My father followed the great leader Do San Ahn from his native province to Shanghai to establish the Korean government in exile. When my father decided to return to Korea after three years of exile, he couldn't go back to his hometown, because the Japanese police force was waiting for him. Instead he went to Seoul to mingle with 1 million ordinary people. Eventually they found him and put him in prison for seventeen months. He never told me in detail about the physical torture he received from the Japanese. He was unable to find a job as a teacher at any government-run school. He ended up in a mission school for a while, until the Japanese government forced the school to dismiss him."

"We were also treated for centuries as second- and third-class citizens by the Japanese occupation," Dr. Kubota went on. "But tell me, Dr. Song, how did you get to be the director of a pathology department and a professor of pathology at Central University Medical School?"

"Well, just by luck, I guess," I answered. "But I had to work very hard and had to be better qualified than the other applicants."

"Wouldn't they rather appoint their own kind?"

"Yes, of course, and I don't blame them for that. Would you blame them?"

"I guess not." Kubota understood.

"I've been in many places," I continued, "including Western Europe and Far Eastern countries. But I'm convinced that the governmental system of the United States is the best one that the human race can create, and it's the only country where foreigners can succeed if they work hard and have perseverance and determination."

As I thanked Dr. and Mrs. Kubota for their hospitality and the delicious dinner, he said, "I'm so glad we had this frank discussion this evening."

Dr. Bob Sudrann and his wife invited me for dinner at their home one evening in the middle of July. The weather was very hot and humid, but the house provided by the University of Hawaii had window air conditioners and was comfortable. During the course of the dinner, I mentioned to Bob the need for an early cervical cancer detection program. He said that he would approach the home office at the University of Hawaii for their comments.

A week later I received an enthusiastic letter from Dr. Gault, who urged me to recruit technologists and train them to read Pap smears from nonsymptomatic women. Bob suggested that he would approach the Okinawa Medical Association through his assistant, John Matthews, to set up a series of meetings. I agreed to give several lectures for members of the Okinawa Medical Association, most of whom were general practitioners.

"I doubt very much, Joe, that they would understand English, so you will have to speak Japanese," Bob said.

"But I haven't spoken a word of Japanese for more than thirty-five years, and I'm not sure that I can communicate with them."

"Well, as you know, all the Okinawans speak Japanese as their official language, although they still communicate with one another in their native tongue."

"I didn't know they had their own language."

"Yes, they do," he said, "but they feel very strongly that they must use the Japanese language as their official one."

A few days later at the auditorium of the Okinawa Medical Association, in Naha, I presented a series of cases of cervical cancer, with the aid of the Kodachromes that I had brought with me, in a lecture utilizing English scientific words and Japanese words. Most of the audience understood, as I saw many heads nodding during the case presentations.

Just three days before my departure from Okinawa for Seoul, Korea, the president of the Naha Association of Medical Technologists visited me at the Central Hospital pathology office. He agreed with the idea that they should establish a project to discover cases of early uterine cervical cancer by means of examining Pap smears. But no trained cytotechnologists were available for the project. He asked me to train medical technologists in Naha and the Central Hospital staff members on my second trip to Okinawa.

At the departure gate of the Naha International Airport, I heard someone calling my name. Turning around, I saw the secretary of the Okinawa Medical Association trying to catch his breath. He presented me with a doll in native costume as a token of appreciation from the members of the medical association.

In Seoul I spent about two hours with Dr. J. K. Lee, at Seoul National University. He praised the groundwork laid by his friend Dr. Neil Gault.

On March 1, 1972, I received a long-distance call from Dr. Gault, in Honolulu, urging me to return to Okinawa in June of 1972 to train technicians for the uterine cancer detection project. He said that they would like to have me back for another month.

When I returned to Okinawa, a series of training programs had been arranged by the Okinawa Association of Medical Technologists, to be held each evening at Naha General Hospital, thirty miles south of Central Hospital, which was located in Gushikawa City. An administrative assistant to Dr. Odom, Mr. Arasaki, was to drive me to the lecture hall every evening. Seven selected technologists and a cytotechnologist from the U.S. Army hospital joined the lectures.

A second lecture was held at the same building for the members of the Okinawa Medical Association, and for about two hours every evening we discussed the histogenesis of the human uterine cervix and the morphological basis for uterine cancer.

Dr. Charles Odom, a new director of education, was a very intelligent, energetic young man from New Orleans, who was dedicated to educational activities for the native physicians. A graduate of Tulane Medical School, Charlie was a board-certified obstetrician and gynecologist, who was an assistant professor at the University of Hawaii Medical School. He possessed a modest and dedicated approach to the education of the Okinawa physicians.

The program kept me busy, as I had to provide routine pathology service and hold teaching conferences for the resident physicians at the Okinawa Central Hospital during the daytime and training sessions for the medical technologists in Naha in the evening. After a month of training, with my use of a mixture of English and Japanese, some of the technologists later became cytotechnologists.

I made my third and final trip to Okinawa in May 1973 at their invitation, to complete the training program. The island of Okinawa had been returned to the Japanese government, and the University of Hawaii residency program for Central Hospital was taken over by Dr. Andrew Chapman, from Harvard Medical School.

The Japanese government made it clear to the natives that there were no funds available for a government-sponsored screening program to detect early uterine cervical cancer. Nonetheless, we continued our training sessions every evening, except for Saturday and Sunday. At the conclusion of the sessions, we had a series of meetings with general practitioners, surgeons, and obstetricians and gynecologists for the screening project. I recommended that the fee for Pap smears and routine pelvic examinations be nominal, as this project was to be a service to the native population.

On the way home I made a brief stop in Seoul to give a series of lectures at Ewha Women's Medical College, changing my subject from sickle-cell anemia to early uterine cervical cancer, since there is no sickle-cell gene in the Korean peninsula.

In the winter of 1974, Mr. Miyagi, a histotechnologist, was sent by the University of Hawaii to our cytology laboratory for intensified cytology training for one month. Our cytotechnology students and cytology staff gave him all the help he needed, including a large number of teaching slides for the Okinawa training program.

The late congressman John E. Fogarty, from Rhode Island, was a gigantic figure in the medical research field. He advocated seeking world peace through the exchange of medical research results, technical aid for cancer research, and medical education. When he died prematurely, Congress established the Fogarty International Medical Fellowships, to be administered through the NCI, of the NIH. Representative Fogarty was a great help to me, and I had much admiration for his philosophy of enhancing world peace through medical research

255

and educational aid. When we did not win the war in Vietnam, in 1975, I felt strongly that normalization of the political situation in Vietnam and in this country would be desirable in the immediate future. In September 1978, I offered my services to Assistant Secretary of State Holbrooke to provide humanitarian efforts in medical education and health service. More specifically, I volunteered to go to Vietnam to train technicians in the detection of early uterine cervical cancer.

In October 1978, I received a cordial letter from Stephen R. Lyne of the State Department, director of the Vietnam, Laos, and Cambodia sections. He thought my suggestion to assist the Vietnamese people was a good one and had referred my letter to Dr. John LeVan, of the University of Chicago, an American citizen of Vietnamese origin. Several days later I received a call from Dr. LeVan asking me to go to Hanoi to launch a cancer detection program for his people. The organization would provide me with an economy class round-trip air ticket from Midtown to Hanoi through Laos, and I was to stay for six weeks of intensified training of technicians in cytotechnology. I accepted the challenge and informed our administrator of my intentions. She felt that this might help in the location of many servicemen who had been reported missing in action. I assured her that I would do my best in any possible way.

Two weeks later, war broke out between Vietnam and Mainland China, and our program was postponed indefinitely.

34
Cancer Chemotherapy Project

"Joe, can you help my young patient?"

I turned from my microscope to see Dr. John Sullivan standing in my office with his characteristic grin. John was a member of the General Practice Section of the hospital, with the reputation of being an honest and competent family practitioner.

"Tell me more about your patient, John," I said.

"He's a twenty-five-year old man with embryonal cell carcinoma to the left testicle. The only effective drug, as I understand it, is Actinomycin D. Can you get some for him?"

An embryonal cell carcinoma of the testis is a highly malignant, rapidly growing tumor that is almost always fatal.

"Where can we get Actinomycin D?" I asked.

"I understand the only source available to us is the NCI. You have some friends there, don't you, Joe?"

"I have a pathologist friend at the NCI."

"Can you call him and ask him to send us some Actinomycin D?" John persisted.

Through a conversation with Dick Miller, head of the Anatomical Pathology Section of the NCI, I learned that we would have to become a member of the NCI-approved investigational team. I then talked to Dr. Paul Carbone, director of the NCI who encouraged me to complete an application form to become an investigator. When I looked at the forms that arrived ten days later, I became discouraged. I was very reluctant to take on another project because of my routine service duties, teaching my residents in pathology, and the manuscript preparation for the book on sickle-cell disease.

I did not respond to the request by the NCI until January 1970, when two more physicians urged me to initiate the project. I contacted the NCI and discussed the matter with their new director, who was less than enthusiastic than the former one because of the size of our institution, with no medical school affiliation. Nonetheless, we completed the enormous amount of paperwork to be submitted to the NCI.

On my first visit to the NIH for the negotiation of the cancer chemotherapy project, I visited Stan Whaley, who was serving as vice president of communications. We spent about an hour talking about the good old days at the University of Arkansas Medical Center.

Negotiations with Dr. Catherine Ross were extremely slow and rather difficult because of our lack of medical school affiliation and the fairly low academic standing of our institution in the state. "Since there is no other fellow of the American College of Physicians besides you, Dr. Song," she explained, "I think you will have to be an independent investigator for cancer chemotherapy."

"An independent investigator? What is that?" I asked.

"Most of the institutions in the Midwest area that are approved for cancer chemotherapy by the NCI are affiliated with the University of Wisconsin. Since your hospital is not affiliated with the university, you will have to be an independent investigator, with direct reports to me. You must complete several other forms for that."

When I returned to Midtown and discussed the matter with key members of the medical staff, they urged me to complete the paperwork for the chemotherapy project. Three months later we were finally approved as an independent investigator in the field of cancer chemotherapy and received several new anticancer drugs and antibiotics, such as Mitomycin C, CCNU, and BCNU.

In June 1972, I was visited by a representative of the Upjohn Company, who informed me of a new drug called Calusterone. This was a modified male sex hormone, testosterone, in tablet form, which was having remarkable results on patients with breast cancer. "To receive this new drug," he said, "you must approach our home office in Kalamazoo, Michigan, to complete some paperwork."

After successful negotiations with the medical director of the Upjohn Company, we received twenty bottles of Calusterone tablets, which were to be used for patients with recurrent breast cancer.

Our first patient, Jean Lockhart, had Stage I breast cancer, which was supposed to be limited to the breast. It was confirmed by left radical mastectomy, which revealed twenty-six left axillary lymph nodes showing no evidence of tumor spread. A year later there was a recurrent breast cancer compressing the left trachea (windpipe), clearly observed by Dr. Don Cook, who had performed the initial surgery. She also developed several small tumor nodules in the left chest wall, which subsequently proved to be recurrent breast cancer.

After six weeks of treating Jean with Calusterone, I asked Dr. Cook to examine her for any significant changes of the tumor site. The report from the Radiology Department of Metropolitan Hospital was exceptionally good, indicating marked reduction of the tumor size at the left trachea, and we were all delighted with such good news. Three months later, however, there was evidence of rapid growth of the tumor nodules at the same location, and we advised Mrs. Lockhart to go to M. D. Anderson Hospital, in Houston, Texas, for more extensive treatment.

Mrs. Lockhart finally died much later, with extensive bone involvement by cancer, despite extensive chemotherapy administered by the physicians at M. D. Anderson Hospital. It appeared that some of the tumor cells were either destroyed or degenerated, and the remaining tumor cells would gain immunity to a certain drug and proceed into a terminal stage by rapid growth.

Mrs. Jane Logan had Stage I right breast cancer, which was supposed to be limited to the breast, but she subsequently developed metastatic foci destroying her left pelvic wing bone, exhibiting an osteolytic lesion (bone destruction) about the size of a quarter. After three months of therapy with Calusterone, it was noted that the bony defect was rapidly filling in. Six months later the formerly recognizable bony destruction was filled in with new growth of healthy bone. The X-ray films showed a normal pelvic wing bone, which was wonderful news for the patient and her husband.

Sitting in my office, she asked, "I'm cured, am I not, Dr. Song?"

"I sincerely hope so, Mrs. Logan," I said. "Let's just say that the drug is working for you."

"I think you're too cautious, Dr. Song. I believe I'm completely cured."

"Well, I wish I could be so optimistic. Let's just keep our fingers crossed."

"I'm sure I'm cured. You won't say that, just to tease me. I'm taking a trip with my husband to visit his parents in Oslo, Norway. Do you think it will be all right?"

"I think that's a very good idea. How long will you be gone?"

"About six weeks."

"Take the Calusterone pills with you," I advised, "and take three tablets a day while you're in Norway."

Twenty-seven months later I was deeply disappointed to see a rampant spread of the breast cancer through Mrs. Logan's spine and rib cage, eventually resulting in her death.

Twenty-seven other patients with recurrent breast cancer were referred to our project from many small towns in Iowa. The administration decided to open up a new chemotherapy unit on West 5, with three full-time oncology nurses on duty.

259

In July 1970, when my secretary mailed the completed manuscript of the sickle-cell disease book to my publisher, I began devoting all my time to cancer patients and routine pathology duties.

Developed by Japanese investigators, Mitomycin C was supposed to be effective on patients with stomach, colon, and pancreatic cancer. However, none of our patients with signs and symptoms of gastrointestinal cancer who received Mitomycin C improved. Most of them died within nine months of treatment. New drugs from the NCI—CCNU and BCNU—were given to many patients with malignant brain tumors, referred by Dr. Frank Johnson, a neurosurgeon at Metropolitan Hospital. Most of the patients did feel some improvement for about three to six months, but all of them died of glioblastoma multiforme, a highly malignant and rapidly growing brain tumor.

Then we received a package of adriamycin, an anticancer antibody, developed by Italian investigators in Milan. Adriamycin showed remarkable results on patients with ovarian and breast cancer and several patients with gastrointestinal cancer, despite devastating side effects, including loss of hair within three weeks of treatment.

I am unable to forget a seventeen-year-old Roosevelt High School senior and football player, Jeff Moran. Jeff had developed embryonal cell carcinoma in his right testicle and was referred to our unit for extensive chemotherapy. After three months of unsuccessful chemotherapy, we were rapidly losing our hope for Jeff. He must have known the probable outcome of the treatment, but he never admitted that he was losing ground. A week before his death, he asked his mother to get his football gear cleaned so that he could play football. When I was told this by an oncology nurse, I was deeply distressed.

The mode of action of various chemotherapeutic antibiotics and chemicals is in the belief that this will inhibit the synthesis of DNA of the tumor cells, leading to their death. The drugs and antibiotics, however, do not have selective action, not knowing which cells to attack and which cells too spare. Consequently, white blood cells and platelets are similarly attacked by the drugs, causing severe anemia (blood loss) and bleeding tendency, due to lack of platelets. Most patients lose their hair and suffer from nausea and vomiting. On the other hand, hormonal preparations, such as Calusterone, having shown significant results through hormonal antagonistic action, retard the growth of tumor cells, having less toxic effect.

A Webster City farmer brought in his eleven-year-old boy, who was receiving chemotherapy at the Mayo Clinic after his leg was amputated because of a highly malignant and fatal tumor, called Ewing's sarcoma.

"I brought you a letter from the Mayo Clinic, Doctor," the farmer said.

"How is your son doing, Mr. Kelley?" I asked.

"Well, he's doing all right for now. But I'm a farmer, you know. I can't take my boy every six weeks to the Mayo Clinic and stay there for three or four days until the treatment is over."

The letter from the Mayo Clinic asked me to take over the planned chemotherapy for his son. I agreed to do so, saying, "We have all the drugs they are recommending for your son. We'll do the best we can, Mr. Kelley. I understand your situation."

"What would be the charge, Doctor?"

"Oh, I think we can forget about that," I said. "Your boy's life comes first."

His face reddened and his eyes filled with tears.

In the middle of October 1972, I attended a tumor conference in Houston, Texas, and decided to visit my old friend Dr. William Russell, chief pathologist at M. D. Anderson Hospital. During our coffee break I was told by one of Dr. Russell's friends that with a combination of chemotherapy and immunotherapy, utilizing BCG vaccine, they were achieving a 70 percent remission rate. A vaccine from BCG (Bacillus Calmett Guérin, a cow strain tuberculous bacillus) would arouse the immune defense mechanism within the body to fight cancer cells. The vaccine was manufactured by the Louis Pasteur Institute, in Paris.

I became intensely interested in persuing BCG therapy for cancer patients and asked Bill Russell to arrange for me to learn the technique of giving BCG vaccinations to our patients. I was to spend two weeks at M. D. Anderson Hospital with Dr. Mark Jordan to learn immunotherapy with BCG vaccine. After one week of training, I was called back to Midtown because of the death of my young associate.

Several weeks later I filed a protocol to initiate BCG vaccine treatment, along with chemotherapy, for 110 patients with recurrrent breast cancer. Several revisions were made to satisfy the officials of the NCI before they sent us a large quantity of BCG vaccine. Each vial contained a small amount of semisolid media in which millions of live but attenuated tuberculous bacilli were present. With 5 cc. of distilled water mixed into the semisolid media, it would become a concentrated vaccine to be inoculated onto the left arm after several small, shallow scars were made, very much like the inoculation method for smallpox. I demonstrated the procedure to my resident physicians and the oncology nurses, Mary Peterson and Paula Newman. Vaccinations were given to approximately sixty patients. To our disappointment, we were unable to reproduce M. D. Anderson Hospital's remission rate of 70 percent with a combination of BCG vaccine and chemotherapy. When I presented our results at the Chicago Symposium in March 1977, showing only 30 percent remission, which contradicted the results presented by the M. D. Anderson Hospital physicians, they were unhappy on hearing our report.

With 171 patients receiving either chemotherapy or a combination of chemotherapy and BCG vaccination, the administrator and I felt that we should import several full-time medical oncologists to take over the unit. Two months later Dr. Sam Brook, from Sun City, moved to Midtown and took charge of West 5, known as the chemotherapy unit of Marymount Hospital.

In December 1977, I received a letter from the NCI indicating that the BCG immunotherapy vaccine for patients with recurrent breast cancer was to be discontinued immediately. The memo also urged me to destroy all the unused BCG vaccine in our stock. With the aid of the maintenance people, we incinerated all the vaccine stored in our refrigerator in the chemistry department.

The treatment modalities for recurrent Stage I breast cancer with chemotherapy or radiation therapy were virtually ineffective, yet all the protocols had been designed by the NCI or various medical centers in this country and the M. D. Anderson Hospital staff. Whenever I faced a patient dying of breast cancer, I felt totally inadequate and helpless. I wondered if we were heading in the wrong direction, destroying tumor cells with poisons or antibiotics, which also destroy the necessary good white blood cells. There must be some other way to help our patients, not by toxic chemicals, poisonous antibiotics, or radiation treatment, but by a new, nontoxic method. Many reports published in the journals by medical oncologists tend to exaggerate their results, which are not reproducible.

Much later the public was shocked to learn through the media that investigators at many Ivy League medical schools falsified their results to gain more research funds from the NCI. An immunologist in New York City was considered by the nominating committee for the Nobel Prize in medicine and physiology. The committee dropped his name immediately upon learning that his technical assistant had been forced to falsify the results of their investigation. It is a known fact that many of the scientists sitting on the review boards borrow ideas submitted by applicants seeking research grants. Many honorable physicians and scientists seem to have no qualms about stealing from research grant applications submitted by those who really needed the funds to continue their independent research projects.

Dr. Jenny Gurkin, of the Will Chase Cancer Research Institute, told me during a trip to South Africa, in 1985, about the case of her friend, the late Dr. Kay Fishbein. "Kay submitted her grant application to the government organization with a diagram of the ox structure. This was stolen by one of the reviewers and given to a young man who subsequently claimed the science prize."

On a Sunday afternoon in August 1976, I was leaving to go to Green Park to play a game of golf when a call came from the university hospital. "We're sending your patient Bob Allen back to you, since there is nothing we can offer."

Bob Allen, a twenty-two-year old man, had been receiving chemotherapy for a testicular choriocarcinoma, a highly malignant and fatal tumor. We followed a regular protocol, administering Actinomycin D and other antitumor antibodies, to no avail. The tumor kept growing fast, involving both lungs. In desperation, we decided to seek aid from the university hospital staff. . . .

"We have nothing more to offer to this young man, since you have covered all the ground, Dr. Song," the voice continued. "Can you hold for a second? Mrs. Allen wishes to speak to you."

"Bob wants to go back to your unit. Can you see him when we arrive there?" she asked.

"Certainly, Mrs. Allen. I'll be waiting for you."

I explained the situation to my friend at the clubhouse of Green Park Golf Course and urged him to go ahead without me. When I entered Bob's room at the hospital, Mrs. Allen was weeping. She said, "Bob wants to see you before he goes, Dr. Song."

My eyes filled with tears. I recalled a remark made by my friend Dick Miller, who said to me once, "Joe, you are not supposed to get involved personally with cancer patients. You are to remain cold. Don't forget—you are a scientist!" But I have never been able to hide my inner feelings.

Eleven years later I was returning to Midtown from a Boston cancer meeting. When the United Airlines jet touched down and taxied to the terminal, a voice called from behind me, "I didn't know you were sitting in front of me, Dr. Song!"

I turned around as I retrieved my trench coat to see a middle-aged woman smiling at me. "You don't remember me, do you? I'm Mrs. Allen, the mother of Bob Allen, from Hinton."

"Oh, yes. I remember Bob."

"He would have been thirty-three years old, had he survived."

"I know. How are you?" I asked.

"I'm fine, she said as we parted. "You look exactly the same as you did before. Not a single gray hair."

35
Resident Physicians

When students graduate from medical school with the degree of Doctor of Medicine, most of them take the traditional rotating internship for twelve months before they specialize in a certain field or become general practitioners. Those who have decided to specialize take additional training, ranging from twenty-four to forty-eight months, depending upon the different branches of medicine. They may begin as straight interns, followed by residency training in a particular field.

In my case there was no debate about specializing in pathology, as I was a student prosector and assistant and had done some cancer research during medical school, for which I was given generous credit toward my board examinations.

The residents and straight interns at the Institute of Pathology of the University of Tennessee were a mixture of good and mediocre physicians. One was extremely lazy, always late for the 8:00 A.M. Wednesday gross conference. One particular morning, all of the organs from autopsy were laid out on the conference table before our chief, Dr. Sprunt, who was to conduct the conference. The first case was to be presented by this lazy resident. Dr. Sprunt never tolerated more than a ten-minute delay and was visibly agitated when the resident was late. Sprunt suddenly threw all the organs from the table into the trash can and walked out of the room without saying a word. My friend who arrived seventeen minutes late, was severely reprimanded.

Several residents were very diplomatic, brown-nosing Drs. Anderson and Sprunt to gain a favorable assignment. One fellow was a typical one, always looking for a shortcut and trying to get credit on someone else's hard work. He was assisting in research on endometrial cancer and received special treatment from his mentor.

Another apple polisher was able to get away with a minimum number of autopsies and very low quality work. Dr. Richard Long, from the New York University was of a different breed, being keenly interested in immunology and cancer research besides the routine pathology service duties. Dr. Sprunt remarked on one occasion that in his fifty years of experience he had never seen anyone who hated performing autopsies with such a passion as did Dick Long.

I must admit that I have never liked to perform autopsies, but it was required as a part of the training and practice of pathology. I had more of a share in autopsy pathology than any of the other residents, but I gained much useful material for investigation and publication of papers.

A senior pathology staff member, Dr. J. Walter Scott, was an outstanding diagnostician, who taught me much surgical pathology during my residency in Memphis. Dr. Scott, a native of Richmond, Virginia, was gifted in bone tumor pathology and later authored a book on the subject. He was a born teacher and a superb surgical pathologist.

Russell Jones was a very energetic and productive pathologist who taught me pulmonary pathology. I found tremendous stimulation for publication of papers and research when I was assigned to Dr. Jones for three months at the West Tennessee Tuberculosis Hospital. He moved to Salt Lake City to become a full professor of pathology at the University of Utah and once visited us in Little Rock when he was studying nuclear medicine at Oak Ridge, Tennessee.

George Changus, an assistant professor and a gifted pathologist, was an excellent teacher. When I had a small paper presentation at the annual meeting of the American Association of Pathologists and Bacteriologists in April of 1970, Dr. Changus walked up to the podium and shook my hand, saying, "Joe, I can't get over how well you presented your paper!" I was surrounded by Dr. Changus and his friends during the intermission, when he said, "This boy couldn't speak much English when he came to Memphis in 1952. Now he's chief pathologist at Marymount Hospital, my sister institution, and surprised me with such a fine presentation of his paper. I'm so proud of this boy!" Dr. Changus was at that time chief pathologist at a Chicago hospital. I was saddened to hear of his untimely death three years later from a myocardial infarction.

It was easy for a foreign medical graduate (FMG) physician to obtain a residency position in pathology at the university hospitals, because many approved positions were unfilled.

During my tenure as an associate professor of pathology at the University of Arkansas Medical School, we had six residents, all of them Arkansas natives and graduates of our school. Some of the good academic residents went to the University of Missouri, in Columbia, when they heard that the newly selected chairman had changed his mind and would not honor the contract with the university.

Many of our residents were mediocre, except for William Hunter and Dick Young, who showed some interest in investigative work and certainly had above-average capabilities. Bill Hunter completed his last two years of residency at New England Deaconess Hospital, under the direction of Dr. William Meissner and Dr. Merle Legg, and came back to Little Rock as associate pathologist at Arkansas Baptist Hospital. He died of stomach cancer several years later.

When the diagnosis of Bill's cancer was made, my friend Sam Sands called me and gave me the bad news. "Joe, this is a very cold and cruel world," he began. "Bill is recuperating from his surgery. They removed his stomach and he doesn't even know the diagnosis yet, but they've already received three applications from pathologists wanting to take his place. Who knows how long Bill can survive? But they couldn't wait."

"They should have waited for another year or so and then approached the Baptist Hospital pathology department," I said. "Jobs must be very hard to come by in Little Rock." I hung up the telephone in disgust.

Until recently the pathology departments of university and community hospitals maintained a large number of pathology residency positions, approved by the American Medical Association (AMA). All the medical school pathology departments desired to fill their positions with their own graduates or other USMGs (U.S. medical graduates), which was quite understandable. If the positions are not filled within a significant period of time, they might offer them to FMGs, not because they are fond of FMGs, but because the departments are compelled to fill the positions in order to maintain approved residency programs. In fact, many professors and chairmen of university pathology departments maintain the view that FMGs would dilute the academic standards, either because of their being poorly trained or because of their difficulty in communicating. In the last fifteen years too many pathologists have been trained for the limited number of positions available.

FMGs are severely handicapped in their search for suitable training positions in pathology, because most of the institutions are eager to fill their vacancies with their own graduates. No one can deny that the selection methods are probably based on racial and cultural prejudice. In other words, the FMGs, when they arrive in this country, either on a permanent basis or on a temporary visa, are destined to carry a heavy cross with them wherever they go and are compelled to demonstrate professional ability equal to or even superior to that of the USMGs. Nonetheless, the FMGs must struggle to search for residency

266

positions in reputable institutions and gain reasonably good positions thereafter.

On numerous occasions I emphasized to my FMG residents that they had to excel and demonstrate their abilities in order to establish themselves in this country. "I really don't blame the Americans for trying to fill the residency positions with their graduates or American physicians," I would say. "I'm just trying to give you all the opportunities, because I, too, was once a foreign medical graduate. To compete with USMGs in the field of pathology, you must demonstrate that you are far better then those graduating from U.S. medical schools."

I have seldom been impressed with my fellow residents at the University of Tennessee Institute of Pathology or those I trained at the University of Arkansas Medical School. Many of them were taking residency training in pathology to land a lucrative position at a general community hospital. Some of the general practitioners who subsequently entered the pathology training program had one purpose—to have an enormous professional income—and they always disregarded the significance of academic accomplishment.

I had many resident physicians who either completed their four years of training with me or moved on to a university setup after two years of basic training in Midtown. Physicians from India, the Philippines, Korea, South America, Pakistan, Iran, and Spain must have tired of listening to my comments. Most of them, however, did well in their training and were able to find gainful employment. On several occasions I heard comments made by fellow pathologists from the East Coast, during the annual pathology conferences, regarding the quality of their FMGs. Even one friend of mine said to me that he would never appoint residents from India or the Philippines because, "They cannot be trusted." I pointed out to him, "Not all of them are bad. Some are very good. It's unfair to make such a generalization on one or two nationalities."

Resident physicians from India had no language barrier and were able to do fairly well. Drs. Gogate and Rajasekharan were above-average residents and secured suitable jobs. One female resident from India, however, was rather conceited. When she left our department, I was called by two members of the housekeeping section to come down to the residents' quarters. "Doctor, we have something to show you." When I arrived at the particular apartment, they took me to the kitchen, where the walls and the stove were smeared with dark yellow-brown stains, which turned out to be the remains of chicken curry. According to the housekeepers, the occupants had not cleaned the kitchen or stove for over a year. They were dismayed to ask the housekeeping people to clean up such a mess.

Two weeks later I was called down again to the apartment of one of our residents from the Philippines. On an unscheduled inspection of the apartments they found a pile of human hair in the garage of Dr. Del Santo. When I confronted him, he said that he was a trained barber before he came to this country, and had been cutting hair for the interns and residents at a discount.

"Look here," I said. "It's your own business if you cut hair after five o'clock, but you must clean up this mess!"

I accepted an application from a physician, from Iran, to become a third-year resident in my department, based on his previous experience and training in pathology. Two days after his arrival in Midtown, I was called down to the office of Sister McGain, our administrator, who was perplexed by a request from him.

"What did he do, Sister?" I asked.

"He wanted to borrow money from the hospital."

"Well, Sister, as you know, many residents and interns have had to ask for an advance in the past," I said.

"I know that, but he wants to borrow five thousand dollars from the hospital."

"Five thousand dollars! What for?"

"He told me that he needs to bring his family from Iran," she replied.

I explained to a resident from Iran that he could borrow up to five hundred dollars from the hospital against his future salary.

"Well, I know a rich oil businessman from my country who lives in New York City," he said. "I could call him to make a loan."

"If you can do that, I think that would solve the problem."

A few weeks later I received a call from the director of the cafeteria, Leo Davenport. "Doctor, we seem to have problems with one of your resident physicians, an Iranian."

I raised my voice. "What has he done now?"

"Well, he developed this habit of drinking afternoon tea while he was in England, and he comes down at three o'clock every afternoon for tea and toast."

"I don't see anything wrong with that, Leo, do you?"

"No, but the number of pieces of toast he desires is always eleven."

"Eleven? Doesn't he eat lunch?" I asked.

"He appears to have a very healthy appetite, eating four meals a day, plus all that toast at three o'clock in the afternoon. When he shows up in the cafeteria my people run to avoid him, because they're tired of making so much toast."

"Well, Leo, you know he's a big man. Maybe he needs to eat that much to maintain his health."

I chose not to discuss the matter with him, who returned to Iran a few months later. He made his decision to leave abruptly, but he criticized the way the hospital people treated him. "When I was in London, I was very impressed with the courtesy and kindness extended to me by the English people, including the constables, who came up to my apartment to check an immigration permit. But these people are rude and barbaric in the way they treat foreigners."

"I disagree with you," I said, "but perhaps you should return to Iran."

The day he left, with his wife and son, I was again called down to see his apartment. "This is the worst pigpen I ever saw, Doctor," the head of the maintenance department remarked with disgust.

A secretary said, "Look at these pieces of furniture, and look at the piles of hospital linens and utensils! How did he get these?"

Two years later one of surgery residents from Oregon, Sam Roberts, moved out of his apartment. I was asked to come down to see it. The floor tiles in the bathroom were all broken, because the Robertses gave swimming lessons to their small children in the bathtub. Every piece of furniture was broken, and the living room carpet was in deplorable condition. I said to them, "I've never seen such a mess in my life! You guys are always complaining about the foreigners' not taking care of the apartments. Now here is your honorable American!"

"Well," they conceded, "I guess we condemned the wrong people."

The wife of a Philippine resident was caught throwing garbage out the window, and I had to caution her husband about that.

The resident physicians from Korea, when they arrived in this country, always had language problems. But they were hard working, diligent people, and when they left their apartments they at least cleaned them thoroughly.

36
Illness of Administrator

At 10:00 A.M. on a September day in 1972, our administrator came to my office requesting a CPK (creatine phosphokinase) enzyme test be performed on her. The form was signed by her physician, Dr. John Johnson.

A CPK test measures the degree of damage of either the heart muscle or the skeletal muscular structures. It is most frequently used to determine the prognosis of a patient who suffers a myocardial infarction, secondary to coronary artery disease. If the coronary artery is completely occluded by a clot, the result is instantaneous death. If the occlusion is incomplete, it usually causes myocardial damage, resulting in an increased amount of CPK in the blood. The enzyme is within the muscular cells, having a normal range of from ten to fifty units per milliliter. If the heart muscle is damaged, the existing amount of CPK is released into the bloodstream, raising the CPK units considerably. When a subsequent CPK test shows a sudden drop or decreased value, it is considered to be a sign of healing of the heart damage. On the other hand, if the CPK value continues to rise, indicating more widespread heart muscle damage, the prognosis of the patient is poor.

"Are you having heart problems, Sister?" I asked.

"Well, lately I have felt some chest pain, and my heart is always pounding."

"We'll let you know the results as soon as they become available," I assured her.

About half an hour after he received the specimen, our biochemist, Joe Jenkins, rushed into my office with the result of the CPK, which was 610 units.

"Joe, this must be a mistake," I said. "I don't think Sister has a myocardial infarction, because her color was good. Why don't you repeat it?"

The repeated value was 742 units. "You must have mixed the specimen with someone else's. Repeat it again!" I ordered.

Forty-five minutes later Joe was in my office again, completely perplexed. "I'm unable to explain this discrepancy. Our third value was 768 units!"

"This is crazy, Joe! Your methodology must be way off. Check all the machines and do it again tomorrow. The normal range, as you know, is between 10 and 50 units. With this kind of CPK value, she should be dead!"

My new associate, Dr. Manuel Punla, a native of Panama and recently discharged from the U.S. Army Medical Corps, stuck his head into my office. "What's going on here? What are you two arguing about?"

When I explained to him the discrepancies of the CPK values on Sister Georgina, he immediately asked, with an appropriate hand gesture, "Is she shooting dope?"

"What do you mean, Manny?"

"I mean is she injecting drugs into her arms?"

His remark angered me. "Look here, Manny, you're dealing with a Sister administrator in a Catholic hospital! How could you possibly imagine such a thing?"

"I've seen them doing it before," he replied with some indignation.

"Where did you see Catholic nuns taking painkillers?"

"In Panama and in the army. Nuns and priests were injecting narcotics into themselves."

"You must be joking," I said. "Maybe in Panama, but not here. You'd better watch how you waggle your tongue if you want to survive here."

"Well, I'm just mentioning the possibility." He walked out of my office with a cynical smile.

Three weeks later I was called into the physicians' lounge in Surgery.

"Joe, I'm going to examine Sister Georgina's esophagus," said Dr. Bob Lewis, a general surgeon.

"Esophagus? Why?" I asked.

"She keeps complaining of epigastric pain whenever she tries to swallow food."

Dr. Lewis found nothing in the esophagus, but Sister Georgina remained in the hospital as a patient. The very next day he told me that he was going to explore her gallbladder in a few days. He further confided in me that her gallbladder had been removed several years before.

"Then why the gallbladder exploration?" I asked.

He explained to me that there might be a stump left inside with a stone. "I'll call you when I locate the stump, and we'll open it to see if any stones are there."

Before and after each surgery, Sister Georgina required multiple Demerol injections to cope with her constant pain. A small nodule, less than one centimeter in diameter, was exposed by the skillful hands of Bob Lewis, and I was asked to open it in the operating room. A nodular sac contained a sharp black stone, measuring 0.5 by 0.3 centimeters. "Look, Bob!" I showed him a tiny black stone, surrounded by a dense fibrous tissue.

"Could that cause such constant pain?" he questioned.

"It could, although I doubt that this size stone would cause a constant sharp pain."

Two days later my resident physician, Dr. Harry Spencer, came to my office and asked, "Why is Sister Georgina requiring so much painkiller?"

"How do you know that? Where did you hear about it?"

"Well, the pharmacy people told me that they are snowed under with so many prescriptions for her for Demerol and morphine."

'As you know, Harry, she just had major surgery. It's routine procedure to sedate the patients with narcotics."

"I understand that. But it seems to me a rather excessive measure, giving her morphine injections every fifteen minutes."

"Some patients require more than others," I said. "I think you should keep that to yourself."

He left my office with a perplexed expression on his face.

Sister Georgina was finally discharged to her apartment in the nurses' dormitory and remained there for six weeks.

The clinical laboratory had entered into the era of automation, requiring administrative decisions on major chemistry and hematology instruments, which were very expensive. The paperwork was stalled in the administrator's office, and no one else had authority to approve or disapprove.

Jim Wilkins, associate administrator, was helpless. The budget hearing sessions were postponed indefinitely. I called him, saying, "Jim, we must have your approval on our multichannel chemistry analyzer right away. The papers have to be signed by administration and returned to the Technicon Company in three days. Can you help us?"

"I'd like to help you, Joe, but I'm not authorized to do so. Can you take those papers to Sister's apartment for her signature?"

"I'd rather not do that, Jim. Would you do it for us?" I asked.

272

"I'm not certain whether or not I should. I'm very hesitant to step into her apartment." Jim Wilkins was cautious and always reluctant to cross the line. "But I believe it's perfectly all right and legitimate for you to take papers to her apartment. Dr. Hale, our radiologist, has done that several times. Why don't you call Mrs. Dickens and arrange a meeting with Sister Georgina?"

Through her secretary I was able to obtain an appointment for 1:00 P.M. the next day. When I stepped into her apartment, it took me thirty seconds to adjust my eyes to the darkness of the room. All the drapes were drawn. Sister Georgina was in bed, weeping. I asked Mrs. Dickens why she was crying.

"My heart is pounding so hard I couldn't get up this morning," Sister Georgina explained, trying to dry her tears.

"Are you taking any medicine for your heart condition?" I asked gently.

"Dr. Taylor gave me several kinds of tranquilizers to take. But none of them are working." I noticed more than a hundred pills on Sister Georgina's bedside table.

When I returned to my office with the signed papers, I called Dr. Taylor, Sister Georgina's new attending physician, who was a very competent internist. "Pete, what's going on with Sister? Why does she have so many tranquilizers? Do you mean to give her several kinds of tranquilizers simultaneously?"

"No, Joe, I want her to try S-tablets first for two weeks. If this particular tranquilizer fails to bring any positive results, then she should try another tranquilizer for ten days."

Unable to determine his logic, I said, "Pete, as you know, her problem is not the right kind of pills. She may be addicted to Demerol and morphine."

"I know that, but I'm sure I can get her off these two narcotics by several kinds of tranquilizers."

"It would be wonderful if you could do that." With a deep sigh I concluded our conversation.

Sidney Wilson, of the Accounting Department, came to my office one afternoon and asked, "Joe, is it true that Sister Georgina is hooked on narcotics?"

"Where did you hear that?"

"Everybody's talking behind her back here in this institution, and the rumors came down to my department."

I had to be evasive in talking to employees in the hospital, although I was deeply concerned that the unfavorable news had spread so rapidly. "Sid, I don't know it for a fact, but let's just keep it quiet."

Because of the rumors flying around the hospital, I asked Bill Rankin to come in to see me. When I explained the situation to him, he was appalled. "You mean to tell me that our administrator is addicted to narcotics?"

"Well, Bill, it appears that way. I wonder what you could do to help us in this situation."

Bill sank down in his chair and was speechless.

West 5, the chemotherapy unit, was filled with patients having all types of malignant tumors. I assigned my four residents and two straight interns to give chemotherapy to the 150 patients in that unit. I persuaded the reluctant residents by emphasizing that contact with live patients would give an added dimension to their training and future practice.

A twenty-six-year-old woman was referred to our unit with a diagnosis of metastatic melanoma in the brain. I instructed Dr. Harry Spencer to follow the protocols designed by the NCI and M.D. Anderson Hospital staff with newly approved antimelanoma drugs and antibiotics. Two weeks later he told me that he was not convinced of the effectiveness of the protocols. "The only thing that is helpful for this patient is cortisone," he stated.

"If that is so, Harry, then we will switch to cortisone," I said.

In three weeks the patient died of massive cerebral metastasis of the melanoma, which was confirmed by an autopsy. We began to have some doubts about the validity of chemotherapy, and I was rapidly losing my faith in its effectiveness.

On the afternoon of February 2, 1974, Mrs. Dickens called me and asked me to prescribe two vials of Demerol for Sister Georgina. "But I don't have a narcotics license," I explained. "You must approach Dr. Taylor for that."

Later I was told that the radiology chief, Dr. Hale, went to see Sister Georgina and gave her two tablets of a new tranquilizer. He told me that he had seen enough pills and capsules around her bed to open a small pharmacy.

On the morning of March 2, I was called to see Sister Georgina in her office. The solemn-faced administrator said, "Dr. Song, I'm having continuous vaginal bleeding, requiring twenty pads a day, and I'm convinced that this is a uterine cancer that I'm suffering from."

"Then we need to do a D and C on you, Sister, to confirm your impression of this being uterine cancer."

She protested, "No, I don't want to go through a D and C. I want Dr. Jim Dean to take the uterus out right away. I want to be admitted to your Unit 5 to receive massive chemotherapy for uterine cancer."

I asked Dr. Dean, a new surgeon, to examine her and explained that she did not wish to have a D and C, or uterine curettings, to confirm the diagnosis. He told me that she had a small fibroid in the uterus, which had to be removed.

Sister Georgina reiterated to me, "I wish to stay in your unit for chemotherapy."

"Well, Sister, we'll cross that bridge when we come to it. Let's not presume the diagnosis at this stage."

Sister's request for chemotherapy was somewhat genuine and convincing, and I felt very distressed to face another patient with uterine cancer. I made several calls to the NCI, Memorial Hospital in New York City, and Dr. Paul Ginsberg, a renowned gynecologist, who had treated thousands of patients with uterine cancer. Ginsberg's suggestion was to wait and see what the tissue diagnosis showed.

Dr. Dean, a very competent gynecologic surgeon, performed a total abdominal hysterectomy, removing both ovaries and tubes. When I examined the specimen, I raised my voice. "Goddamn it! She lied again!" Her uterus was a small, completely normal specimen with a tiny leiomyoma on the anterior wall. The size and shape of the fibroid could not cause the massive uterine bleeding that she had described to us. Both ovaries were perfectly normal, and there was no evidence of any cancer in the uterus and/or cervix. Her postoperative days were filled with repeated injections of morphine in an enormous amount, which worried most of the nuns and my staff. Pam Mitchell, head of the nursing school, told her people that Sister had a very low threshold for pain and should have morphine whenever she wanted it.

After fourteen days Sister Georgina was discharged from the hospital to her apartment and was receiving more morphine injections every day. She did not return to her office for six weeks, claiming that she was too weak. Pam Mitchell called me one afternoon and asked me to give Sister a blood transfusion. "We'll be glad to give one or maybe two units of blood if you will bring her to the emergency room," I said.

"No, Doctor, she wants to receive the blood in her apartment."

"But the apartment is so dark, you would hardly be able to see the veins."

"That is her wish," Pam reiterated.

I asked one of my hematology technologists, Lois Keck, to go to Sister's apartment and obtain a blood specimen for cross-matching for a transfusion. Through the skillful hands of Lois, two units of blood were given, which failed to bring any quick results. Sister Georgina remained in her apartment for an additional three weeks.

During an emergency board meeting with two nuns from the home office, several of the lay board members, anxious to know what was going on with Sister Georgina, tried to probe. Sr. Vera Killion, a supervisor from the province, curtailed the meeting, saying, "We will let you know in time."

"But, Sister, there are so many important decisions to be made. When is she going to be able to attend the meetings?" someone inquired.

"Very soon," was her answer.

The two nuns asked many penetrating questions and finally found out the truth. Two weeks later they came back and told Sister Georgina that they had made arrangements for Delta Complex, in Salem, a well-known detoxification center, to receive her for intensive treatment. Sister Georgina refused to go, saying, "I'll get off this stuff in no time."

I tried to persuade her to go in for treatment. "It's for your own good, Sister. You'll be back here after the treatment."

But she was reluctant to leave her apartment. She was finally told: "If you don't go to Delta Complex, we have no alternative but to fire you now. If you go to the center and receive treatment for one month, you can come back here as administrator."

That afternoon, in talking with Jim Wilkins, the administrator pro tem, I shouted, "I swear to God, I'll never be part of a cover-up scheme again! Nuns and priests are also human beings. They should be willing to go to a treatment center for therapy."

Two weeks later, after my lecture at Central University Medical School, I paid a visit to Sister Georgina at Delta Complex. A coordinator, Dale Green, assured me that Sister was doing fine. He took me to her room. She said that she was happy to see me, adding, "I'm doing by best, but I'm suffering terrific pain in my chest."

Later Mr. Green commented that she was suffering from withdrawal symptoms, but he was quite positive that she would be off the narcotics at the end of the treatment.

The summer of 1975 was unusual in its activity. My new associate, Dr. Henry Kim, a true gentleman and a hard worker, arrived from Newport, Rhode Island, on July 3 and commenced his duties on July 5. Five pathology residents were kept busy with routine pathology training programs and immunochemotherapy projects on West 5.

On August 1, following my lectures at Central Medical School, I was supposed to stop at the Delta Complex and bring Sister Georgina back to Midtown.

She had completed her month-long treatment and was discharged at noon on that day. On our way back from Salem, I casually remarked, "Sister, I'm unable to understand how an important person like you became addicted to Demerol and morphine. When did you start using those drugs?"

She related to me that she had been suffering from an anal fissure (laceration of the anal skin) for a long time. The medication prescribed by Dr. John Cook was not effective in relieving her constant pain, so she went to Dr. Pete White, who prescribed Demerol. And that was the starting point. "I tried to stop taking Demerol, but I was just unable to discontinue the injection in my office."

Dr. Punla was quite correct in assuming such self-administration of Demerol, back in May of 1972. What a naive fool I was! When I carried her suitcase to her apartment at the nurses' dormitory, she mentioned that she had to attend an AA meeting the next day. I had some idea what an AA meeting was, but I asked, "Are you having problems with alcohol?"

"Well, the Delta people told me to attend when they found out that I was drinking too much," she replied. Again I was shocked at such a revelation.

Our maintenance chief visited me when I returned from the New York cancer meeting, in September, and informed me that they were again retrieving an empty bottle of bourbon every day from Sister's apartment.

"Are you positive about that, Scott? I mean, is it from her room? That's disturbing news."

"I know it is, but who else would consume such an enormous amount of liquor in that building? All of them are student nurses."

I had no answer. "Well, Scott, let's just hope that someone else is consuming that bottle of Jim Beam." Later it was confirmed that Sister Georgina was attending the AA meeting every Tuesday evening.

In the latter part of September, I was informed by Jim Wilkins that my new associate Rob Carson, from Mobile, Alabama, was sending a large number of chemistry tests to the Ajax Clinical Lab, in Kansas City, Missouri, some of which could have been performed at our chemistry laboratory. When I confronted Rob, he said, "I know we could do some of that, but we have so many routine chemistry procedures to perform on a STAT basis that I thought it would be advisable to send all the special chemistry tests to Ajax Lab." Both Dr. Kim and I were strongly opposed to this.

A group of nurses working the coronary care unit began complaining to administration that they were working more than eight hours a day and were demanding special treatment from the hospital. Sister Georgina and her associates were having many meetings in an effort to placate the angry nurses.

Administration decided to give a special bonus to the coronary care nurses, and this was supposed to be confidential. When the other nurses found out, they began a revolution against the administration, telling all the hospital employees, including our lab technologists, that it was very unfair to discriminate against other employees by giving a special bonus only to those in the coronary care unit.

I expressed my opinion to Jim Wilkins, calling it a lousy decision, unreasonable and unfair. "If you want to give a bonus, it should be on the all-or-none principle. Everyone should receive a bonus," I declared.

"I agree with you, Joe, but it was her decision."

"You know as well as I do," I said, "that you'll have to give a bonus eventually to everybody."

I left for Korea on October 8, 1975, to present two small papers at a Seoul medical meeting.

On October 30, 1975, I was approached by two members of the medical staff, Drs. Don Swank and Tom Ford, who urged me to run for the position of chief of staff for 1976. I thanked them and asked them to give me forty-eight hours to think it over.

A couple of days later, when I was conducting business with Sister Georgina in her office, she suddenly changed the subject, saying, "Dr. Song, I think you should run for president of the medical staff."

"Oh, do you think I'd make a good chief of staff?"

"I sure do," she replied.

"Well, let me think it over."

The hospital-based physician is by and large under the thumb of the administrator. If the administrator is a Catholic nun who has just returned from a treatment center, it would be difficult to refuse her requests or instructions without jeopardizing the position he holds. There was a rumor going around that Sister Georgina was on the bottle again. I had to consider all the circumstantial complications that might arise if I were president of the medical staff. I decided to decline the invitation. Consequently, Dr. B. Ackerman, of the Department of Radiology, was elected president of the medical staff for the year 1976.

One cold, gray day in March, I received a telephone call from Dr. Jim Kelly, a new attending physician for Sister, who sounded very depressed. "Joe, I've got to talk to you."

"What about?" I asked.

"I got an urgent telephone call at home from Pam Mitchell, who told me that Sister Georgina was crying like a baby and threatening to take her own life."

"How did she plan to do that?"

"She was going to put her head in the oven and turn on the gas."

"So what happened?"

"I gave in and decided to let her have Demerol."

"Oh, my God, Jim! You should never have given in to that kind of threat. You know as well as I do that she would never take her own life."

"Well, I was afraid of having a dead body on my hands."

I sighed deeply. "Now we're back at square one. What do you propose to do in the future?"

"I thought I'd try several different types of tranquilizers to eventually get her off this drug," he explained.

"But we've tried that before, Jim. It never works. One shot of Demerol will bring her back to the original habit, and she'll require more and more. You should never have given in," I repeated.

"What can I do?" He sounded desperate.

"I don't know. But I can tell you this, Jim. All our efforts in the past are down the drain."

In the middle of June 1976, there was a dinner meeting of concerned Marymount Hospital physicians held at West Valley Country Coub. After the dinner they asked Jim Kelly and me, "What's going on with Sister Georgina? She seldom comes to her office for daily business."

I looked the other way and said, "I don't know. I just work in the laboratory."

Tom Ford was especially inquisitive, trying to probe for something. I looked at Dr. Kelly, who said nothing. Everyone was perplexed.

In the early part of July, I was approached by a young medical oncologist at Metropolitan Hospital, Dr. Bob Henderson, who wanted to come to our hospital and take over West 5, the immunochemotherapy unit. I arranged a dinner meeting with Jim Wilkins to discuss Henderson's proposal. Several months before, Bob Henderson had told us that the chief administrator of Metropolitan Hospital, Donald Carter, had come to Central City and made him an offer to open a chemotherapy unit at his hospital, because he could not stand to see the progress being made at Marymount Hospital in terms of an immunochemotherapy project. Carter made all kinds of promises to Henderson, who said that he doubted Carter would fulfill them. Being disgusted

279

with Carter, Henderson wanted to leave Metropolitan Hospital and take over our unit. A detailed discussion of financial requirements and professional activities ensued between Henderson and Wilkins, with a promise by Henderson that he would pursue the matter. We did not hear from him again.

On the morning of August 17, 1976, I was called to see Sister Georgina in her office. She explained that a hard, painless mass had developed in her right submaxillary region, and she wanted to know what it could be. She further explained to me that approximately thirty years before she had received X-ray treatment for inflamed tonsils and adenoids instead of having surgery. I could feel a hard, movable mass, about the size of a quarter, in the right submaxillary region of her neck. "Sister, I think this is a tumor," I said. "Judging from the hard consistency and the nontender, movable character, I would surmise that it is a benign mixed tumor of the salivary gland. How long have you had it?"

"I just noticed it a couple of weeks ago," she replied.

I was puzzled by such a rapidly growing tumor mass, not typical of a mixed tumor, which was a slow-growing benign tumor arising mostly from the parotid gland. "Why don't we go to see Dr. Bob Young, at Lutheran Hospital? He has developed his own technique to visualize the vascular pattern of the tumor mass in the salivary glands."

The next day, after Dr. Young had taken an X ray and examined the film, he called me into his office. "Joe, I think she has a problem."

"What do you think she has? I thought this might be a mixed tumor."

"I don't think so. Because of the rich vascular pattern, it could be a malignant tumor. I think she has a very serious problem."

"Well, let's just keep it quiet for the time being," I said. "She's scheduled to see Dr. Peters this afternoon."

In the latter part of August 1976, Sister was operated on by Dr. Bob Peters, a new surgeon, who found a small but hard lymph node around the right submaxillary gland and asked for a frozen section diagnosis. Five minutes later I went back to the operating room and whispered to him, "Bob, this is a metastatic carcinoma in the lymph node."

"My God, Joe! Are you positive?"

"I'm certain that this is a malignant tumor. It appears to be a very anaplastic and rapidly growing tumor."

Dr. Peters then proceeded to do a total resection of the right sub-mandibular gland and right parotid gland, with the removal of all visible lymph nodes. The final examination revealed a fairly anaplastic and undifferentiated carcinoma involving the right submaxillary gland, with three positive lymph nodes containing metastatic tumor.

The news spread to the province within twenty-four hours. Two nuns flew to Midtown and came to see me the very next day. Srs. Pamela Collins and Mary McCormick sat in my office with grim faces. I explained to them the cell type of the tumor and its possible prognosis. I showed them a chapter in a fascicle published by the AFIP, describing the different types of cancer involving the salivary glands. I called their attention to a statement made by an AFIP staff member in regard to the prognosis of an undifferentiated carcinoma involving the submaxillary glands. Six patients with the same type of tumor all died six months after the diagnosis was made.

"Well, Doctor, this is a simple statement made by a few scientists," said Sr. Pam Collins in an uneasy tone of voice. "We'll make Sister's case an exception. We'll make this a miracle case in cancer medicine, and we will never accept that there is no hope. We shall pray twenty-four hours a day to make this case a miracle." She walked out of my office with indignation.

I recalled a similar statement made by a wealthy Midtown businessman and his wife when their seventeen-year-old son developed acute leukemia. A bone marrow aspiration study confirmed the diagnosis of acute myelogenous leukemia, and when they were told the possible prognosis of this disease they became adamant. "We will never accept the fact that this is a fatal disease. We will do our best to make him recover from the disease and live a normal life." They took their son to Memorial Hospital in New York City, and then to M. D. Anderson Hospital, in Houston. The boy died about six months later.

I truly wish that there were some miracles to save patients from dying of cancer. Many of the cancer victims I knew were the finest human beings I ever encountered in my life. But in my experience I have never observed any exceptional cases or miracles. Cold scientific data would not encourage us to depend upon miracles.

A week after my meeting with the two nuns from Salem, I was asked to explain to Srs. Karen Williams and Mary Quinn, also of the province, the final diagnosis and the possible prognosis for Sister Georgina's tumor. They asked me to take her to some nationally renowned cancer center specializing in tumors of the head and neck. I promised that I would look around and make the necessary arrangements. The head and neck tumor section of Roswell Park Memorial Hospital, in Buffalo, New York, had an excellent reputation as a leading institution in this country. In the middle of September, I made an appointment with Dr. Robert Shedd, director of the Head and Neck Tumor Section there, and we left Midtown for Buffalo two days later, accompanied by Pam Mitchell and Sr. Mary O'Banion.

I discussed the case with the pathologist, Dr. Bill Pickering. He had a nephew at the University of Arkansas Department of Pathology who was a junior state medical examiner for the state of Arkansas. After reminiscing for a few minutes, Dr. Pickering said that he agreed with our diagnosis of right submaxillary gland tumor. Examinations by Dr. Bob Shedd and his associates confirmed our approach, and they saw no evidence of spread beyond the submaxillary gland.

An associate pathologist, Dr. U. T. Kim, who had been two years behind me in medical school, was a well-known researcher in breast cancer. He told me about a recent case of a similar tumor in one of the institute's families. "Dr. Song, I understand that they are going to do a liver scan, but I doubt that it will show any positive signs. This kind of tumor does not spread to the liver. It is very invasive locally and involves the thyroid gland on both sides. This will spread to the other side of the submaxillary gland, and eventually she will be choked to death."

"I appreciate your candid opinion, Dr. Kim," I said, "but we are here to explore all the possible avenues to save this nun."

"I wish you luck, but don't count on it."

When we returned to Midtown, Sister Georgina went back to work, with daily injections of Demerol and morphine. I made no comment about that, as I thought it was a secondary problem.

When we returned to Midtown from Buffalo, with the recommendation that Sister Georgina receive radiation therapy, I approached Dr. Louis Mahon, a radiation therapist at Metropolitan Hospital. I took Sister Georgina to Dr. Mahon's basement office, and he greeted us warmly. "Sister, I always wanted to meet you, but not under these circumstances."

Louis Mahon was a very competent radiation therapist and one of the most sincere physicians I have ever met. With his optimistic manner, he made all of his patients feel as if they were more than patients. It was my good fortune to meet Dr. Mahon, who would remain a good friend for years to come.

In December of 1976, Sister Pamela arrived from Salem to take up her new duties as associate administrator and moved into Sister Georgina's office. Our maintenance crew created a new office for the

head administrator. Sister Pamela had at one time been the administrator of St. Mary's Hospital, a sixty-bed sister institution in Jones-
ville, a town 110 miles south of Midtown with a population of fifty-
five hundred. I had been covering St. Mary's Hospital on a weekly basis
for frozen sections, examining the surgical specimens, and attending
monthly staff meetings with the six physicians who represented the
total medical staff.

Early in March 1977, we discovered that Sister Georgina's cancer
had recurred, involving both lobes of the thyroid, the floor of the mouth,
and the salivary glands of the left neck, subsequently confirmed by
examination of a tissue presented by Dr. Bob Peters. He suggested to
her that since the tumor had spread to involve the other side of the
salivary glands, it meant a radical neck dissection, with removal of
half of the mandible and half of the tongue and total resection of the
thyroid and left salivary glands. He was willing to perform the operation, with a reasonable chance of eradicating the entire tumor. Sister
Georgina would not accept his proposal and insisted that we go back
to Roswell Park for their evaluation.

I recalled a conversation with Dr. Jim Kelly in January of 1976,
when he told me that he would not prescribe any more Demerol or
morphine for Sister Georgina. One month later I was discussing with
her our future plans for the residency program. Watching the traffic
on Popular Avenue, she suddenly turned to me. "Dr. Song, is there
anything else that can be removed from my body?"

"I beg your pardon, Sister," I said. "I don't understand your
question."

"I'm looking for additional surgery. Do you suggest they remove
my spleen?"

It took me some time to comprehend, but I finally understood what
she was driving at. "Sister, you need your spleen. There are several
case reports on patients who had splenectomy and came up with pneu-
mococcal septicemia. The spleen is an important organ to prevent a
fulminating infection caused by either pneumococcus or meningo-
coccus."

In the early part of March 1977, we again saw Dr. Bob Shedd, of
Roswell Park Memorial Hospital. After a thorough examination, Dr.
Shedd told us that there was extensive tumor spread involving the
base of the tongue, the floor of the mouth, the other side of the salivary
glands, and both lobes of the thyroid gland. There was only one way
to deal with the tumor spread, and that was a radical operation, removing half of the tongue and the right half of the jawbone and complete
resection of both salivary and thyroid glands.

Sister Georgina asked repeatedly if he would experiment on her to remove the bulk of the tumor but not disfigure her face. Dr. Shedd insisted, "That would not do the job. Either you go all the way or not at all."

Buffalo was practically buried by snow at this time. We flew out on the last flight to New York City, rerouted our flight to Columbus, Ohio, and Chicago, and finally arrived in Midtown. In a conference call to Dr. Shedd we again asked him about a debulking procedure without going into radical neck dissection. He insisted that even radical neck dissection, with removal of the tongue and jawbone, might not guarantee that the entire tumor would be removed. His suggestion was that we discuss the matter with Dr. Richard Davis, in Texas, who had done a great deal of radical surgery. Dr. Davis made it clear that he would not perform such halfway surgery.

A Midtown plastic surgeon, Dr. Jim Stone, had done several cases in the past, and he suggested that Sister Georgina and Sister Pamela pay a visit to his patient who had undergone similar extensive surgery. The patient was an elderly man who was severely disfigured and needed help with tube feeding and getting around his home. After she saw this patient, Sister Georgina refused to consider any further possibility of such surgery.

A medical oncologist at Roswell Park told me to give sister Georgina methotrexate and adriamycin. We increased the dosage of methotrexate to such a high level that she required renal function tests frequently to ensure normal kidney function. She was admitted as an inpatient because of rather extensive radiation and chemotherapy, and the tumor continued to grow. Her lymph drainage was obstructed by the rapidly spreading cancer. Her face became severely swollen in a short time, giving her a grotesque appearance.

At the Chicago symposium during March of 1977, I met Dr. Robert Donaldson, a medical oncologist from the VA hospital in St. Louis. He had an interesting theory regarding the use of chemotherapeutic agents and BCG vaccination. I paid him a visit in Saint Louis and explained the situation with our administrator. He said, "Joe, I hate to tell you this, but I have never seen any patient who has survived more than six months after the diagnosis of that kind of tumor."

A weekly examination of Sister Georgina's blood picture, however, remained normal. One morning when Dr. Kelly saw the report of the hemoglobin, hematocrit, white blood cells, and red cells, which were all normal, he exclaimed, "We've resurrected Sister!"

"Oh, Jim, don't be silly!" I said. "This hemogram doesn't mean a thing, and you know it."

The next day I was called to visit Sister Georgina in her room. she was visibly agitated. "You haven't been here for two days. I want you to know that I'm not dead yet. I'm so goddamn mad at God!"

I was not prepared for that kind of language. She died three days later at midnight and was buried at Waveland Cemetery. This confirmed the prognosis of that kind of tumor, given in the AFIP fascicle, indicating that no patient had ever survived more than six months after the diagnosis.

Sr. Pam Collins was installed as head administrator in May of 1977. My first meeting with her was in June, to review our educational programs, particularly the pathology residency. I explained to her that half of the nation's pathology residency programs were now disapproved because of the AMA's direction to retain only those at university hospitals. I gave her a brief historical background.

With the help of Dr. Richard Ellis we had decided to combine our program with that of Central University St. Joseph's Hospital in Salem. On March 1, 1976, I met the new chairman of the Pathology Department, Dr. Wayne Benson, at Chicago's O'Hare Airport when I went to visit Dr. William Bishop, AMA secretary of the Residency Review Committee of Pathology. This visit had been encouraged by my predecessor, Dr. Fred Thompson, who was convinced that only a combined and integrated program would survive for the next five years. Dr. William Bishop was impressed with the integration program, and he said that he would recommend approval. Our combined program was finally approved on March 31, effective July 1, 1976, with twelve resident physicians, eight at St. Joseph's Hospital and four at our hospital.

I called Dr. Thompson to express my sincere appreciation for his help and explained to him the detailed arrangements of the combined program. A monthly lecture would be given to our residents by an instructor from Central University St. Joseph's Hospital, while I would do the same for their residents on a monthly basis. One of our senior residents would be assigned to Central University St Joseph's Hospital for two years to complete his or her residency, and the arrangement was quite satisfactory to both parties.

In July 1977, Dr. Sam Brook, a medical oncologist from Sun City, arrived to take over the West 5 chemotherapy unit, with 161 patients enrolled.

During an October picnic at my West farm, held for department heads and key personnel, Sister Pamela announced that her management style was quite different from that of her predecessor. No one had any notion at that time what was coming in the administration of the hospital. In November an administrative team meeting was held, again at my farm cabin, with Dan Cannon, from Salem, acting as moderator.

"What did you accomplish after the all-day session?" I asked Jim Wilkins.

"Well, we justified the appointment of two more assistant administrators, Betty Roush and Caroline Cook."

"But you already have so many assistant administrators. Why do you need two more?"

"That's what Sister wants, and we just went along with it," was his explanation as he continued smoking his Salem cigarette.

I was told in January 1978 that I would be acting as medical director of the laboratory, while all the administrative matters would be handled by an administrative director. "This change is being made not only in the laboratory, Dr. Song, but in the X Ray and the Emergency Department as well."

I tried to explain to her that all administrative matters of the lab are based on medical problems. There would be no sharp distinction between administrative matters and medical problems.

"The decision is final," she said.

The name of the hospital was changed from Marymount Hospital to Marymount Hospital Medical Center, and the administrator's title was subsequently changed to President and Chief Executive Officer of the institution. Two associate administrators would have the title of senior vice president, whereas many assistant administrators are now called vice presidents.

Two of my associates remarked that it sounded very much like a big business corporation, not a health institution. I persuaded them to keep quiet and just go along with the changes.

In January 1979, my hastily prepared manuscript, *Circulating Cancer Cells*, with 270 pages and seventy-six black-and-white illustrations, was returned for the third time from the publishers, rejected because of lack of the latest information and references. It was devastating for me to accept such rejection, and I was deeply disappointed. According to Dr. Bob Wagner, editor of *Human Pathology*, although my manuscript was well written, I needed extensive studies and experiments to prove my point. In retrospect, it was a justified rejection. My subsequent investigation proved three years later that results described in the manuscript were incorrect. Again I was reminded that you can't win them all. But I was depressed for several months.

One of the thirty residents trained by us, Dr. Nguyen Mai Tai, from North Vietnam, was an outstanding physician. A 1974 graduate of the University of Saigon Medical School, he came to this country and secured a position as a pathology resident with us, which he held for three years. Dr. Mai was a hard worker, extremely polite and academic, with publication of two credible papers in national journals. During his assignment at St. Joseph's Hospital he gained a fantastic reputation as a most outstanding resident. Dr. Mai later changed from pathology to internal medicine and oncology and is now practicing in Massachusetts.

During lunch one day in March 1981, Dr. Albert Miller, a pediatrician, commented, "You know, these Oriental physicians are by and large hard workers, but they have such an inferiority complex that they wouldn't be able to answer questions."

"Al, let me tell you something about their inferiority complex," I responded. "It's not a complex per se, but it's the way they are educated during their long years of college and medical school. They are taught not to doubt the professor's decisions or his investigative results. In fact, we were told many, many times not to step on the shadow of our professors—you must always stay six steps behind. This education system was basically wrong, because even professors make mistakes, and quite often they are not correct in their scientific observations. I was marked as a troublemaker during the Korean War because I challenged my professors' decisions. In fact, I was kicked out of the Korean army because of my constant revolt against the system. Physicians from the Far East are carefully selected, possessing great pride and determination. This docile educational system must be changed, but it will take time.

"The second problem is the language barrier. They are hesitant to speak out because of the language difficulty and because of your tendency to laugh at them. The timid character may appear to you as a severe inferiority complex, but they read the journals and publish academic papers while you guys are having difficulty understanding the published articles." With that I walked out of the cafeteria.

In the early part of October 1979, I was approached by two of my good friends, Drs. Tom Ford and Don Swank, to run for presidency of the medical staff against Dr. Eli Peacock. The medical staff secretary, Katie Comito, also urged me to accept the nomination. I was told at the end of November that I had won the election to serve as president for 1980 and chief of staff in 1981.

The St. Joseph's Hospital chairman, Dr. Benson, resigned from the chairmanship of the Department of Pathology in January 1980 and left Salem to take a position at the University of Illinois Research Hospital, in Chicago. I predicted to our residents and the hospital administration that this would be the end of our residency program with St. Joseph's Hospital, and my hunch was correct. In July 1980, we received notice from the AMA canceling our integrated programs, both in Salem and in Midtown.

In April of 1980, three assistant professors from Central University, Drs. Dale Katz, Sam Lee, and Henry Chung, drove from Salem to Midtown and asked me to apply for the chairmanship at Central University St. Joseph's Hospital. That evening they left with a copy of my curriculum vitae, to be submitted to the search committee at Central University. On May 21, after serious consideration, I advised Dr. Louis Sanders, chairman of the search committee, that I would not be interested in the position. However, I recommended three other pathologists for his consideration.

37
Chief of Medical Staff

The president, or chief, of the medical staff, despite such an authoritative title, really has no power of a political or medical nature. His is a thankless job, similar to that of a public servant, with many headaches and very little reward for one's efforts. He is expected to coordinate the medical staff business and the hospital administration's desires. When a hospital-based physician, such as a pathologist or radiologist, becomes chief of staff, the position becomes more difficult. As a rule, pathologists and radiologists are under the thumb of the ruling administration, requiring a delicate balance between the medical staff's interests and the administration's wishes.

When I ran for presidency of the medical staff against a general practitioner who recognized such a precarious situation, I was surprised when he read this statement at a medical staff meeting: "Although Dr. Song is a capable man with reasonable administrative skill, he is still a hospital-based physician who would be unable to stand firm, protecting the physician's interests against the administration's. If I am elected, I will do my best to improve your patients' care and fight the administration to replace many obsolete instruments and equipment and, furthermore, gain more technical help." He campaigned vigorously, making phone calls, sending letters, and approaching members of the staff individually. They all assured him that they would vote for him.

When all the votes were counted, to his disappointment, he received only six votes. When he asked members of the staff, "Did you vote for me?" they replied, "Certainly I voted for you, because you would make a fine chief of staff."

"They're a bunch of damned liars!" he exclaimed. Then where did those votes go?

I have seen one or two physicians in the past who were elected to the presidency of the medical staff suddenly become arrogant, pounding the table and shouting at their colleagues—a sign of immaturity.

Toward the end of January 1981, a serious problem surfaced as the first test of my ability. Two members of the medical staff were found to be addicted to drugs, including alcohol. Pressure from the administration and the state medical examining board was so great that I had to confront the two with an article obtained from the medical board. According to this article, from the *American Medical News,* 14 percent of the nation's physicians were addicted to alcohol and/or other drugs. I was compelled to advise the two impaired physicians to seek professional help and treatment. In our private conversation I emphasized to one that this problem was universal and not unique to our medical staff members. The *State Medical Journal* cited the results of a University of Michigan research team. Of sixteen thousand high school students surveyed, 30 percent reported drug abuse of some sort within the previous thirty days. Everyone is vulnerable to this problem, and these doctors surely needed professional help.

One of the men broke into tears when I talked with him. "I see no future in my case, Joe. My wife left me, and they'll take my medical license away. I'm finished."

"They will only suspend your license," I assured him. "You need to go to a treatment center. I'm sure you'll be able to practice again soon. Think about your patients and your family."

At the end both doctors reluctantly went to a Minnesota institution for treatment. Six months later they were back practicing in Midtown.

The late Dr. Richard Ellis, who was a member of the state medical board, once told me that many physicians were in trouble, citing a large number who needed treatment. Dick had given me such a lift for my sinking morale when I came to this hospital in 1965. I was trying to keep my head above water, and he gave me many helpful suggestions.

Several months later I was confronted with another problem. Dr. Henry Peterson, a skilled surgeon, became intensely interested in abdominal lipectomy and intestinal bypass on obese patients, most of whom weighed more than two hundred pounds. The procedure required removal of a large portion of abdominal skin, with umbilicus, and a massive amount of fat, with intestinal bypass. All the nutrients are absorbed through the small intestine. Bypassing the small intestine (ileum) would add no additional weight to patients who were unable to control their appetite. A portion of jejunum was anastomosed to the large intestine, the main function of which is to secrete water and resecrete minerals back to the lumen, causing a tendency for the patients to have frequent diarrhea. Many of the patients who received this operation lost a significant amount of body weight and retained their normal metabolic rates. A few, however, died of sudden metabolic abnormalities brought on by the intestinal bypass operation.

Our pathology residents hated to handle the grotesque surgical specimens, consisting of a large segment of abdominal skin and a tremendous amount of fat, which reminded them of scenes in meat packing plants.

Dr. Peterson had been performing this procedure at three other hospitals until those institutions outlawed it as an illegitimate surgical operation. He found sanctuary at our hospital, insisting that his patients were unable to lose weight by conventional measures and that the procedures were being performed elsewhere as cosmetic surgery. However, continual criticism by his fellow physicians, who doubted the wisdom of such surgery, and questions concerning its effectiveness persisted for several years.

One of Peterson's patients, a thirty-seven-year-old woman, developed a serious complication following intestinal bypass. A large abscess containing a great quantity of pus formed in the pouch around the gallbladder. The administration seized this opportunity to stop the intestinal bypass operations, and I was ordered to call an emergency executive meeting. All the members unanimously condemned the surgery, and Henry Peterson was notified to discontinue immediately.

Infuriated by such action, Peterson sent his lawyer, Jim Larkin, to my office the very next day, demanding a hearing. I had to call a special executive session with the chiefs of all the branches of medicine and two additional general surgeons on July 22, 1981. Peterson's attorney brought a court stenographer, and our own legal counsel, Dr. Mike Renny, was present. Heated arguments ensued, and the meeting lasted from 7:00 P.M. until midnight. The end result upheld the previous decision reached at the special executive committee meeting.

A week later I received a certified letter from Jim Larkin requesting a final hearing with members of the board of directors of the hospital. Three lay members were absent, while seven nuns attended. Dr. Henry Peterson brought with him four belligerent patients who had each lost more than one hundred pounds following intestinal bypass and lipectomy. They praised Dr. Peterson's service to the community and to obese people. It was intimidating and provoking, but I was able to control my temper for two hours. One male witness addressed me angrily. "Hey, man, what are you trying to do to this wonderful doctor? Do you want to kick him out of the medical staff so poor people will have to suffer more? How can you call yourself a doctor if you have no concern and sympathy for little people?"

There was obscene language, and I was bombarded with silly questions from the four witnesses. Jim Larkin accused me of bypassing legal requirements in making such an arbitrary decision to stop his client's right to perform surgery. Our legal counsel argued successfully and brought the heated session to an end. The final decision by the board of directors was to uphold the previous conclusion to place a moratorium on lipectomy and intestinal bypass. I received several threatening phone calls from Dr. Peterson's patients and angry remarks from his lawyer, notifying me of his decision to appeal and willingness to go to the state supreme court. "You'll have multiple lawsuits on your hands in no time," was his final remark.

Some time later my young associate Dr. Harry Spencer was drinking coffee in my office. "This is your crowning achievement," he commented. "You should stay on for another year as chief of staff."

Exhaling deeply, I said, "You've got to be kidding, Harry. Who would want such a job for another year? Even one year is too long."

During the latter part of September we were extremely busy in the laboratory, with many tests to be performed and a large number of surgical pathology specimens to be examined. The nurse administrator of the hospital's professional review organization came to my office with a brochure describing an administrative meeting to be held in the early part of October. She stressed the importance of the chief of staff's attending the meeting, along with the administrative members. "The meeting will be held at the MGM Grand Hotel, in Reno, Nevada. Have you ever been there?" she asked.

"I have never been to either Reno or Las Vegas," I answered. "I have never been exposed to gambling and haven't had any particular desire to try it."

"You'll enjoy the games at the casino, and you should see Reno or Las Vegas at least once in your lifetime."

Prior to the trip, my friend and associate Dr. Henry Park advised me to take enough money to lose and give some to the nuns. "You're kidding," I said. "Nuns don't gamble."

"You may be surprised. I suggest that you take enough money."

Four of us, Srs. Pam Collins and Mary McCormick, Ann Deluka, and I, left for Reno. On the plane Sister Pamela was playing cards and tried to teach me how to play blackjack. "Sister," I protested, "I have never played this game in my life." The only gambling I had done was in Hot Springs, Arkansas, when my wife and I played a dime slot machine one night and lost thirty-five dollars.

"Well, I'll show you the basic rules for blackjack, and you'll catch on in no time," she assured me.

We checked into the MGM Grand Hotel, and it was indeed a grand hotel. I had never seen so many people gambling, day and night. There was an all-day meeting the next day, which I attended. The nuns disappeared from the meeting room and presumably spent all afternoon at the blackjack table. That evening we went to downtown Reno and saw the rows of gambling houses with their spectacular lights. As previously instructed by Dr. Park, I was very cautious in the blackjack games, and to my surprise, I won about forty-five dollars. In the meantime, the two nuns and Ann visited several gambling houses and lost heavily. When they arrived at my table, I gave all the chips to Sister Pamela, and they spent several hours playing the slot machines while I slept in my room.

While I was attending the morning meeting, I was paged and instructed to go to the nuns' room during coffee break. Sister Pamela was on the telephone, trying to make reservations at Caesar's Palace, in Las Vegas.

"Are we going to Las Vegas?" I asked in surprise.

"Yes, we are," she replied. "I want to take care of you because of your contributions to the institution for so many years."

When we arrived at Caesar's Palace, there were no vacancies except for one small corner room, which was given to me. It was noisy, and a thirty-mile-an-hour wind blew relentlessly throughout the night. I could not sleep a wink.

There was a serious problem awaiting me when I returned to Midtown. Two doctors of osteopathic medicine (D.O's) had applied to become members of the internal medicine section of our hospital. The general rule was that an osteopathic physician must have received AMA-approved residency training before he could submit his application to the medical staff office. The two osteopathic physicians had completed their internal medicine residency at osteopathic hospitals, so they were not eligible to become members of our staff. Problems dealing with osteopathic physicians were chronic; there had been a long-standing dispute between M.D.'s and D.O.'s.

The distinction between the MDs and DOs was marked, requiring approval of the county medical society when DO's requested consultation by MDs. Generally speaking, the issue was so confusing that I had never fully understood it. Having osteopathic medical schools created a unique malformation of the medical education system in this country, in my opinion. I have never heard of such a duplication in the medical profession in other countries. In my native country I remember seeing signs advertising osteopathic treatment for fractured bones and misplaced joints. Patients were treated by osteopathic technicians, not osteopathic physicians.

I was told that there were about one dozen osteopathic medical schools throughout the USA, producing hundreds of osteopathic physicians. My friend Dr. Ron Goodman, of Minneapolis, once said, "These guys ended up in osteopathic medical schools because they were rejected by medical school admission boards, so it's a second-class medical school."

"That may be true," I said, 'but I have found that some of the osteopaths are very good and well trained."

"Why do your medical people and the AMA let osteopathic physicians practice medicine and surgery with all the privileges reserved?" he asked.

"I don't know. They're allowed to practice at the osteopathic hospitals. But we have many osteopathic physicians on our medical staff. I believe they should be promoted to MDs after having taken so many courses and special training, and all the osteopathic medical schools should be absorbed by the university medical schools, as they are in California."

The administrator instructed me to admit the two osteopathic internists to the Department of Medicine. "Sister," I protested, "our bylaws indicate that they must receive residency training approved by the American Medical Association, and it is clearly stated that they are not eligible otherwise for membership at this hospital."

"That may be so, but I want them to join us in the Department of Medicine, and they are requesting a hearing with their lawyers attending."

The opinion of our medical legal counsel was that if they sued our hospital and medical staff, the court would grant them membership on the staff. "We might as well just accept them without going to court."

"I disagree with that, Mike. Bylaws are bylaws," I insisted. "Either we have regulation or we don't have it at all. Let's go to court. I'm sure I'm speaking for all the members of the internal medicine section and the medical staff."

At the end the osteopaths were admitted to the internal medicine section because of the administrator's desire. Four months later the board of directors officially approved their membership, opening a "can of worms." Unqualified osteopathic physicians who had no AMA-approved training began joining the medical staff every month like a flock of birds. It is true that some of them are good physicians, with excellent training, but they diluted the academic standard of this hospital, which was not much to begin with. By and large, osteopathic physicians are not academic, according to Ron Goodman.

Two days before Thanksgiving, in 1981, twenty-six nurses, pump technicians, therapists, anesthesiologists, cardiologists, and cardiac surgeons left the Midtown airport for Rome, Italy. As chief of the medical staff, I was briefly informed by the administration that they were sending a team of nurses, technologists, and surgeons to perform bypass surgery at the University of Rome Hospital. When these people arrived in Rome and took up residence in twenty-six units of an apartment complex, they learned that the physicians and administrators at the university hospital had no prior knowledge of their arrival.

My investigation revealed that in the summer of 1981 an Italian-American physician, sold a bill of goods to physicians and administrators at the hospital, stating that a large number of patients in Italy were on the waiting list to receive coronary bypass operations. The physicians' fees and the compensation for nurses and technicians would be paid by the Bank of America in Italy (BAI), and the bank was to be reimbursed by the Italian government. During successive meetings he painted such a glowing picture that everyone was euphoric, and several physicians asked if they could form a partnership arrangement in this venture. The hospital was to act as a general partner, and the physicians were to buy one or more units as limited partners. Each unit would cost $360,000, with the provision that the physicians were to be responsible for future financial needs. Several groups of physicians invested their pension money, and a few also bought a half-unit, costing $180,000. The equipment was to be leased through the BAI, and they were ready to perform the first coronary bypass. But University of Rome physicians were unaware of such a venture and refused to let them operate because of their lack of medical licenses to practice medicine in Italy.

A senior vice president of the hospital, Dick Dunn, proceeded to negotiate with officials of the Italian consulate in Chicago. He made numerous trips to Chicago, with piles of papers and documentation, in an attempt to substantiate their qualifications. In the meantime, our people were waiting patiently in their Rome apartments, and administrators and vice presidents were flying back and forth to Italy every week to try to solve the problems. I soon heard it said around the hospital that "they had better buy their own 707—it would cost them less."

The University of Rome Hospital Staff rejected the idea of having a group of people from America perform coronary bypass surgery, and the reception of the communist Italian government was also very cool. There were more than fifteen thousand unemployed physicians in Rome, and the government refused to even consider allowing people from the USA to perform the operations.

The planning director of the project, Ken White, was dismissed suddenly by the administration, and the nurse in charge was asked to carry on negotiations. When the equipment arrived, the Italian customs officers refused to hand it over to the nurse coordinator, Susan Drake, because Ken White was still listed as the receiver. Consequently, the twenty-six nurses and technicians had to wait, and many of them spent their time sightseeing in Europe.

They were dealing with the second medical school of the University of Rome and decided to remodel the operating rooms of St. Anna's Hospital, which cost them at least $1 million. Numerous negotiations took place, none of which was productive. Eventually, after one year, the hospital had to bring the twenty-six people back to Midtown, and most of them were able to regain their old jobs. All the money from the investors, including many physicians and some laypeople, was wasted. Several agonizing years passed, resulting in the hospital's loss of approximately $3 million—$1 million for the remodeling of St. Anna's operating rooms and $2 million for the equipment lease agreement.

The term *Roman fiasco* was used by the people of Midtown, and the hospital became a laughingstock. The BAI subsequently filed a lawsuit against the hospital, claiming $2 million for the equipment lease agreement, and the lawsuit was still pending. Six hearings were held in Midtown with the lawyers representing the BAI and the hospital. The BAI was subsequently sold to a West German bank, which continues to pursue the lawsuit against the hospital.

Entering the Walker Club for dinner with two out-of-town guests, I heard someone call out from a neighboring table, "Hey, Joe, how much have you lost in your Roman fiasco?" I turned to see two grinning physicians from Metropolitan Hospital and Lutheran Hospital. I intensely disliked the term *Roman fiasco* because of the hospital's many dedicated employees. The whole venture should have been carefully planned and checked and double-checked before so many people were sent overseas for nothing.

I was talking with my administrative director, Dick Paul, one day. He said, "In spite of the Roman fiasco loss, the hospital's net profit was still 6 million dollars for the year."

"What are they going to do with such a profit?" I asked.

"They should take care of their little people here," he answered.

"Dick, I think the prudent thing to do to contain the rising cost of medical care here would be to reduce the room rates and the lab and X-ray fees. Why don't you suggest that at the team meeting?"

"I might do that," he said. "But this whole thing was motivated by greed, not by humanitarian endeavors."

A few days later Dick told me that when he suggested reducing the room rates, he was immediately silenced.

In April of 1982 the hospital's board of directors upheld the decision by the executive committee to suspend abdominal lipectomy and intestinal bypass surgical procedures. Members of the executive committee and an ad hoc committee worked hard to put a moratorium on these procedures, which I thought was the end of the matter.

During the early part of January 1983, I received a telephone call from Dr. Ken Miller, chairman of the institutional review committee. The major functions of this committee were to review all the research protocols submitted by the medical staff, investigate in depth the new surgical and medical procedures that were still in the investigational stage, and approve or disapprove the use of investigational drugs.

Dr. Miller said, "Dr. Song, I was asked to call a special meeting for noon today to discuss the resurrection of the intestinal bypass."

"You must be joking. We went through several hearings, not too long ago, to conclude that issue and suspend the procedure."

"I know that. But I was ordered to call a special meeting to discuss a protocol submitted by Drs. Oliver Pratt and Tony Johnson."

"What to they want you to discuss?" I asked.

"They want to perform a modified version of intestinal bypass, called biliopancreatic bypass, on their patients with morbid obesity."

"Tell me more about the procedure."

"Well," he went on, 'it consists of resection of the stomach and division of the small intestine at two meters from the ileocecal valve, which would create a selective malabsorption of fats and starches. It's a nonreversible procedure, due to the gastric resection, and a very delicate operation!"

"This is a modified version, but it's still an intestinal bypass. I don't think it makes sense, Dr. Miller. Why don't you come to the meeting and try to talk them out of it?"

Heated arguments ensued at the special meeting, and I spent approximately half an hour emphasizing that approval would defeat our purposes in suspending these procedures. "You people must remember the difficult time we had in dealing with legal hearings and lawsuit threats in 1981."

"I know that, Joe," remarked Tony Johnson, "but this is a modified bypass, which would create tremendous results for obese patients."

"Your point is well taken, Tony, but this is still intestinal bypass. You're trying to drive backward, which doesn't make any sense at all."

Despite my vigorous opposition, the committee approved the bilio-pancreatic bypass procedure. Later I was told by Helen Gregory, of the utilization review committee, that an order came from the top requesting the members of that committee pass the proposed procedure without further delay.

The surgeons performed the procedure on seven patients. One died of pneumonia following respiratory distress syndrome, which was unresponsive to the most aggressive treatment. The distress was brought on by an excessive amount of abdominal surgery. Finally the procedure was discontinued in June of 1984.

During the battle I consulted two past presidents of the medical staff, Dr. James King and Dr. Don Baker. Both men were deeply perplexed by the administration's decision. A few days later Jim called me and said, "Joe, this is a medical decision. She is not supposed to make such decisions without consulting members of the medical panel or getting advice from the board and the medical staff. What motivated the administration to make such a medical decision?"

"I don't know, Jim. I can't understand their reasoning. I was hoping you could find out the background of their reaching such a drastic decision against the previous ruling."

Another comment by Dr. King was also interesting. "It's historically true that you can perform any operation at your hospital and get away with it, regardless of the outcome of the surgery."

"That may be true," I said, "but those days are gone, as you know."

Several days later I was visited by three indignant cardiologists, Drs. Bob Keaton, Charles Condon, and Abdul Hussain. "Gentlemen, please sit down and tell me what I can do for you," I said.

"We wish to appear at the next executive committee meeting to present our view on who can perform PTCA and who cannot." PTCA (percutaneous coronary angioplasty) was a new procedure, which opened up a coronary artery by the insertion of a metallic instrument or a balloon into the obstructed area.

"What seems to be the problem?" I asked.

"A cardiologist from another group told us that we can't perform the procedure because we lack training."

"Is he trained for that procedure?"

"He went to Switzerland and spent a couple of weeks with a physician who invented this procedure, and he keeps saying that we're excluded because of lack of training."

"Can you people receive training from the same physician or take any workshop elsewhere to learn how to perform it?"

"That's the reason we're here, Dr. Song. We wish to express our dismay at the exclusion of our group, but we have already been attending seminars and meetings to familiarize ourselves with the procedure."

At the next executive committee meeting, a cardiologist and three other physicians of different cardiology groups appeared and presented their views. After five minutes I interrupted. "Gentlemen, I believe this is a problem that you people should get together on and solve by the give-and-take principle. I think you can resolve this without taking the committee's time. If you should need a mediator, I'll be more than happy to serve in that capacity, but I'm positive that you can find some compromise." Six days later the matter was settled to everyone's satisfaction. Many problems presented to the committee were based on economic gain rather than improvement of patient care.

The state bureau of criminal investigation set up a meeting with Bob Reed and me. Mr. Reed had many photographs depicting child abuse reported in the state. Five days prior to this meeting, we had performed an autopsy on a handsome blond six-year-old boy. He had been beaten by his stepfather, who had stepped on the boy's abdomen, causing rupture of the liver. Many cigarette burns were clearly visible on the boy's back, and it was a disgusting case to perform and certify.

Mr. Reed explained to me that every year more than a million children in the United States were abused severely by their parents, guardians, or others, and between two and five thousand children died as a result of their injuries.

"Mr. Reed, I don't know what to say to you, nor do I know of any way to prevent this kind of abuse," I said. "All we can do is make people aware that this is going on."

"Doctor, do you have such an epidemic of child abuse in your native country?" he questioned.

"I can't say that I have seen any cases of child abuse there," I replied, "but I'm certain that a lesser degree of child abuse exists in other parts of the world."

I do not regret choosing pathology as my career, and I would probably take training in pathology if I were to begin again. The only time I curse myself for being in this branch of medicine is when I am called in, always at midnight or early in the morning, to examine a female

299

child to certify sexual abuse. I have examined many female children who were brought to the emergency room by the police or the rescue squad. Each time it sickens me to see the indescribable trauma to the genital area caused by a violent attack by a male guardian or sibling, even the father.

According to the *State Medical Society Journal,* sexual abuse of children is a silent epidemic, a situation frequently hidden from the treating physicians. It is mind-boggling to responsible adults. Society is just now beginning to come to grips with the problem and its excruciating dimensions: How and why does it occur? How can it be dealt with? How can it be prevented?

Despite various studies, the actual incidence of child sexual abuse is not fully known, according to this article. The Department of Human Services reports that one in four females will be sexually abused by age eighteen. One of ten boys will be similarly mistreated by age eighteen. The state child protective services estimates that possibly one of seven boys are unknown victims because of the reporting taboo on the part of the victim, parent, or health provider. Experts estimate that up to 250,000 cases of intrafamily sexual abuse occur annually in the USA. Another estimated 250,000 cases of child abuse and extrafamily abuse occur annually, considering that only 30 percent of the cases are reported. Cantwell reports the incidence of 1:1000 total population. Kahn and Sexton report this age distribution: 53 percent under six years; 29 percent, six to nine years; and 18 percent, ten to twelve years. DeYoung and others report that 14 percent of the sexual assault victims in their study were males under eighteen. Statistics from the state department of human services show 106,000 child abuse cases reported from 1979 to 1983, with 21,415 substantiated.

Is this a problem unique to this country? I do not believe so. Are we dealing with beasts or sadistic animals? I have no answer to those questions, nor do I have any constructive measures for preventing the occurrence of sexual abuse of children. I believe this is a worldwide problem that we must face eventually.

A survey by a University of Northern Iowa (UNI) researcher showed that one in five students on campus, men and women, have been involved in incestuous relations, causing intense pain for some but satisfaction for others. A clinical counselor on the UNI campus said that he was not surprised to find such a high percentage of abuse in families with college-bound students and that the rate was likely to be comparable elsewhere. "I don't think any religious, race, or economic background offers any protection against this abuse. It cuts across all lines," he commented. "I thought that there might be a greater incidence of abuse among religious fundamentalists, since they tend to be more isolated, with more rigid value systems that don't allow them to have sexual expression, but I didn't find that to be true." *Incest* was defined as "sexual relations between persons so clearly related that their marriage would be illegal," or sexual relations involving a parental figure who was not necessarily related.

I always intensely disliked responding to a call from the emergency room to certify a case of rape. But when it was a case of sexual abuse of a child, I really hated my own profession.

On April 16, 1982, my mother passed away after a lengthy illness, at the age of eighty-five. She had a stroke in 1977 and had been bedridden ever since. She was indeed an extraordinary person, one of the greatest human beings who ever lived, in my opinion. Rev. Hume Ward, of Westside Presbyterian Church, officiated at the funeral ceremony. She was buried at Resthaven Cemetery, although her wish was to be buried in Seoul, Korea, next to my father, who had died in 1965, at the age of sixty-five. She would be missed by many at Westside Church. Reverend Ward gave the following tribute to her in one of his messages:

> The Minute for Missions reminds us of the way we are ministered to by those from other lands. There was a delightful little lady from Korea named Mrs. Wha Soon Koh, who was Dr. Joe Song's mother. Her life is much like one of the journeys of Paul, but it spanned far greater distances. Born in what we now call North Korea, she crossed the thirty-eighth parallel in 1946 with her son, Joe, who went to South Korea for medical school. Then in 1960, after living through the Korean War, she came to this country . . . to make her home. Everywhere she went, she carried with her the sturdy Christian faith in which she was raised.
>
> Mrs. Koh would often be in church here at Westside. She spoke a lot more English than I speak Korean, but her son or daughter-in-law would often come to the church with her on Friday or Saturday to get a church bulletin, so that she would have a better understanding of what was happening in the worship service.
>
> One day she asked her son why they didn't have Bibles in the pew racks at Westside. She said, "Joe, you ought to get Bibles for the church." Drs. Joe and Kumsan bought 250 pew Bibles, which we use today. So from far-off Korea we have been ministered to by those who walked in faith without fainting. And Mrs. Koh, though physically dead, speaks, in a way, each Sunday when we turn to our pew Bibles.

38
Extra Session

Daniel S. Longo, M.D., director of medical education at Marymount Hospital, was an honest physician. He had retired from the VA hospital as chief of surgery years before and went into private practice in Fort Denny before accepting his current position. His secretary asked me to come down to his office.

"Joe, I have some important matters to discuss with you." He told me that our administrator, Sister Pamela, was planning to set up a rotating internship to train osteopathic physicians graduating from the College of Osteopathic Medicine and Surgery (COMS).

My immediate reaction was surprised and dismay. "What for? What do we get out of this internship?"

"Nothing I can hope for, Joe," Dan replied with a sigh.

"You mean to tell me that she made such an important medical decision against your advice?" I probed further.

"It looks that way. I tried to persuade her not to make such a decision without consulting the physicians."

Several days later I was called to see Sister Pamela in her office. As soon as I sat down, she demanded, "I need your support in this internship for D.O.'s for the community."

"May I ask why this internship is so important to this community?"

"As you well know, Dr. Song, the COMS is here to stay, and they provide more physicians for family practice in small towns and communities. If we train them well, so much the better for rural health care. Don't you agree?"

"Well, that may be true and has considerable merit," I conceded. "But it will also give the impression that you're turning this institution into an osteopathic hospital, requiring many unqualified D.O.'s from COMS to teach the interns. As you may know, your predecessor once tried to do the same thing."

"I didn't know that." She was surprised. "What happened to her programs?"

We had to be approved by the AOA [American Osteopathic Association] to have a D.O. teaching program. Two D.O.'s and an administrator from the Cleveland osteopathic hospital came to inspect our hospital, and their main purpose was to find more deficiencies in our institution than in osteopathic hospitals."

"What was the outcome of their inspection?"

"All the M.D.'s were thoroughly disgusted with their inspection and reached the conclusion that it was demeaning to pass their osteopathic inspection. We withdrew our application even before they completed their inspection, and that was the end of it." I gave her a complete rundown.

"Nevertheless, I'm determined to set up this program for D.O.'s." She was adamant.

"I think it would be well for you to ask each section to respond to your proposal. After all, the members of our medical staff will have to get involved. It's the only prudent thing to do," I said.

A pained expression came over her face.

Dr. Longo notified me, two weeks later, that all the sections of the medical staff had rejected her idea, with the recommendation that she should approach the university school of medicine. During the medical staff meeting I mentioned to several members of the staff that we should give her credit for her previous efforts to become affiliated with Central University Medical School. She had approached Dean Joe Hoffman, of Central Medical School a year before. Dean Hoffman brought Dr. George Gillman, chairman of the internal medicine department, and Dr. Claude Oyan, of the Surgery Department, to inspect our facilities. Both physicians were very cold, to begin with, and when they learned about the lack of a sufficient number of board-certified internists and surgeons, they flew back to Salem. They also cited that we had too many D.O.'s who were not trained in AMA-approved programs. Again and again we were reminded of our deficiency in not having enough qualified physicians for teaching.

Several weeks later I was told by Debbie Swanson, a secretary in Administration, that I had to attend an important team meeting at 2:00 P.M. on that day. "Debbie, we're shorthanded today, and I must read all the surgical slides to render a diagnosis on the specimens we received yesterday. Could I send my administrative director to attend the meeting?" I asked. I explained to Debbie that all the diagnoses had to be made before 3:00 P.M. so that patients with benign diseases could be discharged from the hospital.

303

"You must attend the meeting, along with your administrative director," Debbie insisted.

When I arrived at the meeting, twenty-five people, including all the department heads, a radiologist, and several secretaries, were already there. Five minutes later four people walked in, with various charts, and began emphasizing how important it was to have our own condominiums in the Denver area to secure two weeks of vacation for our families. "You can rent them out through our management team for the rest of the year when the condo is not used by you and your family," a young saleswoman stated.

We looked at one another, perplexed.

"You must have your own place to relax for two weeks instead of having an Einstein vacation!"

"Einstein vacation? What is that? I've never heard of that before," commented a radiologist.

"An Einstein vacation is a visit to your relatives as a vacation. You know, his relativity theory!" a salesman explained jokingly.

I left the meeting, as I had to complete my work before 3:00 P.M. A head nurse on North 5 later told me that I was criticized for leaving before the completion of the presentation.

"Jill, you know as well as I do that patients come first in this hospital. Doesn't the patient's life mean anything to you? Whose idea was that, to waste an hour listening to those salespeople?" I asked.

"A sister of our administrator, Mrs. Carolyn Murphy, runs a construction company that builds and sells condos in Colorado. You should have bought at least two units," she said sarcastically and laughed.

39
Trip to South Africa

On March 2, 1985, members of the U.S. cancer research delegation, consisting of fourteen physicians and Ph.D.'s who were engaged in cancer research, and two laypeople, left the John F. Kennedy Airport for Johannesburg, South Africa. This delegation was organized by the People to People International organization and Dr. Rolf Barth, a research pathologist at Ohio State University. On the plane I went over my notes, containing a brief history of South Africa, given us by Daan Fourie, a representative of the South African consulate in New York City.

White settlement began in 1652 with the development of a supply base in Cape Town by the Dutch East India Company. The British conquered the Cape Colony in 1806. Dutch people from the Cape Colony founded republics in the Transvaal and the Orange Free State. As a result of the Boer War (1899–1902), Britain conquered the Afrikaner republics, and in 1910 the Union of South Africa was founded, formed as a white-controlled British dominion. Politically, the Nationalist Party has held power since 1948 and has progressively taken power from the nonwhite population until the promulgation of a new constitution in 1984, which set up legislative assemblies for the Indian and colored (white and black mixed) populations.

On March 4 we visited the site of the first gold strike by an American, George Harrison from New Jersey, and then made a stop at an African medicinal shop in the middle of the city of Johannesburg. Dr. K. M. Naidos, proprietor of the shop, offered herbs, bones, and animal skins to "cure" any ailment. We were perplexed by his explanation of "voodoo" medicine and by the large shop in the middle of downtown Johannesburg.

A visit to the Johannesburg Hospital, a clean 2,000-bed institution, was in sharp contrast to the medicinal shop we had visited two hours previously. Although this enormous teaching hospital served a total population of 5 million people, half of its 2,000 beds were empty.

305

We were told by the administrator that because of the constitution, they had to turn black patients over to Baragwanath Hospital, a 3,000-bed hospital for blacks in Soweto, a southwestern township with a population of approximately 1 million.

As in many other countries, the major cancers in the white population of South Africa were (1) lung, (2) breast, and (3) head and neck. There was very little oncology (chemotherapy for cancer patients) practiced by private physicians; most were referred to Witwatersrand University Hospital, where the staff was overworked and had little time for clinical research. Chemotherapy programs at Pretoria University Hospital were still in the developmental stage, as I saw it, demonstrating only one young boy with Hodgkin's disease.

I was struck with the extremely high incidence of hepatoma (liver cancer) among black South Africans. The same worldwide distribution of the hepatoma virus (HBsAg) has been found in 11 percent of blacks and only 0.16 percent of the white population. In the patient population all blacks displayed the serum HBsAg antibody, causing very high incidence of liver cancer.

Our tour guide told us that blacks prefer their witch doctors to modern physicians. It takes six years of training to become a qualified witch doctor. They use contaminated or unclean knives to drain wounds, make skin incisions, and perform circumcision on growing boys. Perhaps this kind of surgery, with rusty and unclean instruments, had created such a prevalence of the virus infection causing hepatoma. In South Africa hepatoma requires fifteen years to develop following the initial viral infection.

We learned that there were seven major black tribes and fifty-two subtribes in South Africa, each tribe having its own language and culture. According to our guide, Inger Hamilton, Zulu men were legally allowed to have five wives, but most of them had six or seven, or maybe more, with an average of between twenty and thirty children. A man's wealth was measured by the number of children he had. This was abundantly clear when we visited Baragwanath Hospital. More than fifty young black women, mostly teenagers expecting a third or fourth child, were waiting at the obstetrical outpatient clinic. Each patient was required to pay a nominal fee, ranging from 8 to 15 rand ($4.00 to $7.50) for all the obstetrical care. Population control was indeed difficult, yet it was an urgent problem for the South African government.

During the scientific session at the South African Research Council, I learned that South African blacks had a 50 percent higher incidence of cancer of the uterine cervix than women in the United States.

306

All patients with Stages III and IV cancer (spread outside the uterus) were treated with radical surgery and radiation therapy. Dr. Leiman, a cytopathologist, told us that twenty five thousand black women were screened annually by the Pap smear method. I commented to her that they should screen at least seventy thousand or more women annually to control uterine cervical deaths, and it would be cheaper for the South African government to treat patients by early cancer detection than with surgery and radiation therapy.

Dr. Leiman said, "I agree with you completely, but the South African government is reducing the number of cytotechnologists and the budget every year."

Professor Metz, director of the Research Council, agreed with Dr. Leiman, saying, "There is no long-range planning in the health field by the South African government. Dr. Leiman used to have sixteen cytotechnologists. She now has only seven. It's impossible for us to screen more than twenty-five thousand women annually."

We also learned that the high incidence of cancer of the esophagus was a basic problem in another tribe, while the Zulu tribe's main problem was coping with liver cancer. The tendency to drink more home-brewed beer, which allegedly has a high iron content, might be responsible for inducing such a high incidence of esophageal cancer.

In Umtata we were told that although the Republic of Transkei was supposed to be a self-sufficient state, the people depended on a yearly grant of 3 to 10 million rand from the central South African Government.

A general surgeon at the Baragwanath Hospital remarked during our luncheon break, "You may not know that 5 million white people are feeding 22 million blacks and 3.5 million colored and this is a heavy burden on the South African government. In this hospital compound," he continued, "we find two to three thousand people every year who are murdered by their fellow blacks, mostly stabbed to death. American blacks use handguns to kill, but here they use a sharp knife."

He was the only physician in South Africa who carried a German pistol in his waistband. "When I pull this pistol," he told us, "I mean to shoot and kill any blacks. We produce everything here in South Africa. We don't need any U.S. help, nor do we need trade with any Western countries who are critical of our government. We really don't care what they say about us. But I want you to keep in mind that we have a heavy burden to feed 25 million blacks and colored."

We visited the University of Medunsa, a South African black medical school admitting students not only from South Africa, but also from

307

Kenya, Zambabwe, and Sudan. The dental school was under construction at the time of our visit. After a lecture we asked several black students if they would seek medical advice from well-trained Western doctors or go to witch doctors. To our surprise, all of them said they would prefer to go to the witch doctors first and then try Western medicine if the witch doctors failed to heal them. We again felt the heavy burden of the South African government.

I enjoyed an hour-long conversation with Dr. Hans Keller, a West German pathologist who was head of the pathology department at the University of Medunsa. His major problem was lack of help at the senior and junior pathology staff and technologist level. He formerly had five cytotechnologists and a number of qualified medical technologists, but because of the reduction of the budget, his technical staff had been cut in half. He was overworked with teaching duties and service pathology and asked me if I would be willing to come over for a period of one year. "I'm sure we could pay you 65,000 rand and an automobile allowance if you would come and spend a year here."

Dr. Rolf Barth, overhearing the conversation, said, "How about it, Joe? You can help them out."

"Well, I have a moral obligation to help my own country and my own people," I explained. "If I could take one year off, I would be heading for Seoul, Korea. But I think I can send you some teaching material, Dr. Keller, in both cytotechnology and general medical fields. We have three excellent cytotechnologists and close to a hundred first-class medical technologists in my institution. But I doubt that any of them would be willing to come over here for a year to help you." I cited the names of some fine technologists who had made contributions to their own fields in Midtown.

On the bus from Skukuda Airport to Kruger National Park, we saw baboons and kudu. The ride over dirt roads was uncomfortable because of the hard seats. The temperature was warm, and we retired to the veranda at Mala Mala Resort for a cool drink. As we sat facing a small stream, two elephants came for water. Early on Sunday morning we rode around the reserve in a Landrover to see the wildlife.

After two days of rest we flew to Durban. King Edward III Hospital, in that city, was a 3,700-bed institution that had been established in 1935. It was a teaching hospital for the University of Natal Medical School, which admits a large number of Indian and black students. The superintendent, a Greek physician, gave a summary of the activities of the hospital, which receives patients with all kinds of diseases, from typhoid to cholera to psychiatric problems. After a brief discussion of their big problem, viral hepatitis in epidemic proportions, he said to me, "I understand you speak Russian."

"I know a few Russian words. Why do you ask?"

"I spent some time in Russia during World War II," he replied.

"Oh, how interesting! How did you end up here in Durban?"

"Well, that's a long story. Let's hope we can get together later." Then he walked off with the other delegates.

During lunch break I was approached by an Indian physician, Dr. K. Rao, who was born in Durban and finished his schooling at the University of Natal Medical School. He told me that they had a copy of my sickle-cell book in their library. "How did you find time to undertake such a project? Did you have much help from your residents or associates?"

"As a matter of fact, I didn't even ask them to help me with the book. However, I must say we had a very efficient librarian who gathered all the necessary information."

Treatment at the King Edward III Hospital was free to everybody, and the patient most likely to accept the treatment was the black (Zulu) from the rural areas. However, the problem of transportation prevented follow-up, and many patients simply did not return to the hospital. The oncology section served 6 million people of the province of Natal and offered all forms of treatment, including radiation therapy. King Edward III Hospital handled forty thousand deliveries a year. With wealth indicated by the number of wives, it must be very difficult to control the birthrate, and the population was increasing by gigantic proportions.

On March 13 we visited Kwa Mashu Township, made up of five hundred thousand Zulu people. The housing units normally had four rooms with brick walls and tile roofs. To show ancestral respect, the people placed animal horns on the roof. It was obvious that there was a lack of care of the rental units.

The main industries in the province of Natal centered around sugarcane and tea. To harvest sugarcane, the South African government had imported three hundred thousand Indians on contract for a five-year period, and many of them settled in the Durban area. Approximately 1 million Indians were residing in the province of Natal around Durban. Many of them were wealthy businessmen and merchants. Our guide took us to a Durban shopping center, where all of the shops were run by Indians. Some of them were living in large mansions.

Judy, our tour guide, told us that when a Zulu man spots a girl whom he would like for his sixth or seventh wife, he goes to her father to negotiate in terms of the number of cattle he will have to give for her. If a girl is heavyset and able to do hard work, she will cost seven or eight cattle. If on the other hand, the girl is slim, he may give only three cattle for her. Judy, a slender white woman, was once the object of an offer of half a cow. When she protested with indignation to her husband, he said, "Judy, take the offer! After all, one half-cow is better than nothing!"

The famous Mahatma Gandhi once lived in Durban, and his house was preserved by the Indians as a historical site. The house was burned to the ground by an angry black mob during a recent race riot because of their resentment toward the wealthy and successful Indian merchants.

We made a short stop at Butterworth Hospital, in the Republic of Transkei, a black national homeland and an independent nation in South Africa since 1976. The facilities and sanitary conditions of Butterworth Hospital were less than satisfactory. There were a large number of male patients with terminal esophageal cancer. One of them was in his third year of witch doctor training, and his body was heavily painted. We were told later that 70 percent of the Transkei budget was provided by the South African government, and the soil erosion of the Transkei republic was appalling.

Our visit to the University of Transkei, in Umtata, was not worthwhile. The buildings were beautiful, but the equipment within each college was generally obsolete, and the quality of the students was not impressive. We took a scenic bus trip down to Cape Town along the Garden State Highway, enjoying the views of the South African west coast. We switched buses at Port Elizabeth, a coastal town, on March 16, when the South African police killed three black demonstrators.

At Cape Town our delegation visited the National Accelerator Center. They were building a huge neutron facility to treat patients with head and neck cancer. It was being shared by physicists and clinicians, and the radiation therapy involved an isocentric beam capability for cancer patients.

Dr. Ralph Kirch and his wife, Beverly, were very kind to invite us for dinner at their home. Dr. Louis Morgan, of New York City, and I attended, along with three South African physicians and their wives. I mentioned that the research papers presented at the Cape Town Research Council meeting that afternoon were generally good and we were impressed with the quality of cancer research. I asked them if they had a national tumor registry in South Africa. When they said no, I emphasized the necessity of having such a registry and spoke proudly of our tumor registry, which was built up by Mary Johnson.

They asked if she would be willing to come over there to help them in setting up a national tumor registry. "I doubt it," I said, "but maybe you can send someone to Midtown for training."

There was a heated political discussion after dinner, touching on Bishop Desmond Tutu's press conference in Johannesburg, in which he declared that the apartheid policy of the South African government had to be abolished in thirteen months or there would be a bloody revolution. His emotional announcement reminded me of the decision reached by the representative of England, the United States, and the Soviet Union in December 1945 in regard to the postwar treatment of the Korean peninsula. Their decision was to have a five-year trusteeship for the Korean people, to train the additional engineers, government officials, and scientists needed for independence. It became an emotional issue overnight, and thousands of people demonstrated against the decision reached in Moscow. I was one of thousands demonstrating in the streets, shouting, "After thirty-six years of Japanese occupation, we're sick and tired of any kind of trusteeship! We want our independence now! Independence or death!" The fact of the matter was that not enough Koreans were trained to take over the government, heavy industry, and the educational system. It was logical for the negotiators to reach that agreement, since there were very few people qualified to govern our own country. If we had accepted their decision to put in a trusteeship for five years, we could have avoided a bloody war throughout the Korean peninsula and it was not impossible to hope for a peaceful establishment of an independent nation.

I suggested to my South African friends that the slave system and colonialism were dead. They should have a long-range plan to integrate their society by training more blacks in all segments of South African society. To do that they should seek a dialogue on both sides, not make excuses, saying, "We really don't know who is representing what tribes." I said to them, "I really hope you people will seek a dialogue between the two races and make a workable long-range plan." It was the most significant evening, as far I was concerned, of the whole three-week trip to South Africa.

On our way back to New York, as I was going over my notes on the trip, one of our party, Dr. Roy Smith, of Cleveland, came to me and asked, "Joe, did you enjoy your China visit, in 1983, more than your visit to South Africa?"

"It was a wonderful trip, Roy. I think you should go to Mainland China for a visit. You should see the Great Wall, the Ming tomb, and the Forbidden City, the emperor's residence. And try to understand the depth of their culture."

311

"Did you present any papers during your visit to China?" he asked.

"I presented a paper regarding cervical cancer detection at the Nanking University Hospital. About three hundred people attended. I also visited the pathology lab, reviewing several cases with three women pathologists who were very good but were hindered by lack of books, modern instruments, and microscopes. I sent some books to the Nanking University Hospital and a large number of Kodachrome slides illustrating lesions of various kinds of tumors."

"Did they receive your help with grace?" Roy questioned.

"I have never heard from them since I shipped the books and slides, but I hope they received them and put them to good use. I believe they are afraid to send me a letter of acknowledgment or thanks unless the government urges them to do so. But I think you should go over there and try to help them."

On the evening of March 26, when I returned to Midtown, I called Jim Wilkins and asked him if he had received the postcards I sent him from South Africa.

"I did receive them and enjoyed them," he said, "but I've been anxiously waiting to talk to you when you got back from your trip."

"What's going on, Jim?" I asked.

"I'm being forced to resign from the hospital."

"Forced to resign? I don't understand."

"I'd rather talk to you in person," he replied, and I told him to meet me at the Diner's Club on March 29 for dinner.

In the meantime I asked my associates if they had heard about Jim's dismissal. They said, "Yes, we heard through the grapevine that he was forced to resign. That makes the thirteenth vice president fired by Sister Pamela."

At dinner I remarked to Jim, "I wasn't aware that you were on Sister Pamela's famous hit list."

"Well, Joe, to tell you the truth, I didn't know it either."

"Give me a complete rundown since I left for South Africa." I was eager to learn the details.

According to Jim, a group of clinic physicians, mostly osteopaths, and an administrator, took a trip to Mexico City for a few days. During that trip the administrator rounded up enough support to present a case to Sister Pamela that Jim Wilkins was a major obstacle to the future progress of the clinics and the clinic physicians.

"Did she agree to that?" I asked.

"Apparently she bought that story. Three times in ten days she told me to move to another office and take up a different assignment."

"My God! They must be crazy! You're the brains of the whole institution. How could she change her mind so often in such a short time?"

"She told me to think it over for two weeks. But the very next day she stuck her head in my office and told me that she needed to know my decision that very day. I was so mad that I left my office before 11:00 A.M."

I could not believe my ears when Jim presented his story regarding his pending dismissal. He had done a great deal for the hospital, saving them millions of dollars, and this is the way he was paid for his decision.

"Jim, why such a sudden change of atmosphere in administration? Have you done something wrong?"

"Well, Joe, perhaps I did upset Sister Pamela because I didn't support her Rome heart project. I was skeptical from the beginning, and I didn't hide my feelings. It was too good to swallow."

"My associate told me that you are the thirteenth vice president fired by Sister Pamela in a short time," I said.

"That's right. She never gives anyone the benefit of the doubt. When a vice president makes a trivial mistake, she cuts off his head. You remember Sidney Kent, a vice president who was hired and fired six months later?"

"Yes, I do. I thought he was a capable administrator."

"Yes, indeed, he was. But he was hired because he had a nice smile, and when one of the department heads complained about his way of conducting business, that was the end of him."

"What is your plan now, Jim?" I asked.

"I decided to retain a legal counsel, George Rankin, of West Town."

"George Rankin?" I raised my voice. "You know she hates his guts."

"Exactly. That's the reason I hired him to represent me."

Four weeks later Jim Wilkins left the institution after thirty years of dedicated, distinguished service. He was able to obtain a satisfactory arrangement, receiving continuous compensation for years to come.

It became a joke among the hospital employees that the longevity of vice presidents at this institution was anywhere from six months to two years. As I anticipated, Sister called me from Las Vegas on April 7 urging me to join her at the Flamingo Hotel. I politely declined her invitation, citing an extreme physical fatigue from a long trip to South Africa.

40
Health-Planning Session in Vegas

"Doctor, Betty from Sister's office is on the telephone and wishes to talk to you!" Donna, my secretary, called out.

I turned around from my microscope to pick up the phone. "Yes, Betty, what's up?"

"The Midwest Health Corporation [MHC] is having their annual planning meeting at the Sahara Hotel in Las Vegas in September, Doctor. Sister wants you to attend with the nuns from here."

"Betty, I have been at several such meetings in the past. It's a waste of time! Can I send Dr. Spenser or Dr. Park in my place?" I asked grimly.

"No, you must attend, I'm afraid. Two well-known speakers will discuss the philosophy of patient care."

"I know all about their philosophical approaches to health care problems. In fact, I can teach them from here, Betty," I said jokingly.

She giggled and said that the hospital would pick up the tab for air transportation and lodging at the Sahara Hotel in Las Vegas.

I frowned and went back to my microscope.

Just as I predicted, the three-day meeting was a complete waste of time, producing no significant results. I saw many administrators, some physicians, and nuns betting money at casino tables, sitting at the tables for hours day and night.

When I returned from Las Vegas following the meeting, I found a message to call a member of the board of directors of Marymount Hospital. He wanted to know the diagnosis of lung biopsies on a friend of his.

"Who operated on him?" I asked.

"He was operated on three days ago by Dr. Jim Hinton."

"Have you called Dr. Hinton? He will tell you the diagnosis."

"I want you to tell me the diagnosis, Dr. Joe," he snapped.

"I suggest you call Dr. Hinton and ask him the diagnosis and prognosis," I said fretfully.

The man was adamant. "I want you to explain to me the diagnosis now! I am a member of the board."

"I know you are," I said, "but I cannot reveal the tissue diagnosis to anyone except the attending physician, Dr. Hinton. There are medical ethics involved."

"Don't give me that ethics stuff!" he snorted. Within a minute, the sister administrator was on my back.

"Why can't you give him the diagnosis?"

"I can't, Sister. That would be unethical. He should call the attending physician," I said, raising my voice.

"I want a copy of that pathology report immediately," she insisted.

I asked my secretary to take a copy to Administration. When I explained what had happened to Dr. Jim Hinton, a thoractic surgeon, he exploded.

"That goddamned shit-kicking board member! Who the hell does he think he is?"

I knew that my name was now on Sister's famous shit list. When Jim asked me with a concerned voice whether I was in trouble with the administration, I stated, "I don't care! I go by the book!"

On October 1, I left for Seoul, Korea to visit my youngest sister, who was practicing family medicine in a small city twenty miles south of Seoul. My sister and her husband and I visited the large cemetery where my father was buried in 1959. After two medical lectures at Seoul University Medical Center, I paid a visit to Mrs. Francesca Rhee, widow of former president Syngman Rhee. She was very old, frail, and gray-haired. She was speaking German, her native tongue, very quickly, and I was unable to understand her except for a few words. She was under the care of the government at Ewha Mansion. Mrs. Francesca Rhee, a native of Vienna, Austria, had helped me when I was trying to come to Memphis, Tennessee, in 1952. Now she was senile, unable to recognize me. My heart sank and I turned around and left.

After the completion of my last lecture at Pusan, I was joined by old classmates and our mentor, Prof. J. H. Chun at a resort town, Song-Do. I then returned to Seoul and drove to the east coast. I stood on Hill 1179 and Bloody Ridge, old battlefields during the Korean War. Both sandy hills had absorbed so much blood in the summer of 1951 that they had turned into red clay. Both regions were covered by heavy vegetation and thick foliage giving the appearance of lushness. No battle scars were observable, and no signs of the thousands and thousands of casualties were visible. On the very spot where I was standing, many of my colleagues and corpsmen had been killed. Unable to stand any longer, I turned and quickly went to my car with misty eyes. They had died in vain. Few lucky ones were left lingering on. Many undisputed geniuses in medicine and science perished in such a useless war. My stomach felt as though it had been twisted in a knot.

When I returned to my office I found a letter from Dr. Jane Wright of New York Medical College inviting me to go to Eastern Europe and the Soviet Union as a member of a cancer delegation in March 1987. I accepted her invitation.

While I was on the telephone informing Dr. Wright of my intention to present two papers at the meetings in Czechoslovakia, Hungary, and Moscow, my associate Dr. Harry Spenser walked into my office with his coffee cup in his hand and sat down. When I finally finished the conversation, Harry said with a cynical smile, "Have you heard the latest news around here?"

"I just got back from a tiring trip, Harry. What has been going on here?"

"Another vice president, Jim Klein, got fired yesterday."

"What?" I was surprised. "Why? He was a good man!"

"He was. Klein was a financial wizard, saving millions of dollars for this institution."

"Then why was he canned?" I could not comprehend.

"There is no job security for anybody around here, you know."

"I know that, but this is going too far, Harry. There must be something else involved for Jim to get canned."

"When you find out something I don't know, let me know, Joe." Harry went back to his office. I talked to several people in the accounting office, who were also saddened and severely depressed.

"He was such a good and capable man. We are equally puzzled," said one employee. "We are all scared to death."

Two days later, I received a phone call from my friend Dr. John Bain, a pathologist at Midtown General Hospital.

"Joe, while you were in Seoul, Korea, your sister administrator sent her two vice presidents to Windsor for negotiation."

"What negotiation, John? What are you referring to?"

"Well, apparently she wants to buy the Union Medical Laboratory in your area, Joe. Has she discussed this with you?"

"No, no one told me about it. Are you positive about this, John?"

"I was told this morning by Dr. Barry Johnson, who works at the Union Laboratory, at their home base. Barry and I were together at Northwestern Hospital for our residency training."

"I know of Barry Johnson, John. Why don't I call him now?"

"I wish you would find out soon from your sister administrator. We are worried about you, Joe."

The UML, a commercial outfit for a profit-seeking company, was based in Windsor, with several branch laboratories in three other states. The one in Midtown was three blocks west of Marymount Hospital with ten laboratory technicians employed. They offered discounted laboratory tests for blood chemistry, bacteriology, and tissue pathology drawing numerous specimens from clinics and physicians' offices. It was a thorn in the flesh, and I wished they would disappear one day. The UML, however, was thriving and yielding significant profits.

I called a meeting with the administrative people, including the head administrator, Sr. Pamela Collins: Jack Fenton, a new vice president; and a senior vice president, Bob Baker.

"I understand you people are buying UML here!" I asked, looking at them queerly.

"Well," Sister said with an apologetic smile, "we are making a feasibility study into such an acquisition."

"Isn't it true that you sent Jack Fenton and Bob Baker to Windsor twice to make an offer?" I persisted.

Jack and Bob looked at each other uncomfortably.

"We went to feel them out for such business transactions, but nothing has been decided," Jack said hoarsely.

"And it never occurred to you that you should discuss this with me beforehand?" I raised my eyebrows.

"We intended to tell you after we acquired the UML and make you a partner," Sister said wryly.

"A partner? Let me ask you one basic question. Who is going to do the extra work or take on more responsibilities? You or us?"

After no response from them, I continued wrathfully, "What was your offer for the UML?"

"We offered $2.7 million to acquire!" Sister replied in almost a wail.

"And they accepted?" I snapped.

"We don't know yet," Baker murmured.

"Let me tell you something," I said in an outraged tone. "There is a thing called professional courtesy. You people should have had the decency to consult with me in this matter before you should approach the home office of the Union Laboratory to make an offer. Who do you think will have a task to absorb additional work to include the UML once it is bought? We pathologists and our medical technologists must carry an additional burden, not you laypeople."

Both Jack and Bob looked at each other in silence.

I called a former hospital attorney, Jim Kelly, and gave him a complete rundown. Jim sighed dejectedly and said, "Joe, you are absolutely right. They should not have pulled these shenanigans. She is getting worse every day. Why don't you have a stiff drink and forget about it?"

"Forget it? Are you joking?" I snapped.

I informed Dr. John Bain, a pathologist at General Hospital, of what I had found out, saying, "John, you were right. They are trying to buy UML for $2.7 million. The bastards will pull the rug from under anytime, I am afraid."

"Yeah, too bad, Joe. Watch out for yourself. She is very dangerous."

Two weeks later John Bain called. "Joe, it looks like they just blew another of her half-assed ideas out of the water."

"What do you mean, John?"

"They turned her offer down, the UML home office, I mean."

"Oh, they did? I thought the $2.7 million offer was more than they asked for!"

"Apparently not, Joe. It appears that your headache is gone."

"You will never know in this place, John," I said evenly.

41
To Moscow

On March 16, twenty delegates representing M.D.'s and Ph.D's in the cancer research field arrived in Prague, the capital of Czechoslovakia, and were met by a guide. The airport was dirty and there were no chairs in the waiting lounge. It took forty minutes to go through customs and passport control sections.

Our guide explained that there were 10 million Czechs and 5 million Slovaks. We saw many houses and buildings with bullet holes, reminders of the Soviet invasion of 1968. Several large buildings in the downtown area were badly in need of repair and cleaning. The general expression of the people was not happy, as far as we could tell.

Our hotel was a small and old establishment. We went out into the streets in the downtown area to buy some fruit but were unable to find any. Consumer goods were very scarce. Each store was filled with Soviet-made vodka and canned goods such as herring and sardines. Small, shriveled oranges, flown in from Cuba, were available at our hotel.

At the Cancer Research Institute of the Slovak Academy of Medicine, I was asked to present a paper on colon cancer detection. I spent a few minutes showing the U.S. map, focusing on the Midwest and Midtown, then presenting my Kodachrome slides depicting farm scenes. Then I proceeded to a scientific discussion of colon cancer and its detection.

At an evening reception given by the U.S. ambassador, Mr. Nemecek, it was abundantly clear that the economy of Czechoslovakia was depressed, but there was very little they could do about it. At the reception we met many warm and friendly Czechoslovakian physicians, and I spent some time discussing cancer statistics and research projects. I promised Dr. Jiri Kanka, chief of the obstetrics and gynecology department at Charles University, that I would send him a number of slides for training of cytotechnologists in detecting cervical cancer and uterine neoplasms.

The visit to the Children's Oncology Hospital was an experience that I would never forget. Many sick children with acute leukemia were housed in a hospital where nurses and physicians were devoting themselves to the children's care in facilities that needed much improvement.

At a roundtable discussion at Charles University, the dean of the medical school told us that their problem was to distribute young physicians equipped to care for rural people in the health care system. Most of the physicians wished to stay in large cities, instead of going to small towns and villages. Many of them were successful in obtaining suitable positions because of their political connections with influential government members.

The ordinary people of Prague were very friendly and open and did not hide their hardships under Soviet occupation. For example, there were eighty thousand Russian troops in Czechoslovakia, reminding them of their obligation as a Warsaw Pact nation.

In the afternoon we were taken to Prague's Jewish ghetto and saw a cemetery of two acres in which thirty thousand Jews were buried. Because of the limited amount of land, they had to dig deep and bury their dead in nine different layers. Thousands of headstones stood on the ground, those of rabbis being much larger than those of the ordinary Jewish people.

Officials of the Ministry of Health presented their figures on three major malignant tumors—namely, cancer of the lung, cancer of the stomach and gastrointestinal tract, and lymphoma and leukemia. I was struck by the figures indicating a high incidence of stomach cancer among the Czechoslovakians.

Members of the delegation were delighted to see the expressions on the faces of the people in Budapest when we arrived there on March 22. Private enterprise appeared to be working well, as the people were better-dressed and looked well fed. The downtown area of the Pest section of the city was full of merchants and shops. Young street musicians were performing everywhere, even around the Budapest Hilton Hotel. We gave a small amount of money to each group. The Hilton Hotel had been built on a destroyed monastery with its characteristic architectural design and offered the first-class facilities of a modern hotel. Air pollution was extremely bad in Budapest, being much worse in the Pest section, where some industry was located.

At the National Institute of Oncology at Semmelweis University, I gave my presentation regarding Stage I breast cancer.

We visited Castle Hills, in the Buda section, followed by an afternoon tour through a cathedral, the Basilica, where we met a large number of Soviet soldiers who were also sightseeing. We subsequently learned that there were eighty thousand Soviet troops in Hungary, and I was advised not to risk provoking them by taking pictures. As they were leaving the cathedral, however, I took several shots from a distance.

At an evening reception held by the university people, we felt the openness and honesty of Professor Lapis, chairman of the Department of Pathology at Semmelweis University. Professor Lapis readily admitted that their biggest social problem was alcoholism, citing that 60 percent of autopsy studies showed alcoholic-type cirrhosis of the liver. He also asked me to look up his friend, a professor of pathology at the second medical school of the University of Moscow. I was pleased to see the freedom they were enjoying in the field of medical research and pathology studies.

Before leaving Pest, we dined at a fairly large Japanese restaurant, where we saw many friendly people enjoying themselves.

Arriving at the Moscow airport on March 27, we went through passport and customs inspection without difficulty. In fact, it took such a short time that everyone was puzzled. When I reached a large tourist hotel in a suburb of Moscow and was led to my room, I was very disappointed with the facilities and substandard service. With painstaking effort, I tried to replace a burned-out light bulb, without any success. My room was dark for the duration of my stay in Moscow.

The delegation leader, Dr. Jane Wright, attempted to contact the Soviet authorities through our guide for permission to visit the Department of Cancer Epidemiology, Oncological Research Center, and Department of Chemotherapy, but her request was denied without any consideration.

No organized evening receptions were held in Moscow or Leningrad. Each person was on his own, and I was advised to purchase my own theater tickets for evening shows. I particularly enjoyed the musical programs that I attended at the Bolshoi Theater. Their performance of *Swan Lake* was excellent.

On Monday morning the U.S. delegates were allowed to visit the Moscow Cancer Center, approximately thirty miles from the Moscow city center. It was an impressive building with exquisite interior design. We were led to the Department of Endoscopy, headed by Professor Podogony, who had previously been at M.D. Anderson Hospital in Houston. Photographs of Lenin were everywhere, and a political seminar was held faithfully every Monday, we were told. The endoscopic department was fairly well equipped with Japanese-made instruments. Professor Podogony tried to demonstrate a Soviet-made laser machine, which broke down three times. He finally gave up his demonstration.

I approached the interpreter in an effort to meet Professor Lapis's friend at the second medical school of the University of Moscow. Later I was told to make written application to the Ministry of Health for a short visit to the laboratory of pathology. I gave up the idea after being informed that it would take three days to process my application.

The subway system, called Metro of Moscow, was very efficient. For a fee of fifteen cents any citizen of the Soviet Union could ride thirty to forty miles in any direction. The subway station was very clean, with many paintings on the walls and beautiful chandeliers hanging from the ceiling. Several small boys were running around, asking the visitors for cigarettes and chewing gum. We were told that the KGB agents were trying to catch them but had never been successful.

The gray-and-black office building housing the KGB headquarters was an imposing sight in Dzerzhinski Square, exhibiting an awesome silhouette to the visitors. Before I left Midtown, I was warned by many of my friends who thought I was taking a tremendous chance in going to Moscow, since I was an escapee from the Soviet police in Pyongyang, North Korea. I dismissed such caution by saying, "That was forty years ago, and I was a very small fish." But whenever our bus passed the KGB building, I got goose bumps. One fellow delegate, in warning me not to go into the building, said, "Joe, if you went into the first floor, they would give you a one-way ticket to Lubianka Prison, and we would never see you again." A massive iron gate in the backyard apparently led into the basement of the most notorious jail for political prisoners in the world.

At the Moscow museum I took pictures of the paintings and sculptures. Our guide later informed us that they were all copies of the originals, done by students of the Moscow Art Institute. I wasted a whole roll of film capturing the fake works of art.

Many members of our delegation had prepared papers to be presented, but the Soviets did not wish to exchange information in the cancer research fields. Unfortunately, we had no chance to exchange ideas with our Soviet counterparts.

Consumer goods were scarce. We saw long lines of people waiting to buy fresh fruit and ladies' shoes made in East Germany. Photographs representing Soviet heroes from various factories were displayed everywhere in the city. Among them were three workers in vacuum cleaner factories who had produced over and above the quota and received the title Workers' Hero.

On a cold morning of early April, we joined several hundred Soviet citizens to visit Lenin's mausoleum. The lines moved slowly, inching its way across the rough cobblestones of Red Square. The tomb itself was built of blocks of reddish-brown and black marble in the shape of a ziggurat. The upper level served as a reviewing stand for the Kremlin leaders on state occasions. Wreaths of flowers had been placed along the front wall of the tomb; on either side of the doorway two soldiers in gray greatcoats, blue caps, yellow belts, and white gloves stood motionless, facing each other, rifles at rest. We went down a flight of steps, then up some more steps to the right and into the center of the mausoleum. Lenin lay on a raised red bier, bathed in a blaze of very bright white spotlights. The rest of the room was dark, increasing the dramatic contrast with the two solemn-faced soldiers guarding the tomb. Lenin's right hand was clenched, his left hand open, a balding little man with a reddish beard and hair, the waxy face chalky white. There was no time to study the waxen figure more closely; the guards kept the crowd moving silently around the bier and out the door. Once outside again, we were routed along a path that ran behind the tomb and directly beneath the Kremlin wall. In the grass strip between the wall and a line of fir trees we saw statues of dead Soviet leaders, not including Nakita Khrushchev.

The group left Moscow, arrived at the Leningrad airport, and was taken to a first-class tourist hotel where many East and West Germans and Japanese visitors were staying. The next day I spent about three hours at the Petrov Institute of Oncology, in a suburb of Leningrad. My wish to visit the cancer patients' ward was flatly denied, and the Soviets showed no interest in hearing the group's papers or exchanging cancer information. The director of the Oncology Institute told us that all the antitumor drugs and antibiotics were manufactured in the Soviet Union, but later he slipped by mentioning a contract between the Soviet Union and Japanese chemical companies.

I visited the pathology department at the Petrov Institute of Oncology and found that the department was outdated, with poorly equipped and illuminated laboratories and office space. There was only one pathologist, who was trying to screen more than twenty-five thousand Pap smears a year by himself. No cytotechnologists were available at the Oncology Institute. I questioned the pathologist regarding the problems of alcohol and drugs, and the answer, according to the interpreter, was that the Soviet system has no problems with alcohol or drugs.

At the Helsinki airport, however, I read articles in a German magazine concerning the acute social problems with alcohol, drugs, and 120,000 moonshiners in the Soviet Union. There were forty-two thousand deaths a year attributed to drug addiction, and many Soviet citizens were now alcoholics. The KGB arrests over 150,000 moonshiners a year and puts them in different labor camps, but they will have to cope with increasing numbers of illegal alcohol manufacturers.

The delegates whispered to each other, "How lucky we are to live in the United States!" I repeated this story later to the laboratory staff, hospital employees, and members of my Presbyterian church, saying, "You people should thank God that you are citizens of this country."

Epilogue

When my late father retired from his teaching job at age sixty-three, he said to me, "Everybody should write his or her memoir because everyone's life history is unique." When he died of a stroke at age sixty-five, he was on the third chapter of his biography. In 1986, after reaching the decision to write my story, I went to Seoul, Korea, to obtain black and white photographs of my guardian angels who had helped me during the darkest days of the Korean War. I was dismayed to find that most of them had died earlier. Through my friends, the children and grandchildren of people to whom I owed so much, I was finally able to obtain small snapshots or black and white photographs to include in the book.

Indeed, without their help I could not have survived the war and reached Memphis, Tennessee, in 1952. After donating several thousand Kodachrome slides to a medical school in South Korea, I began my lecture tours to teach medical students about breast cancer and cancer research. I frequently stopped during the lectures and asked whether they understood my language as I had not lectured in my native tongue for forty years. Students nodded and said, "We can understand what you are saying despite your heavy northern Korean accent."

My father advised me on numerous occasions that I should go out to play with other children and find out the meaning of life. "Son, you are a bookworm! An imperfect person! You should mingle with the people and be a normal boy!" Indeed, he was right in referring to my tendency to shut myself away from the real world. In this regard, I am a failure in many ways.

I have much admiration for a famous Canadian physician who once remarked, "If a man has no enemies, he is a nonentity." Indeed, he was right. It would be unwise, however, in this complex world for a man to make more enemies than he can afford.

In closing my career after forty-five years of practice, I am constantly reminded that I have made so many stupid mistakes repeatedly. I beg forgiveness from my former associates, colleagues, and friends. If I had another chance to do it over again, I would have done it differently. I am thankful to God that remarkable progress is being made in South Africa and wish to praise the farsightedness and political courage shown by many politicians. My keen disappointment in life, after thirty years of association with religious people, is that I found more racial bigots among the nuns of this particular order than among ordinary people. When a group of novice nuns arrive at the convent, they should go through multiple sensitivity sessions to lessen their racial prejudice before they undertake anything else. After all, they are there to serve God, and he may not approve of their racial bigotry.

Before closing, I must make one comment in regard to cancer chemothcrapy. With many qualified oncologists, medical oncology has made a remarkable progress in the last twenty years. Many patients with various types of cancer are now achieving remission after remission to survive for longer periods, which was impossible years age. It is hoped that medical and radiation oncologists will further advance their skills in the field of cancer treatment to save many patients with cancer.